MURDER at DUSK

How US soldier and smiling psychopath
Eddie Leonski terrorised wartime Melbourne

IAN W. SHAW

hachette
AUSTRALIA

hachette
AUSTRALIA

Published in Australia and New Zealand in 2018
by Hachette Australia
(an imprint of Hachette Australia Pty Limited)
Level 17, 207 Kent Street, Sydney NSW 2000
www.hachette.com.au

10 9 8 7 6 5 4 3 2 1

 A catalogue record for this
book is available from the
NATIONAL
LIBRARY National Library of Australia
OF AUSTRALIA

ISBN: 978 0 7336 404 52 (paperback)

Cover design by Luke Causby, Blue Cork Design
Front cover photographs courtesy of Getty Images (51538432/Bettmann: Eddie Leonski); State Library
    Victoria (H86.98/230: 'Collins Street from Treasury'); and State Library Victoria, Newspapers
    Collection (Gladys Hosking, Pauline Thompson, Ivy McLeod)
Back cover photograph courtesy of National Archives of Australia (A472, W7493/Arthur de la Rue)
Map by Kinart
Text design by Bookhouse, Sydney
Typeset in 12/17.25 pt Simoncini Garamond by Bookhouse, Sydney
Printed and bound in Great Britain by Clays Ltd, Elcograf S.p.A.

In memory of
Sergeant Winton Rex Shaw, RAAF, and
Sergeant Delia Mary Shaw, WRAAF,
who lived through this and much else besides.

CONTENTS

Inner Melbourne, 1942

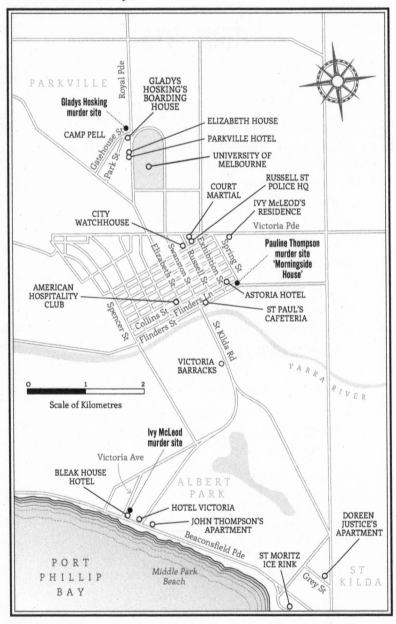

It is sweet to dance to violins
When Love and Life are fair:
To dance to flutes, to dance to lutes
Is delicate and rare:
But it is not sweet with nimble feet
To dance upon the air!

Oscar Wilde, The Ballad of Reading Gaol

PROLOGUE

2 A.M., 3 MAY 1942, ALBERT PARK, MELBOURNE

Ivy was cold and tired. It was two o'clock in the morning and she was alone, waiting for the tram. Three hours ago, she had caught one from the other side of the city to visit John, the man she thought she might spend her future with.

Now, though, she huddled in the shop doorway across the road from the beach. There would be a tram arriving sometime in the next twenty or thirty minutes, and while she was still cold and tired, she would also soon be home and warm.

●

His name was Eddie and he, too, was cold and tired, and a little bit annoyed. He was an American, a soldier in the US Army, but he was also a long way from his home in New York City. The day had started more promisingly. His duties at the army camp were over by mid-morning and, by lunchtime, he had showered and dressed up, and was drinking with a group of other servicemen at an old hotel across the road from the beach by mid-afternoon. They had eaten – he thought it might have been fish and chips – before continuing to drink in the hotel and then across the broad esplanade on the low beach wall.

Eddie recalled that two of his new buddies had gone off to find more beer, leaving him alone with Patricia, an Australian girl who had been drinking with them and who now insisted that he call her Pat, but not Pattie. They had kissed a couple of times, but she wasn't his type and when the others returned, they had given him a bottle of beer and headed off into the dark.

He didn't mind being alone, as it gave him time to think about things. About his mother, in particular, and how she would be coping with her wayward sons with only her daughter, Helen, to help. His mother had problems in her head and needed him there. Both his brothers also had problems in their heads, but there was not much he could, or would, do about that. One was already locked up and the other probably would be soon. That would leave his sister-in-law footloose and fancy-free. Eddie had been there, but was not yet ready to go there again.

And so Eddie threw the empty beer bottle onto the sand, listening for the soft thud as it landed. He fixed his uniform, tucking in the tie and adjusting the overseas cap on his head before crossing the darkened road towards the tram terminus that he knew was somewhere around here.

•

Eddie sensed there was someone in the alcove before he actually saw the figure in the shadow.

'Jeez, ma'am, you sure gave me a fright,' was the best he could come up with.

'I'm sorry,' came the reply in broad Australian. 'I'm just waiting for the next tram and thought it would be a bit warmer in here.'

As his eyes adjusted and the woman stepped a little forward, Eddie saw that she was well dressed and several years older than him. She seemed wary, rather than alarmed, at meeting a man, and, to provide some reassurance, he enquired about her handbag, which seemed large and also looked to be specially tailored. She said that, yes, she had bought it especially for its size and utility; in her work, she often had to carry many different things.

'And what work would that be?' asked Eddie.

'Sorry,' was the reply this time. 'The name's Ivy and I am a lady's companion. I live with an older lady, and I take her shopping, on outings to the city, and generally just assist her with her life.'

Eddie smiled and then explained how he had met up with but then lost a group of other soldiers and some Aussie dames. It was getting very cold and, if she didn't mind, he asked if he could stand with her in the alcove as they waited for the next tram. There was more than enough room for two, Ivy said, and stood towards the side away from the beach.

Eddie stepped into the alcove and smiled at Ivy. As he did so, he casually draped his right arm across her shoulders.

1.

HE'S COMING SOUTH!

Sometime in early 1942, the Australian government began to print and distribute large numbers of a new patriotic war poster. At the top was printed, 'He's Coming South', and written across the bottom was, 'It's fight, work or perish.' Between the printing and the writing was a stylised painting of a Japanese soldier, tommy-gun in hand, with a Japanese flag as a backdrop. Like a colossus, the soldier was astride the South Seas. One foot was out of the picture, presumably planted firmly somewhere in China. The front foot was about to land in the centre of Western Australia. It was not a subtle poster: the Japanese were coming and Australia had just three options – fight, work or perish.

•

Until 8 December 1941, the war that Prime Minister Robert Menzies had taken Australia into in September 1939 had made a relatively limited impact on Australian society. There had been an initial rush of young and not-so-young men volunteering for active service but, as with World War I, the fighting took place overseas. Japan's entry into the war changed that.

Prime Minister John Curtin – who replaced Robert Menzies in October 1941 – had been desperately trying to bring all Australian ground forces home to protect the country from a possible Japanese invasion. He was doing so in the face of some determined opposition from Winston Churchill and the British War Cabinet. It was a fight which Curtin would win, but that victory came at a cost, stretching the Imperial bonds to breaking point. Britain could not and would not protect Australia, so Curtin turned his country towards the United States and asked for assistance. They are coming south, Curtin said, and we don't think we can stop them. Will you help?

Australia, and Melbourne in particular, did not really seem to know how to deal with the possibility that the country could become a war zone. The closest that most Australians had been to the realities of war was from the comfortable seats of their local picture theatre. There, they could see both the horrors of the London Blitz and the heroics of the Battle of Britain interspersed with footage of wiry diggers in foxholes and pillboxes at Tobruk, or our sun-bronzed infantrymen climbing a palm tree on a pristine beach 'somewhere in Malaya'.

It was not as if nothing had changed physically though. The major cities of the south-east of the continent gradually moved to something approximating a war footing. As well as posters warning about the inexorable advance of the Japanese hordes, federal and state governments introduced and encouraged a range of more practical measures. Air-raid shelters for both public and private buildings were constructed, plate-glass display windows were taped against possible bomb and shell blast, and tens of thousands of sandbags were filled and stacked. Slit trenches for use during air raids scarred playgrounds and there was serious talk of evacuating all women and children from urban centres

– certain targets for bombers – to the comparative safety of the countryside.

And then there was the brownout, which was enacted in all the coastal capital cities. A total blackout was neither necessary nor practical, and a brownout would save energy while engendering both a sense of sacrifice and some discipline in the civilian population. In Melbourne, street lamps were screened and in some places every second light globe was removed. Those who wanted to take it further took out the other globes and painted up to ninety per cent of their surface area black before returning them to their sockets. Motor vehicle headlights were to be covered, with just a thin section left clear to provide a kind of pinhole light. To compensate for the dangers caused by the lack of vehicular illumination, the speed limit for all motor cars and trucks was reduced to thirty-five kilometres an hour.

Public transport was not overlooked in planning the brownout. Hoods were provided for all tram headlights, while their interior lights could be turned off completely when the trams were moving. Tram conductors in Melbourne were given special ticket bags containing a small interior light which enabled them to identify coins and notes. Elsewhere, dimmer lights were installed in all railway carriages and all lights at railway stations were screened.

In Melbourne, there were a number of unforeseen consequences to the brownout. At the beginning of 1942, Victoria Police officials were complaining bitterly and publicly that the new regulations were receiving little more than lip service and that drivers of motor vehicles, in particular, seemed to think that brownout measures, including speed restrictions, applied to everyone but themselves.

More worrying for some was what appeared to be an imminent breakdown in public morality. At the outbreak of war, Melbourne, like the other capital cities, had become a magnet for young people. For young men from regional and rural Victoria, it was where they went to enlist in the services or where they took their initial tests and training. If you were successful in all of this, Melbourne then became where you tried to go on weekend leave, to either catch up with your family or to carry on with your mates. For young women, Melbourne was where jobs and other possibilities were. With so many young men in the services and so much work to be done, there were opportunities for almost everybody and almost everything.

An essentially staid and conservative Melbourne political establishment struggled to cope with the stresses and pressures that the young people's war brought. One of the early flashpoints was the perceived abuse of alcohol and consequent problems with street offences. The Victorian premier, Albert Dunstan, was so concerned that he asked the Chief Secretary, Henry Bailey, for a police report on excessive drinking in Melbourne. A preliminary report was delivered to the premier three days later. Among its statistics were figures which showed that 128 arrests were made in the City of Melbourne over the first weekend of March 1942. The equivalent figures for the corresponding weekends in 1938 and 1939 were 63 and 44 arrests.

It was all stuff and nonsense. Young men and women who have volunteered to fight – and possibly die – for their country rightly expect to be treated with at least a modicum of respect. And young men and women who are earning as much in a week as their parents earned in a month expect to be able to spend that money when and how they choose. This was the real cause of many of the issues which so perplexed Victoria's senior politicians in early 1942.

For those who wanted to drink, there were plenty of opportunities. In the state's hotels, trading hours were from 10 a.m. until 6 p.m. All alcohol served prior to closing time had to be consumed on the premises, leading to the infamous 'six o'clock swill' – the unedifying spectacle of grown men ordering several drinks just before closing time and then trying to down them all in a fifteen-minute sprint. Licensed clubs were at least a little more discreet. They were generally allowed to serve alcohol with meals until 8 p.m., and after that time could sometimes be prevailed upon to serve champagne in fine bone china tea cups.

On Sundays, the hotels were, in theory, closed to all but bona fide travellers. The generally accepted definition of such a traveller was someone who had travelled at least eighty kilometres that day. If nothing else, this gave young people the opportunity to both study geography and learn the distances between towns.

Most nights of the week during the early brownout months of 1942 the city centre of Melbourne and parts of certain inner suburbs were thronged with people. Picture theatres were so popular that their opening times were staggered to allow dedicated filmgoers to progress from one cinema to another.

It was the hotels, though, that drew the biggest crowds, followed at a distance by the clubs and cabarets that sprang up to cater for the men and women in uniform. From early 1942, some of those men in uniform really stood out from the rest. Their uniforms were better, their wallets were bigger and their accents were broader. But – officially at least – they did not exist until 19 March, when Prime Minister Curtin stated, 'It is gratifying to be able to announce that there are substantial American forces in Australia . . .'

•

Within a few weeks of the opening of the Pacific War in 1941, and well before the fall of Singapore in February 1942, there were a number of American servicemen in Australia, although the government chose to keep their presence in this country a secret. At the same time as the attack on Pearl Harbor and the invasion of Malaya, substantial Japanese forces attacked the Philippines, then an American protectorate. This other surprise attack destroyed most of the US combat aircraft stationed there, while substantial numbers of Japanese troops also gained a foothold on the main island of Luzon.

The destruction of a significant part of the US Navy's Pacific Fleet at Pearl Harbor, coupled with the loss of most of their air force on the ground in the Philippines, had an immediate impact on American strategy. In the changed circumstances, and facing a rampaging Japanese Navy and Army, US military planners looked for a safe and stable location from which they could both supply the Philippines and build up the men and equipment they knew would be necessary to push the Japanese all the way back to their home islands. Australia, being a large and friendly nation, was the logical and obvious choice for this.

Staff for both planning and operational logistics arrived in Australia in December 1941, but it was not until early in the new year that Americans in any numbers arrived Down Under as part of the new US strategy. The first arrival of large numbers came in what was known as the *Pensacola* Convoy of combat ships and transport vessels that arrived in Brisbane on 22 December 1941.

The USS *Pensacola* was a heavy cruiser and in December 1941 it was escorting a convoy containing army units destined for service in the Philippines. Midway across the Pacific the flotilla was redirected – reportedly on the direct orders of President Roosevelt himself. After a refuelling stop at Suva, the convoy proceeded directly to Brisbane where its four transport vessels were unloaded. The 4600 servicemen those ships carried included infantrymen, artillerymen and air force ground-support units.

The troops in the *Pensacola* Convoy were under the command of Brigadier General Julian Barnes, who assumed command of all US troops in the Australian theatre upon his arrival in Brisbane. Barnes was succeeded by Lieutenant General George Brett, who arrived in Australia on 28 December. Barnes remained with Brett as his chief of staff, accompanying him to Java before they returned to Melbourne where Brett established his headquarters.

With the establishment of this headquarters, combat and support troops began to pour into Australia. Two more convoys filled with troops arrived on 1 February 1942, one sailing into Brisbane and the other into Melbourne. The second was known as the *Mariposa* Convoy, after the pre-war luxury liner that carried most of the troops; it and a second transport, the *Calvin Coolidge*, were escorted across the Pacific by the heavy cruiser USS *Phoenix*. After a two-week voyage from San Francisco, 4550 American servicemen disembarked at Port Melbourne and marched, via Dandenong Road, to their temporary camp at Caulfield Racecourse. One of those who marched was US Private No. 32 007 434, Edward Joseph Leonski of New York City.

•

As bizarre as it may now seem, in early 1942 the average Australian probably knew as much about the Trobriand Islands as they did about the United States of America. Australia was part of the British Empire, and while this may have brought benefits, it also brought restrictions. Because there was fierce competition for world markets, the United States and Great Britain were as often in a competitive relationship as they were in a cooperative one. There were implications for Australia in all of this.

In the early 1930s, the United States had small consulates in Melbourne, Adelaide and Newcastle and a Consulate-General in Sydney. Australia had only a Trade Commissioner in the United States and he was based in New York rather than Washington. All Australian diplomatic issues were handled on Australia's behalf by the British Ambassador in Washington. This somewhat convoluted form of international representation and diplomatic interaction meant that Australia often viewed America – and American priorities – through the prism of British interests.

Throughout the 1930s, there was a general dissatisfaction with the United States felt across Australia, primarily because of an unfavourable balance of trade and a belief that the Great Depression had been a direct result of American fiscal policies. By contrast, in the early 1930s, Japan was regarded as a good and reliable trading partner, especially important for its annual purchase of Australian wool. The relationship between the two countries had soured towards the end of the decade but for many years the Japanese had seemed to be better friends of Australia than the Americans.

Most Australians who laid claim to some knowledge of Americans probably gained that knowledge directly from Hollywood or indirectly from newspaper and magazine articles about Hollywood. Cinema attendance was at its peak, America's movie industry was churning out hundreds and hundreds of films each year and Australia was enthralled. The lives of Clark Gable and Carole Lombard were scrutinised more closely than those of prominent Australians like Joseph and Enid Lyons, and locals who had only limited knowledge of Squizzy Taylor could recite the life and crimes of Al Capone.

In early 1942, the Japanese were coming but the Americans were already here. The peaceful invasion had started.

•

For an invasion it was. By February 1942, the American war planners were in the process of diverting two full infantry divisions, the major part of the 5th Air Force, anti-aircraft units, tank battalions, surface vessels, submarines and a wide variety of support units to Australia. The 41st Infantry Division would arrive in Melbourne in early April and would be followed almost immediately by the 32nd, which would initially be based in South Australia.

On 21 January 1942, Australia had agreed to a US Navy proposal to establish an 'Anzac' naval area covering Australia, New Zealand, Fiji and New Caledonia. Fleet units would primarily operate out of Brisbane, drawing thousands of Australian and American servicemen there.

For sound strategic and tactical reasons, US Army Headquarters was established in Melbourne at Victoria Barracks on St Kilda Road, just on the other side of the Yarra River from the city centre. Although those headquarters would later be relocated to Brisbane, for the first six months of 1942, Melbourne was the nerve centre for the prosecution of the Pacific War. Estimates of the total numbers despatched to Australia vary quite widely, but by March 1942 there were probably 30 000 American servicemen in Australia, a figure that grew to 120 000 by November of that year. The numbers would peak in mid-1943 when there were in excess of 200 000 based in Australia, meaning nearly three per cent of the nation's population was American. While Melbourne was hosting US Army headquarters, there were never fewer than 15 000 in and around the city.

The invasion was initially a visual affair. Australians all over were used to seeing soldiers, but not soldiers like these. Physically, most of them looked like our soldiers – young and white – but everything else about them seemed different and alien. The Australian Army, for instance, had pretty much two basic uniforms, summer and winter, and both had changed only marginally since the landing at Gallipoli. Drab khaki colours, poorly designed and cut and usually uncomfortable to wear, they made the Australians look like country cousins alongside the smartly tailored dress suits and work uniforms of the Americans, with their colour coordination, overseas caps and bright braid and badges.

For the rest of her life, one young Melburnian woman would always recall the 'otherness' that the American soldiers represented: 'There are so many things that are different from now, and men had buttoned flies, all army uniforms had buttoned flies, and then along came the Yanks and they had zippers – and you found yourself trying not to look.'

There were several other things equally obvious about the Americans. One was that they possessed a 'can do' culture which emphasised getting things done with a minimum of fuss and red tape. Australians were genuinely amazed at the speed with which the Americans could get things done. Open parkland would become a new army camp, complete with facilities that Australians could only dream of, in a few short weeks. Equivalent works by Australian contractors could take up to a year to complete.

It was also obvious that the Americans were paid more than their Australian counterparts, and that they were prepared to spend what they earned. At all levels of service, beginning with the lowest private, an American soldier was paid at a rate that was approximately double that of their Australian equivalent. It was a differential that increased with rank, and it was a difference accentuated by an exchange rate that was favourable to the American dollar. Even if they ran out of those dollars, the Americans had access – through their PX (Post Exchange) canteens – to a range of goods that most Australians could neither find nor afford. As a medium of exchange, in Melbourne's pubs and clubs, American soldiers began to sell off cigarettes, chocolates and stockings they had purchased.

A long way from home, those soldiers also wanted to be entertained. Astute picture theatre proprietors in Melbourne added 'The Star-Spangled Banner' to 'God Save the King' when opening their film sessions, while a variety of entertainment venues opened specifically to address an almost insatiable American desire to go out and do something. In Melbourne, local girls were recruited to act as hostesses at special dances organised for American servicemen. They were known as 'Victory Belles', and they wore small silver bells with their first names engraved on them.

It was this desire for entertainment, for something to do before heading off to battle, which led to the first of what would be several clashes between the visiting Americans and the country and society that was hosting them. Some of these clashes would be philosophical, while others had a distinctly physical bent. The first major clash of philosophies was over Sundays and what could or could not take place on the Sabbath in Melbourne. American authorities, concerned about morale, wanted entertainment of all sorts allowed. The Victorian Council of Churches fought hard against this, applying real pressure to the government, but eventually agreed to a loosening of the regulations which forbade most forms of public entertainment being offered on Sundays. 'Entertainment' would be allowed, but all activities were to be in keeping with the dignity of the day. There was to be no profiteering involved either.

A second flashpoint was the Americans' treatment of Australian women or, more accurately, how that treatment was perceived by Australian men. The pejorative phrase, 'over-paid, over-sexed and over here' was probably coined by a young Australian in an ill-fitting uniform watching through an open doorway or window as laughing young Australian women danced the night away with good-looking Americans in their fancy tailored uniforms. The relationship between Australian women and American servicemen would cause tensions at several levels wherever and whenever there were significant numbers of both present.

Compared to the general stoicism and reserve of many Australian men, most Americans were regarded as outgoing and fun to be with. 'The Americans were so much more attentive . . . very attentive, very considerate and apparently very loving,' and, 'The Americans grinned broadly and brought a new dimension of manly courtesy towards women. Flowers and chocolates were not yet in the standard courting armament of the young Australian male.'

There was always an air of ambivalence about what was happening, elements of jealousy disguised as genuine moral concerns, with a sometimes overwhelming belief that many Australian women were powerless in the face of the personal charm – and silk stockings and chocolate – that the average US soldier could bring to bear on his selected female target. Coupled with this was a degree of resentment that America and its soldiers had stood by for two years while British and Imperial troops stood alone against the might of Nazi Germany.

A number of anecdotes reveal these underlying tensions. Many American officers thought that Australian women were promiscuous, one offering the following observation: 'American soldiers never meet the higher type of Australian girl because our men have carried on in such a way that to be seen with an American uniform . . . practically identifies a girl as a whore.' A somewhat contrary view was espoused in one of the many stories that circulated at the time. 'What do you think of us stealing your girls?' an American asked a digger recently returned from the Middle East. 'Aw, you didn't steal them,' came the drawled response. 'You just sorted them out for us.'

•

As the massing of American forces in Australia continued, it became clear to all that the build-up was one of the preliminary moves for a massive response to the Japanese onslaught. The only things missing were a strategy and a leader. Both arrived in the person of General Douglas MacArthur.

The jury of history is probably still out on the enigmatic figure that was Douglas MacArthur. A vainglorious man constantly seeking private reassurance, the public figure was almost larger than life. A tall, somewhat stooped man in his late middle age, the General MacArthur of February 1942 appeared to be floundering in the Philippines, where he was in command of all American and Filipino forces.

However, his President and Commander-in-Chief, Franklin Roosevelt, saw something in MacArthur that many others consistently overlooked. Roosevelt recognised that MacArthur was a man of destiny. Roosevelt saw a man with a fine military record, but moreover saw a man whose ambition would continue to drive him on long after the Philippines campaign was gone and forgotten. He also recognised that MacArthur was a master of the relatively new art of public relations. His plain uniform, a battered cap and a corncob pipe all spoke of a man of the people, an image MacArthur reinforced every time he interacted with someone from the media. A decision was made. MacArthur was ordered to leave the Philippines to take up a new position in Melbourne, Australia. He would take command of all Allied forces in the South West Pacific Area.

A measure of the man can be taken by charting his escape from Corregidor to Australia. It was not without danger: a Patrol Torpedo Boat dash to the southern Philippines, followed by a suspenseful flight aboard a B-17 Flying Fortress through skies controlled by the Japanese, before a final touchdown at Darwin, at the northern extremity of the world's largest island.

MacArthur had been ordered to escape taking only essential personnel with him. This included his much-photographed (and much younger) wife, Jean, and their little boy, Arthur. It also included little Arthur's Chinese nanny, several of MacArthur's Filipino cronies and – perhaps – some important deposits from the Philippines' National Treasury. High-ranking officers, technical specialists and intelligence officers with detailed and important knowledge of the Japanese were left behind.

Until their arrival, there had been a formal media ban on the reporting of the presence of US servicemen in Australia, a ban that was respected despite their obvious presence in Melbourne, Brisbane, Darwin and Townsville. With MacArthur's spectacular and successful escape to Australia, Curtin himself lifted the ban, announcing both the presence – but not the number – of

American troops in Australia as well as MacArthur's safe arrival to take up his command role in Melbourne.

When the MacArthurs arrived at Melbourne's Spencer Street station on the morning of 21 March 1942, 6000 Melburnians gave the general and his family a hero's welcome, recognising that the 'great fight for civilization' now had a worthy leader in the south. Three hundred and sixty spit-polished American soldiers formed an honour guard for the general and his family, and Douglas MacArthur was formally welcomed to the country by the deputy prime minister, Frank Forde, as he stepped, waving to the crowd, from the train.

The MacArthurs remained in Melbourne for four months as the general and his aides plotted the campaign to destroy the stranglehold the Japanese had established over South-East Asia and on into the South-Western Pacific. In those months, they were treated like royalty, and behaved accordingly. The family took over a suite in the Menzies Hotel, then regarded as Melbourne's finest, and had a grand piano installed so that Mrs MacArthur could practise the scales. General MacArthur, and sometimes his wife, travelled around Melbourne in a black limousine with number plate, 'USA 1'; it was applauded everywhere it went, irrespective of whether or not it was occupied.

The general and his wife enlivened the social scene and generally made good copy for the Australian newspapers. For most of those four months, the MacArthurs were the most famous Americans in Australia. They only really had one serious challenger.

2.

PRIVATE LEONSKI

Edward Joseph 'Eddie' Leonski was born into a world that he would never quite understand. The circumstances of his birth and growing years were just one variation of the kaleidoscope which was the Great American Dream. Eddie's parents were migrants who had left the confines of the Old World for the freedom and promise of the New. His father, John, had been born in Russia in the late 1860s and his mother, who later anglicised her name to Amelia, in Poland in 1888, then part of the Russian Empire. They had met and married in New York City and then moved across the Hudson River to New Jersey, where John Leonski found work as a stevedore and made just enough money to support a growing family.

Eddie's parents were damaged before they met and, if it was not a good marriage, it at least was a productive one, with three boys, Vincent (1909), John (1911), Walter (1914) and a girl, Helen (1916), arriving at regular intervals; Eddie was the youngest and arrived into the world in 1917. The main problem in the marriage was that John Leonski was an alcoholic, and moreover an alcoholic who seemed to lose a lot of social control when drunk. He would regularly assault his wife and children and when doing so seemed to ooze hatred, not only towards them, but towards the world in general, a world that never quite gave him what he thought it should. His alcoholism slowly spiralled out of control, and in 1924 Eddie's mother took the children back across the Hudson to New York, to a fifth-floor apartment in a brownstone building at 425 East 77th Street, a working-class neighbourhood in Manhattan. John Leonski stayed in New Jersey and died there, killed by his alcoholism and his bitterness sometime in the late 1920s.

Eddie had disliked his father only because he was too young to understand fully what hatred is. The dislike was over the abuse heaped upon his mother rather than any physical beating he may have suffered, and the move to Manhattan came as something of a relief in his young life. That relief was short-lived though, because his mother took up with another man in New York. This man was also from Eastern Europe, and they may even have married. If so, it was a continuation of a pattern which had been established earlier. The new man was another alcoholic and a giant who would throw his weight around in the family home. He would also disappear for extended periods, and then the family was happy. But he always seemed to return.

Eddie idolised his mother, who returned his love with interest. As a young boy, this love was tempered with the reality of some of the things he witnessed and some of the things he suffered in the family home. They would play on his mind for the rest of his days. Not unsurprisingly, his mother skated along the edges of alcoholism and could only work intermittently to support her young family. Disaster struck in 1928 when Eddie's mother suffered two serious nervous breakdowns. Confined to a New York hospital, she was initially diagnosed with a manic-depressive illness. One of her doctors suggested that she was also exhibiting symptoms of schizophrenia. It was an episode that took them all a long while to get over.

•

Growing up, Eddie was always full of energy and was in love with physical activities, with a particular interest in competitive sports and games. Baseball was initially his favourite, but then he discovered handball, a game based around rebounding a ball off a wall, which quickly went from being an interest to being a passion. He would play and practise alone for hours at a time; Eddie was never one for half-measures.

As he entered his teens, Eddie also became interested in bodybuilding and in sports which required strength as well as technique. His first love was weight lifting, an interest he shared with his older brother John. As John's interests moved into other areas, Eddie took up boxing and wrestling and became very good at both. As he moved through his teenage years, Eddie's physical interests narrowed to two main elements, his strength and his physical appearance. He would spend many long and lonely hours working on both.

Eddie's compulsory education ended when he finished junior high school in New York, but he continued his education by enrolling in a three-year secretarial training program at a vocational college in Brooklyn. Eddie enjoyed his time there and moreover was successful, graduating twentieth in a class of 291. He was especially proud of his writing and of his ability to take shorthand. After college, he worked in several small department stores before settling into a job with Gristede Brothers, a large chain of grocery stores stretching across the Bronx and beyond.

Eddie was presentable and worked hard and was soon promoted to Gristede Brothers' new flagship store, where he again charmed the other staff with an open and engaging smile that could light up a room. Some other, stranger characteristics soon started to emerge. When asked about either his strength or his physique, Eddie would pick up a forty-kilogram bag of sugar in one hand and hold it above his head as he continued the conversation. He also quickly learned the various techniques of short-changing customers, and on occasion would boast of his finesse at this to his supervisor, as if challenging him to do something about it.

The petty infractions developed into something more serious, and Eddie became involved in outright criminal activity. Sometimes alone, and sometimes with his brother John, Eddie would break into warehouses and stores to steal items of value to sell. On one occasion, he was challenged by a night watchman, but simply ignored the challenge. A shot was fired, but missed, and Eddie walked off. With strength of body and strength of purpose, he learned that you could get away with just about anything.

●

As Eddie Leonski reached adulthood, things at home also started to change, and not for the better. Most of the time there were just five Leonskis living in the Manhattan apartment: Eddie, his brothers John and Walter, his sister Helen and his mother. The stepfather was rarely seen in the late 1930s as the Leonski boys grew up. Eddie's mother had seemingly recovered from the mental illnesses of a decade earlier but was still 'delicate.' Eddie believed he still had a special relationship with his mother, who doted on him in return. It grieved him when she went missing mentally.

While the eldest Leonski brother, Vincent, had disappeared from the scene, Helen Leonski was becoming the stable rock around whom the rest of the family swirled. She was hard-working and she was honest, attributes which were becoming increasingly rare in the Leonski family. Walter Leonski was showing increasing signs of serious mental disturbance – irrational behaviour and inappropriate responses became increasingly common and reached a point where he had to be treated. Diagnosed with paranoid schizophrenia, Walter Leonski was confined to an institution in August 1940 and would remain there for the rest of his life, living, and eventually dying, quietly in a world of his own. It was a path that made a lasting impression on Eddie.

John Leonski junior's behaviour was also changing, and he seemed determined to carve out a career as a small-time criminal. The inevitable happened, and he was caught and sentenced to two years imprisonment. Before that happened though, he had married a native New Yorker named Mae Black. Mae was big and blonde and full of sass; after John was put away, she and Eddie began a sexual relationship, which was fun for her, but which obviously meant a lot more to Eddie.

Part of the problem was that Eddie remained deeply in love with his mother, who he saw as representing everything that was good and proper about womanhood. Through the trials and tribulations of two tempestuous marriages and her own mental issues, Eddie's mother had remained true and faithful to her own children and to Eddie in particular. Both believed that, in some way, Eddie was destined for greatness. It was their secret and one that they protected and nurtured. Throughout his teenage years and into his early twenties, Eddie had an active social life, though there were no particularly serious relationships.

Eddie never took a girl home to meet his mother. Perhaps he didn't want either his mother or his girlfriend to make comparisons of one another, or perhaps it was important for Eddie to keep all the various parts of his life separate. Or maybe it was because, in Eddie's world, women were either a Madonna – like his mother – or a whore, like his sister-in-law. Maybe, indeed, they were a mixture of both. He loved them for what they were. He hated them for what they were.

•

In January 1941, Eddie Leonski appeared to be an excellent example of American manhood. At six foot, he was above average height, and he was blond – even if it was a dirty blond – and blue-eyed, with a sallow complexion and a wonderfully open face, unlined and youthful, and possessing a radiant smile. He had broad shoulders, a powerful chest and a narrow waist. He looked like a bodybuilder – overdeveloped biceps and forearms in particular – but he carried himself well. He was also more than happy to talk to people and, if prompted, would even show off some feats of strength.

Aged twenty-three, Eddie was approaching his physical peak, which was precisely what his country needed. War clouds were gathering all around, and America might need to become something more than the Arsenal of Democracy. In February 1941, Edward Joseph Leonski was called up for compulsory military service and was inducted into the United States Army. One day he was a civilian; the next he was Private Leonski, No. 32 007 434.

•

The union of Eddie Leonski and the American Army was not a match made in heaven. Despite the evidence of the destruction wrought by alcohol all around him, Eddie had begun to drink in his late teens. During 1940 with so many things happening to his family, Eddie started to abuse alcohol heavily. He would always recall that the drinking made him feel good, but there was a lot more to it than that. When drunk, he could release some of the little demons that had started to live within him. Like his mother had intuited, Eddie felt he was a person capable of achieving great things, but he also understood there were standards of behaviour that society expected of people, and that there may come a future conflict between the two.

Eddie's army induction took place at Fort Dix in New Jersey, and after satisfactorily completing all the tests and trials there, he was sent south for further training, to Fort Sam Houston in San Antonio, Texas. There, Eddie joined the 52nd Signal Battalion with hundreds of other new inductees all going through weeks of basic training followed by the specialised training many would need to fulfil the requirements of being a trained signalman. Eddie did not follow that path though, his general clerical background saw him drafted into the battalion's Headquarters Company. In these early months, Eddie developed his army persona which, like many other aspects of his character, was increasingly complex.

To begin with, Eddie was not a particularly good mixer, beyond a superficial level, and he seemed either incapable of or unwilling to form the close personal relationships that military service encourages and promotes. In part, this was a conscious decision by Eddie who understood that he had very little in common with his fellow GIs. But it was mainly because he was so obviously different from most of those around him. Take, for instance, the physical exercises that were part of the training. Boxing was part of the curriculum, and Eddie was very good at boxing. So good in fact that he soon ran out of sparring partners and opponents. Everything would be all right until Eddie took a hard punch. If that happened, he would lose control and would try to tear his opponent apart. It sometimes took several people to restrain him until he had calmed down. Eddie always claimed that he was not a bully, but he did take obvious pleasure from the fact that others were scared of him.

Those around him also noted that Eddie may have been developing a real dependence on alcohol. As the months passed by at Sam Houston, the role of hard-drinking soldier settled on Eddie's shoulders and also became increasingly well known around the 52nd. Private Isidore Bernstein had known Eddie from the beginning, with both having arrived in the same draft to the battalion. Early in the year, Bernstein was a fairly regular drinking partner of Eddie's and, during one of their sessions in a San Antonio bar, Eddie confided to Bernstein that drinking helped him to deal with the issue of his brother's wife. Bernstein did not push for further information, and Eddie was either unwilling or felt unable to provide further details.

Private Henry Jacobi became another of Eddie's early drinking partners. Like Bernstein, Jacobi had been drafted into the 52nd at the same time as Eddie, although the two had never been especially close. On several occasions when the two went out drinking together or with others, Eddie would add condiments like salt and pepper, tomato sauce, chilli, or even ice-cream to his drinks. Jacobi assumed that Eddie was just doing it for effect, a bit like walking across the bar on his hands to show everyone how strong he was.

It was also common for Eddie that a drinking session concluded with a visit to the red-light district of San Antonio, located on the west side of the town. It was during one such visit that Eddie made by himself, that a potentially career-ending incident occurred. On the night of 13 April 1941, Private Edward Joseph Leonski was detained by the San Antonio Police Department and charged with assaulting a local girl named Beatrice Sanchez. As well as striking her, Sanchez reported that Leonski had also tried to choke her. She had escaped and told her story to passing police, who then arrested Eddie. The story ended there, with no apparent follow-up, and just the frightened statement of a young woman who may or may not have been working the streets of San Antonio.

Eddie was a prodigious drinker and a normal session would see him consume between twenty to thirty drinks with little apparent intoxication. And he never seemed to have a hangover; the only effect that Eddie would ever admit to was a temporary loss of memory about some of the finer details of his previous evening's activities.

The closest Eddie had to an army buddy was Private Anthony 'Joey' Gallo, a fellow New Yorker who made the same trip south as so many others and first met Eddie in March 1941. While it was not an especially close friendship – Eddie didn't have any of those – and seemed to be pretty much a one-way affair, the two had shared living quarters and occasionally did drink together. The little Italian-American was not the smartest guy in the unit and was occasionally bullied because of this. When Eddie let it be known that he would personally take on anyone who picked on Gallo, the bullying stopped immediately.

On most occasions Eddie proved to be a reliable and competent army clerical officer. He regularly said that he was looking forward to the opportunity to serve in a combat unit, and also let it be known that he was not averse to hard work if there was some that needed to be done. In the Headquarters Company, he was generally regarded by his superiors as a friendly, talkative and cheerful individual who did not cause any real concern. Some believed that he was a little bit obsessive about his personal appearance, especially the cleanliness of his hands, but concluded that he had the makings of a good soldier. There was no reason to transfer him out, so he stayed despite his run-in with the law.

Those who lived and worked and played with him might have thought differently, but it was not their opinions that counted. That Eddie was in some kind of difficulty was patently obvious at times and, as the date drew near for the outfit to move out of Sam Houston, Eddie's drinking and associated behavioural problems became a lot more apparent. It all came to a head on the day the 52nd was scheduled to decamp. Early in the day, Murray Cooper, a sergeant in Eddie's company, came across Eddie outside his hut. Eddie was trying to cross a street while walking on his hands. When ordered to stand up straight, Eddie seemed unsteady on his feet. Cooper thought that he was drunk.

Two of Eddie's hut mates that day were Harold Votaw, who had only known Eddie for three weeks, and his old friend, Isidore Bernstein, now promoted to Private First Class. When the time for the actual move came, Eddie refused to do anything, and simply sat on his bunk, crying. He kept saying, almost as a mantra, 'I don't want to go. I don't want to go.' Votaw and Bernstein had to dress Eddie in the appropriate uniform, pack his bags and help him to the truck that would take all of them away from Fort Sam Houston forever.

•

The various components of the 52nd Signal Battalion were brought together in San Francisco in the days following the Japanese attack on Pearl Harbor, and Eddie found himself confirmed as a general duties enlisted man in the Headquarters Company. He certainly had mixed feelings about the army on the eve of his departure for active service overseas. One part of him was resentful; the army had already taken him a long distance from his mother and was about to take him even further, and that was bad. It had also closed off some of his favourite pastimes; handball, for instance, was something he just couldn't do anymore. In some ways he felt that this was limiting his potential, and this was all disappointing.

On a more positive note, the army was looking after him and paying him a decent and steady wage. While it had taken him away from his mother, it had also taken him away from his loser brothers. Also Mae, who he could not really resolve his feelings about. She was sluttish, yes, but she was a good-looking woman who had told him that she thought about him all the time. He certainly spent a lot of time thinking about her. That was probably a break-even. The army had also promised him the opportunity to prove himself on the field of battle. He didn't really know how he was going to get there from his formal position of clerk in Headquarters Company but, then, stranger things had happened.

On balance, he thought that he was better off than he might have otherwise been. The only ongoing issue was the restrictions that army life placed on his newly expanded social life. It was this very thing that gave Eddie his first brush with army law, the system of legal jurisprudence known as the Uniform Code of Military Justice. It was Christmas Eve in San Francisco, the soldiers all knew they would soon be heading overseas to face the Japanese and they were all confined to camp, awaiting a Japanese onslaught on the West Coast. Eddie wanted a drink and some entertainment, so he simply walked out of camp and into town. When he returned several hours later he was detained and charged with 'breaking restriction', fined fourteen dollars, and confined to camp for several days.

Shortly after this confinement ended, on 12 January 1942, Eddie Leonski was one of 4550 American servicemen who boarded the luxury liner *Mariposa* in San Francisco harbour. Most of his camp mates had wanted to go out for one or two drinks the evening before. Eddie said that he wouldn't go with them because if he started to drink, he would never want to stop. Like all US Navy vessels, the *Mariposa* was a dry ship, alcohol-free, and it is not certain whether Eddie would have changed his mind about pre-departure drinks if he had known that. It was presumably a trial for Eddie and others to last two weeks without a drink. There was only one stop on the trans-Pacific voyage. That stop was at Tonga, but none of the enlisted men were allowed ashore. On 1 February, the *Mariposa* docked at Port Melbourne and soon afterwards, Eddie Leonski disembarked from the longest voyage he had ever made. He knew the city was called Melbourne and the state was called Victoria; what he didn't know was that he would never leave either of them alive.

3.

CAMP PELL

Major Floyd Pell was an army aviator. A native of Utah, he had always wanted to be a pilot, and after graduating from US Military Academy at West Point in 1937, was commissioned into the United States Army Air Forces. When the Pacific War broke out, Pell became part of that great movement of men and supplies despatched to Australia. Shortly after their arrival in Brisbane, Pell and his squadron flew out again to Darwin via Adelaide. Pell and his men were at readiness at the main air base in Darwin on the morning of 19 February when the Japanese launched a massive air raid on the port and all the defence facilities clustered around it.

Floyd Pell was one of the first to reach his aircraft when the alarm sounded and was quickly strapped in and airborne. He had reached a height of barely thirty metres when his Kittyhawk was hit by sustained machine-gun and cannon fire. Pell reacted instinctively, putting his aircraft on its side and bailing out. He had just enough height for his parachute to open fully and slow him down before he hit the ground. Pell landed at the edge of the runway and was struggling to get out of his parachute harness when a second wave of attacking aircraft swept in. He was cut to pieces in a rain of machine-gun fire from one of those aircraft.

•

Floyd Pell may have been killed, but his sacrifice was remembered and his name was given to a large new American base being built in Royal Park, just to the north of the City of Melbourne. It would be known for the next decade and more as Camp Pell. It was certainly situated on prime real estate. Royal Park itself was almost a century old and its 180 hectares contained many playing fields and walking paths. It also contained the Royal Melbourne Zoo, with its own railway station, while the parklands themselves were crisscrossed by roads and paths. Among Royal Park's several claims to fame was the fact that it was the starting point for the ill-fated Burke and Wills expedition, which set out to cross Australia from south to north in 1860.

In March 1940, the Melbourne City Council had agreed to hand over more than ten hectares of Royal Park to the Australian Army to be developed as an army camp. Located in the south-eastern corner of the park, almost abutting the edge of the city, the area was chosen because it had tram lines on either side, giving those who would be stationed there cheap and easy access to the city centre. Originally, the Australian Army's Provost Corps and recruit reinforcements were to occupy the site after amenities and ablution huts had been constructed and the whole area connected to Melbourne's sewerage system. The final touch was the digging of V-shaped slit trenches for protection against possible air attack. These were situated near the eastern border of the camp.

The major works were completed in early 1942, but Australian troops were only ever visitors to the site. Handed over to the US

Army, the site was open for business by the end of February when a formal ceremony at the new parade ground saw the American flag hoisted over the complex. That flag, a gift from a Melbourne Ladies' Auxiliary, fluttered and waved in the fluky breeze as the first American soldiers to march in snapped to attention. Among those young men were the soldiers of the 52nd Signal Battalion.

•

Eddie Leonski's new home was Tent 16, Row 4, part of a group of rectangular tents which housed the members of the 52nd Battalion's Headquarters Company. Like all the other accommodation tents on the site, Eddie's had a wooden floor with a stout coal stove in the middle with a flue disappearing through the roof. Again like all the other tents, Eddie's had four occupants: himself, and Privates Joseph Occiogrossi, Vincent Tuzzio and Pat Forino. All were New Yorkers and all were in Headquarters Company. Eddie didn't particularly like any of them and none of them particularly liked him. Eddie's iron-framed camp bed was the first on the left as you entered the tent. That suited him, too, as it meant that he didn't have to speak to anyone as he entered and left unless he wanted to. He rarely did.

The ablution blocks – toilets and showers – were about forty metres away, and a little further on were the main camp buildings, cafeteria, assembly hall, parade ground, work areas and the like. In the northern part of the camp was the Provost Corps area, fenced off and containing a lock-up, office and Military Police (MP) huts. This was all some distance from Eddie's tent, which was located in a part of the camp known as Area One, towards the eastern end of Camp Pell.

Eddie did not have to work hard for his thirty dollars a month. Most of the thousands of troops in Camp Pell were up early in the morning and, after breakfast, would work through the morning on various drills or on those tasks in which they specialised. After lunch, for most, their time was their own. In a camp where most of the enlisted men had it fairly easy, Eddie had it easier than most. He was permanently assigned to the kitchen, on Kitchen Patrol (KP) duty, and within that broad area his responsibilities began and ended with breakfast. When the last breakfast dishes had been cleaned and stowed away, and the last benches, chairs and floors had been swept and cleaned, Eddie was his own man. More importantly, he was his own man with a Class A pass – issued to all KP staff – which meant that when he was not on duty, Eddie and the other catering staff were free to go on leave. Potentially, there were thousands of young men who were required for military service at Camp Pell for just a few hours each day. Potentially, there were thousands of young men with a lot of money and a lot of free time in a city that was foreign to them all.

This was, potentially, also a cause for concern. One of the senior officers posted to Camp Pell was Colonel A. L. P. Johnson, and part of his role there was to oversee the provision of recreational facilities for the thousands of troops who would be based there. Johnson had, early on, identified boredom as being the biggest threat to morale and the major trigger for the kind of behaviour that could give Camp Pell's residents and, by extension, the entire US Army, a reputation it did not wish to be saddled with. He therefore planned to introduce a recreation program which was both comprehensive and, moreover, would cover not only weekends but any periods when the soldiers had spare time.

Johnson's vision was nothing if not expansive. His program would include: 'sports events, theatrical and musical entertainments, movies, the provision of canteens and welfare centres and the establishment of information and hospitality bureaux to serve the troops and their hosts and to provide a means of communication between the troops and the people of Australia'.

There were suggestions that the US Army might also look at establishing hostels and canteens away from the camps while permanent recreational facilities would be constructed in the larger camps. Those camps might also contain permanent cinemas, complementing the mobile cinemas that would be introduced almost immediately. Until then, a large entertainment marquee would be erected at Camp Pell.

All this was for the future, though, and at the beginning of March 1942 the facilities available to the troops within the confines of the camp were limited and those that were available were voluntary; only those particularly interested were inclined to join in any of them. Leave was not automatically granted, but most acted as though it was, and hundreds of GIs travelled into the city every day, generally returning before midnight, although there were always exceptions to this as well.

•

Even by the low standards that characterised the early regime at Camp Pell, Eddie had a very cushy job. If this was not the kind of army career Eddie had envisioned, he had no one but himself to blame. During his time at Fort Sam Houston, his secretarial and business training and experience were recognised and, with clerical responsibilities, he was promoted to Private First Class on at least two occasions. Each time this happened he would eventually do something – usually connected with his drinking – that would lead him to again being reduced in rank.

He had the opportunity to make a fresh start at Camp Pell. There he met a Headquarters Company sergeant named Joseph

Stagg who believed that Eddie had a lot more to offer than what he was contributing as a mess hand in the kitchen. Stagg had seen Eddie's file and knew about his educational qualifications, his shorthand and typing skills, and all the other clerical skills that Eddie had picked up at vocational school and in the years of work with Gristede Brothers. Stagg proposed to the company commander, Captain Christian Kauffman, that Eddie be appointed to one of the company clerk positions and the captain agreed.

It was Fort Sam Houston all over again; Eddie lasted one day in the position. He did not turn up for work at all on the second day and when Stagg went looking for him on the third day, he found him drunk and passed out in his tent. Stagg continued to keep an eye on Eddie for a short while before finally giving up on him. He saw him around the camp a few times, but more often than not Eddie was drunk. Stagg did, however, believe that Eddie liked him because he would always flash that winning smile and speak to him in a clear and somewhat cultured voice.

Just as Eddie was beginning to let the army down, that army was also beginning to let him down. The results would be terrible.

•

Eddie's drinking was coming to increasingly dominate his life. This was an issue in itself, but it was accompanied by more serious acts that ranged from the mildly entertaining to the confrontational, and then went beyond even that. Eddie's demons were beginning to eat him up from the inside, and he simply didn't have the skills to exorcise them. The army did not acknowledge Eddie's behaviour, let alone the advance of whatever condition was driving it, and so Eddie carried on, alone, as he always had and always would.

His tent mate, Vincent Tuzzio, attempted to extend the hand of friendship, but was rebuffed. Any chance of an enduring friendship was totally extinguished when Vince saw Eddie pummel an opponent into insensibility in the boxing ring. What started out as a simple spar turned nasty when Eddie took a solid shot to the body. His response was a flurry of vicious head and body punches, followed up with knees and elbows. Eddie had to be physically restrained until his breathing and his behaviour returned to normal.

Joey Gallo was still the closest thing Eddie had to a friend. Joey looked up to him and thought that Eddie may indeed have saved his life. But Joey could be a little bit simple at times and didn't really understand a lot of what Eddie said and did. For instance, Eddie had told him about the affair he had conducted with his brother's wife, adding that they were deeply in love and that Mae – the woman – was still sending letters to him in Australia. Yet Eddie also said that he had not made allotments from his pay for any family members despite the fact that he knew his mother in particular was doing it tough back in New York. Eddie figured that he earned the money and it was therefore his to spend as he saw fit.

The drinking itself didn't worry Eddie. He was very well aware of the alcoholism and mental instability that lurked in the dark corners of his family's history, but that was the others and he knew he was different. He felt good when he drank, and others seemed to like the Eddie he became. The mixing of drinks, the feats of strength, the laughter and the camaraderie were good things, positive things in Eddie's life, and the occasional bad thing – the fights and blackouts – were a small price to pay for feeling good. Just about everyone knew that if you wanted a few drinks and a fun time, you went out on the town with Eddie Leonski.

In late February, soon after their arrival in Melbourne, Eddie's drinking partner from Fort Sam Houston, Harry Votaw, caught up with him and the pair went into the city for a mid-afternoon drink. At 2 a.m. the following morning, Votaw realised that he was Absent Without Leave (AWOL) and that he was also physically incapable of drinking any more. He told Eddie that he wanted to return to Camp Pell. Eddie wished him well and continued drinking with a group of Australians. Votaw kept out of Eddie's way after that.

•

By the end of March, Eddie's behaviour when drunk was becoming offensive to even some of his hard-drinking army colleagues. He would force kisses onto girls he met on the streets of Melbourne and would also attempt to corral them in pubs and clubs. Drunk or sober, he was also always looking for opportunities to show off his strength and masculinity.

At times, his behaviour in camp was no better than his behaviour outside. In the mess, Eddie was now answerable to a supply sergeant named John Wiseman. Around the middle of the month, Wiseman found Eddie and one of his regular drinking buddies, a private named Carlson, sitting in a storeroom, obviously drunk, and swigging something Wiseman could only describe as 'plonk.' Wiseman ordered some other soldiers to take them back to their tents and put them to bed. No further action was taken.

Officially at least, Eddie Leonski was no better and no worse than any of the other hundreds of soldiers at Camp Pell. An examination of the extant records would not have revealed a string of penalties or even warnings for being AWOL, for public and private drunkenness and for a range of anti-social acts from holding and forcibly kissing women on the streets of Melbourne through to assaulting other soldiers in camp by entering their tents, lifting up their beds and tipping them out, then challenging them to a fight if they felt aggrieved. And there were many other things the authorities just didn't know about.

Nothing would have been done to curb Eddie's increasingly erratic behaviour had an Australian soldier not stepped in. That soldier, as anonymous today as he was discreet back then, contacted the Camp Pell authorities to inform them that Eddie Leonski, an American soldier, was keeping 'bad company' in Melbourne and was currently in a well-known city café with a group of Australian civilians. An examination of relevant records and non-commissioned officers revealed that Eddie had in fact been AWOL *for six days*!

The officer in command of Headquarters Company, Christian Kauffman, was informed. He immediately ordered a taxi and, when it arrived, directed it to the café which the Australian soldier had named. Eddie was there, just as predicted, sitting with a group of what appeared to be shady characters. Kauffman walked up to him and told Eddie that there was a taxi waiting outside to take the two of them back to Camp Pell. There was no argument; in fact it appears that no words were exchanged at all.

Eddie broke down during the trip back to camp, crying almost uncontrollably and telling Kauffman that he felt that his life was spinning out of control. After getting out of the car, Eddie seemed to change once more and he asked Kauffman, with no apparent irony, if it was all right for him to go back into town now. Kauffman said it certainly wasn't all right and that Eddie would now be taken – under arrest – to the stockade. Kauffman would later order thirty days detention for Leonski's various infringements. It was a punishment that Leonski had, once sober, requested, in order to help himself 'stay out of trouble'.

Eddie's time in the stockade passed quietly except for one curious incident. Somehow Eddie gained access to alcohol, which he drank alone in his confinement cell. Drunk, he forced his way out of the room and out of the stockade. He completely ignored the MPs calls to stop and the warning shot fired over his head which followed. In an eerie reprise of the incident in New York when he and his brother broke into a warehouse, Eddie continued walking calmly to the PX canteen, where he stood in a queue, purchased some chocolate and returned to the stockade, which was by then in something of an uproar. No further penalty was added to the term he was already serving.

Eddie was released from the stockade on 20 April. It was as if the enforced break had never occurred because, almost immediately, he returned to precisely the kind of behaviour that had put him in the stockade in the first place.

•

In late April a young married woman returned to the flat she was renting at 80 Grey Street in the bayside suburb of St Kilda. That woman's name was Doreen Justice and, although she had grown up in the area, she was now resident in Sydney and was therefore just a visitor to Melbourne. Six months earlier, Doreen, her husband, Percy, and their one-year-old baby had moved to Sydney where they rented a home in inner-city Glebe. Doreen fell ill, however, and her doctor recommended that she return to Melbourne for her health, suggesting perhaps that time with family and friends in an environment she knew well would aid her recovery. Doreen and her baby had travelled to Melbourne in late January and, after staying at the Federal Hotel for two weeks, had taken a flat in the apartment block on Grey Street.

Doreen decided to spend a day in the city, primarily to do some shopping but to also move around in the open air by herself. She dropped the baby off with her mother at the family home at Ferrars Place in Albert Park and had a wonderful day wandering between shops in the city centre. Around five o'clock in the afternoon, feeling a bit weary, Doreen caught a tram from the city to a stop near where she was staying.

As she walked from the tram stop to her flat, Doreen was accosted by an American soldier, who she noted was very well mannered and nicely spoken; just what most Australians had come to expect from American servicemen. Almost apologetically, the American asked her if she could direct him to a nearby suburb. To help him, and to make sure that he understood her directions, the young woman and the soldier walked some distance along the footpath past her block of flats. As they walked, the American commented on how friendly and hospitable the people of Melbourne were, and how interested he had become in Australia. He thanked her, and they parted ways at an intersection, the American standing and looking, while the young woman returned home.

As she opened the front door to the flat she realised that the American soldier she had spoken to had actually followed her back to her flat and was now close behind her. She had no time to respond in any way before his shoulder crashed into her back, propelling both of them into the flat. The soldier spun and shut the door behind them, then forced the woman down onto a couch in the front room.

She was not going to be cowed. Standing up, she told the man she didn't know what he was thinking, but that it was time for him to leave. The soldier's response was equally forceful: he told her to shut up, and said simply that if she screamed he would choke her. Exerting every moral fibre she possessed, the woman refused to back down and simply snapped back at the soldier. In a blur of movement, the soldier grabbed her by the throat and squeezed; she blacked out almost immediately.

She regained consciousness as the soldier was carrying her into the bedroom and dropped her onto the bed. Without taking his eyes off her, the soldier undressed quickly. The young woman, by now very frightened, noted that the man had an erection and that there was a large birthmark or mole on his penis.

While she may have been frightened, she was certainly not panicked and – speaking hoarsely – she told the soldier that she was having trouble breathing and asked if, before they did anything else, she could please have a drink of water. The reply was a grunt, but the naked soldier lifted her by the arm and continued to hold onto her as he led her into the kitchen. He stood behind her as she poured, then drank, a cup of water.

Spinning suddenly, she dashed past the soldier and ran to the front door, shut but unlocked. She threw it open and was halfway through, screaming at the top of her voice, when she was grabbed around the waist by the enraged soldier. As if on cue, the door of the adjoining flat opened and an older woman emerged. Doreen recognised her as Mrs O'Neill, a relative of the apartment block's owner who, with her husband, lived next door. What O'Neill saw was a naked man struggling with the young woman; she understood instantly what was happening, and called out for her husband as loudly as she could.

Several things then happened all at once. The naked man released his grip on the woman, turned and stepped back inside the flat, shutting and locking the door behind him. The two women ran into the O'Neills' flat and also shut and locked its front door. The older woman shut and locked the back door as well, just in case. The two women talked, the younger one saying that her attacker was an American soldier and that she thought he had been drinking quite heavily. The older woman wanted to contact the police immediately, but the answer was an adamant 'No!' The younger woman explained that her husband had an almost morbid dread of the police and would not countenance any contact with them. Besides, she said, no real harm had been done, and by the time the police arrived her assailant would be long gone.

•

Next door, as he quickly dressed, Eddie Leonski cursed his luck and thought about what he could have and should have done. He had made some mistakes, he realised, but he was smart and would not make them again. Dressed, he let himself out of the flat's back door and walked off quickly into the gathering gloom.

•

An hour later, the front door of Doreen's flat opened and the two women and the older woman's husband entered cautiously. There was no sign of the soldier and no indication of the drama that had so recently occurred there. Except for one thing. Crumpled up in the corner of the bedroom was an American army singlet with the initials 'E. J. L.' written on it in permanent ink. After their neighbours left, the young woman discussed with herself what she and her faraway husband could and should do. Doreen was loath to have any contact with the police, and she was also loath to put herself into a position where she would be compelled to describe what had happened to her. While some would believe her story, many others would question the circumstances of the attack, suggesting that she may indeed have invited the American soldier into her flat, and only reported the attempted rape to protect her reputation.

While she would not report the assault to the police, she would keep the singlet and take it with her the following day, when she was returning to Sydney, to her home and her husband. It would serve as a reminder of what could happen if you were either careless, unlucky or simply in the wrong place at the wrong time. It would also give her a reminder that things were not always what they seemed.

•

Eddie's downward spiral continued and, if anything, may have even accelerated a little bit. There were occasions when Eddie didn't turn up at the mess in the morning; he was either drunk and passed out on his bunk or simply hadn't returned to camp after an all-night drinking session somewhere off-site. Even when he did report for early morning duty, there was no guarantee that he would be sober.

•

Around the same time as Doreen Justice survived an attempted rape, at the St Moritz Ice Rink in St Kilda, close to the beach and close, too, to the site of Doreen's ordeal, a young woman just skating happily around on the ice was approached by an American soldier who asked her to skate awhile with him. The soldier was visibly annoyed when the offer was declined.

Later, in the early darkness of the brownout, the same young woman was waiting alone at a nearby tram stop when the soldier who had spoken to her earlier reappeared. Without any real preamble, he hissed, 'I'm thinking of choking a dame and it might as well be you.' In one swift movement, he grabbed her by the throat and squeezed. The woman felt an enormous pressure and blacked out immediately, falling to the ground as she did so. As the soldier stooped down, a tram rattled into the stop. The soldier ran off into the night. The woman was helped to her feet by the tram's conductor. Uncertain about what exactly had happened, the young woman decided that there was nothing to be gained by reporting the matter to the police.

•

As Eddie was finishing his official duties in the early afternoon of Thursday, 30 April, Melbourne was hit by a severe thunderstorm, with vivid flashes of lightning and tremendous peals of thunder providing a backdrop to a torrential downpour. Within half an hour of the storm hitting, several Melbourne roadways became major torrents. One of the city's main streets, Elizabeth Street, had been a dry creek bed when European colonisers arrived and now became one of those torrents. Shortly after the first crash of thunder, water started pouring down Elizabeth Street from Queen Victoria Market and from Parkville and Camp Pell beyond.

At the lower end of Elizabeth Street, where it forms a T intersection at Flinders Street at Melbourne's main railway station, the waters flowing down met other floodwaters from the eastern side of the city and immediately started to back up. They reached a depth there of almost a metre, but the drainage system worked well enough to ensure that it got no deeper than that.

The floodwaters brought with them elements of real drama. A small boy was swept into and through a stormwater drain that emptied into the Yarra River where he was rescued, apparently unharmed. Elsewhere in the city, a woman was swept off her feet at the intersection of Swanston and Little Collins streets, but was grabbed as she struggled in the water by a policeman who had been directing traffic in bare feet. Many small cars stalled in the water and some were pushed, or floated, downstream. Their drivers waded after them. A large, official-looking lorry took on the water, and lost. It was towed out by a US Army jeep. Trams, looking like ferries, pushed out bow-waves and, when they passed another moving tram, made certain that the passengers near the doors copped a soaking.

By the time many of the downtown shopkeepers had finished sandbagging their premises, the storm had passed. An hour after Melbourne had been covered up by clouds, the sun emerged again, and all that remained of the storm were the high-tide marks of litter and mud and a number of stranded motor vehicles. That and a massive clean-up job.

•

Eddie never needed an excuse to drink, but the storm, its power and its aftermath, certainly provided one and, later that afternoon, Eddie and another of his regular drinking partners, Private Ben Moncrief of the 52nd's Medical Detachment, invited another private named Smith to join them for a drink in the city. They found a hotel and settled in for an extended session. Unusually, Eddie did not drink beer on this occasion, but switched between wine, gin and rum. By the time they had consumed around twenty drinks, Moncrief and Smith realised two things. The first was that they were both extremely drunk, and the second was that Eddie still seemed sober. They had one more drink, then left to return to camp. The last they saw of Eddie was him walking around the bar on his hands.

Sergeant John Ardito went out drinking with Eddie and another soldier named John Hajducsak in early May. The three men started drinking at Carlyon's Hotel in the city centre before Ardito and Eddie caught a tram to Luna Park, on the foreshore at St Kilda. There, Eddie grabbed several girls and asked each to kiss him.

From Luna Park, the two soldiers walked up the Esplanade, past the St Moritz Ice Rink and to the Esplanade Hotel where they continued drinking. At that hotel, the two soldiers met two Australian girls. For some reason, Eddie spent a lot of time trying to teach the girls to say the word 'prunes' with an American accent, giggling at their attempts to do so. At one stage, Eddie and one of the girls left and went outside; Eddie returned a short time later, alone. He and Ardito returned to Camp Pell not long after.

On another occasion, in early May, Ben Moncrief heard that Eddie and Private Carlson had a bottle of Scotch whisky in Eddie's tent, and were slowly working their way through it. Moncrief joined them and watched as Carlson downed two large whiskies in succession before passing out and falling across Eddie's bed. Moncrief and Eddie simply picked him up and carried him to his own tent, where they dumped him in a rain shelter.

By early May, Eddie had also found a new favourite drinking spot, and he tried to spend some time there every day. It was called the Parkville Hotel and it was on Royal Parade, just a short walk from Camp Pell and opposite the university. He especially enjoyed sitting in the public bar and drinking with the regulars. The bar counter there was horseshoe-shaped and was covered in a rough red material which provided a good grip when he did his favourite bar trick, walking on his hands from one end of it to the other and back again.

Those regulars all knew him as Eddie and regarded him as a big drinker and a bit of a character. If asked, they would say that Eddie was a 'swell guy'.

4.

MRS IVY VIOLET MCLEOD

Ivy Violet McLeod was thirty-nine years old and well aware of the weight those thirty-nine years carried and what they signified. To begin with, that name was legally correct but was her name in name only; she laughed when she thought of that. For the last five years she had used her maiden name of Dargavel in everything but legal documents, because she and her husband had separated those five years ago. She had heard from someone that her husband was now living in New Zealand, but that was really of little interest to her now, and someday she would initiate the process that would legally end her marriage and allow herself to become fully Ivy Dargavel again. All that stuff represented the past though, and now Ivy Dargavel/McLeod was looking firmly towards the future. On the cusp of forty, Ivy remained a good-looking woman, seeming much younger than her years, and a person who quickly made others feel comfortable with her.

Five years ago, she had broken with more elements of her past than just her husband. She had left a job she liked as a hostess at the upmarket Wentworth Café in Collins Street to take up a permanent position as a lady's companion. It was a job that involved looking after an older lady and her home. It was not too demanding, the hours were good, and Ivy got to live in a beautiful old house on Victoria Parade, East Melbourne, next door to the imposing Eye and Ear Hospital. There was a major tramline a few metres from the front gate of her home and a tram stop just a few more metres beyond that. One of the trams that ran past went all the way to its final stop opposite the bayside beach at the intersection of Beaconsfield Parade and Victoria Avenue in Albert Park. That particular tram would sometimes carry Ivy to her parents' home in South Melbourne. Her mother had been seriously ill, and Ivy was able to help her father out around the home; the family had remained very close.

The trams would also take Ivy to the home of a new and special friend. His name was John Thompson and Ivy had known him for just five months. He was a good deal younger than her – Ivy guessed the difference would be about ten years – and he too had reasons to look forward rather than backwards. John had been a member of the 2/12th Field Regiment and had joined up when news of Hitler's crushing victories in France had filtered through and the very fate of the British Empire was at stake. He had fought with his regiment in North Africa – Tobruk, in its own way, had been a highlight – and had returned to Australia with the rest of the 9th Division when they were needed to prop up the home defences against the advancing Japanese.

John's health had suffered though, and shortly after his return to Australia he had been given an honourable discharge on medical grounds. He had not been idle since, and after mustering out had sought and gained employment at the Commonwealth Aircraft Corporation's factory at Fishermans Bend, a relatively short tram ride away from the small flat he had found at Albert Park. John was from Portland in Victoria's Western District, and he had enlisted in the army while living down there. He would be happy moving back to the country one day. It was something he and Ivy talked about a lot. They discussed jobs and locations and the two of them had pretty much agreed that someday, perhaps soon, they would move to somewhere in New South Wales to start a new life, together.

•

On Saturday, 2 May 1942, Ivy had finished all that she wanted and needed to do by the middle of the afternoon, so she dressed up and headed off to have a bit of fun. Choosing the clothes to wear was the easiest task; it was almost winter, so everything would be black, with a dash of contrasting colour. Had it been summer, she would have dressed in white, again with a dash of contrasting colour. Today, she chose a black suit and overcoat, with the special splash of colour being a light blue scarf. She also chose a pair of black shoes, a black handbag and a pair of black gloves.

Around 4.30 p.m., Ivy caught a tram at the stop outside her lodgings and half an hour later was knocking on the door of a girlfriend's house in Albert Park. The pair chatted for an hour over a cup of tea before Ivy said her thank-yous and left. She walked a couple of hundred metres to another girlfriend's house, where the process was repeated: cups of tea, snacks and a lot of talking. Amongst that talking was Ivy's revelation that she was planning to move to New South Wales and that she thought she might even take a brief holiday in Sydney.

Ivy McLeod's movements for the next three hours remain a mystery; she knew the area very well and had a lot of friends there. Whether she called in on any of them would never be revealed. It is possible she caught another tram into the city for a meal or maybe even a meal and a drink. It is also probable that sometime during the evening she started to feel lonely, so she made a snap decision to visit John.

John Thompson was sitting up in bed, reading, when a tapping on his bedroom window broke his concentration. It was 11 p.m. He pulled an overcoat on over his pyjamas and went to the front door, beaming a smile when he found that it was Ivy on the other side. He ushered her through to the kitchen and pulled out a chair for her to sit on before seating himself on the opposite side of the table. After the usual small talk, Ivy asked John if he thought they might have a drink. An apology was followed by a bottle of beer and two glasses.

They had settled on where their future together would be: somewhere in New South Wales, close enough to be able to stay in touch with family and friends, yet far enough away to leave all their baggage behind.

For there was quite a bit of baggage: John having been a gunner in the heat of battle in North Africa and invalided out, around the time they had met, six months earlier.

For Ivy, it was a lot more complicated. John only knew a little of her past. He regarded her as Ivy Dargavel, a spinster who worked as a lady's companion to a much older woman who lived in a large house in East Melbourne. She was sweet and kind and considerate, and he believed they were growing close enough to perhaps marry before they moved away. But Ivy was really Ivy McLeod, a married woman now separated. She thought of divorce, and she too considered remarriage in another state, with John. Only when their future together became clearer would she tell him of her hysterectomy and of all that the surgery implied.

Theirs was not yet a physical relationship, and she suspected there might be complications if and when it became one, but in other ways their relationship was like that of an older, married couple. They were happy to just sit and talk across the kitchen table, whether it was at her place or his. And that was what they did for the next two hours. At one stage, John produced another bottle of beer and was also able to put together a supper of leftovers and biscuits.

They both realised that it was getting very late, and Ivy said that she should be getting home. It was after 1.30 in the morning. Ivy told John that she would walk to the tram terminus and catch the all-night tram, which would take her almost to her front door. She knew the trams left the terminus at about a quarter to each hour, and thought she had enough time to catch the next service as the terminus was only a brisk five-minute walk away, directly down Beaconsfield Parade. John offered to dress and go with her, but she was not concerned about travelling alone in the brownout. There was also a taxi rank around the corner from the terminus. If she missed the tram, she had enough money to catch a taxi.

The tram must have departed early. It was certainly only one or two minutes after 1.45 when Ivy arrived at the terminus, yet there was neither sight nor sound of a tram. Equally, there was no sign of a taxi, which caused something of a problem. If she waited where she was, it could be fifty minutes before she could get transport home. If she went back to John's, he might be asleep or he might think she was becoming a bit pushy. It had been a good night though, and there was an alcove between two shops near the pub on the corner – she knew it was called the Bleak House Hotel – where she could shelter from the cold.

It was just a minute or two later that she heard footsteps and saw a figure jump back a bit when he realised that there was someone in the alcove. There was enough light for Ivy to see that the figure was an American soldier, and that he was now smiling broadly. 'Jeez, ma'am,' he said with a little giggle, 'you sure gave me a fright.'

●

Eddie Leonski had not enjoyed a particularly good day and, so far, the night was only marginally better. Although it was a Saturday, it could have been any day of the week; for Eddie, they were all pretty much the same now. He had worked in the morning or rather, he had watched the work of others, doing little more than standing by as other people did other things. His responsibilities in the provision of breakfast were well and truly over by ten o'clock, which was good, as it gave him time to change out of his working clothes and into his going-out clothes. He was at the Parkville Hotel shortly after it opened at 10 a.m.

He stayed there, drinking with his new acquaintances, until mid-afternoon, when he felt it was time to move on. He knew the when and where of Melbourne's tramway system and two short rides took him to one of the places he found most exciting about the city – the nearby bayside suburbs. His favourite spot had been St Kilda. Not so much for the beach – sand is sand and water is water for Chrissake – but for the feel of the suburb, the slightly seedy excitement of the place. Luna Park was sweet, the Esplanade Hotel was cool, and the Fitzroy Street precinct reminded him of some of his favourite parts of New York City and San Antonio.

But there had been a couple of incidents in or near St Kilda, and Eddie did not want to go back there anymore. Besides, there were always plenty of MPs and cops cruising around the area.

A bit closer to town, but also near the beach, were two pretty good hotels, the Victoria and the Bleak House, both of which were popular with GIs. So that was where Eddie headed. He arrived at the Victoria before the notional closing time of 6 p.m. and was inside when the doors were shut and locked, and the blinds pulled down. Once that had been done, the drinking continued. Eddie drank with a group of American servicemen, but it was leading nowhere and doing nothing for him, so Eddie left, crossed the beachside boulevard that was Beaconsfield Parade, and sat on the low wall that separated the footpath from the wide, sandy beach.

He sat on the low wall and he let his thoughts wander, and wander they did. Firstly, they drifted back to New York and to his mother, who he knew continued to worry about him. Walter and John were disappointments to both Eddie and his mother, but not great disappointments, because neither of them was ever going to amount to much anyway. Unlike them, Eddie did not carry the seeds of failure and inconsequentiality around with him. He was going to be better than all the others but, gee, it was taking a long time to get there.

From thoughts of his mother, he drifted to thoughts of Mae and the impact she had made on his life. She was a powerful woman and sex with her had been, almost literally, a heart-wrenching experience. Boy, could she put out. But she was married to his brother, that poor bastard John, and as far as he knew there had never been a word about a divorce. Back home Mae had told him that she loved him and that she loved the way he did it to her, and she had repeated the same words in the letters she had sent to him in Australia. It just didn't feel right, though, and somewhere at the back of his mind he *knew* that she was doing the same things with some other poor Joe behind everyone's backs.

The question, 'Are you OK, buddy?' snapped him out of his reverie. It was asked by a GI who had another soldier alongside and a young woman in tow. He was also carrying what appeared to be several bottles of beer. After establishing that he was, yes sirree, OK, and re-establishing names after realising that they had all been in the Victoria earlier in the evening, the group got down to the business of drinking. The two Americans were from a base nearby – Eddie thought he heard something about an old football ground – while the woman, on closer inspection, proved to be a little older than he had originally suspected, maybe even in her thirties. He remembered that her name was Pat and she spoke a little too loud, her makeup was a little too thick and her lipstick a little too red. She reminded him of many others and he did not want to go there.

Then the beer was all but gone and the conversation started to falter. One of the other Americans said he thought they may be able to buy some more beer down at the Bleak House Hotel and they wandered down towards there. He gave Eddie the last bottle as they walked towards the darkened hotel. Pat and Eddie sat on the beach wall as the others crossed the road and dis-appeared somewhere around the back of the hotel. Pat told Eddie he was a good-looking man and kissed him on the lips a couple of times. Eddie thought she had bad breath and smelt of cigarettes. He did not return the kisses and was saved from having to do anything else by the reappearance of the soldiers from across the road.

They called out that the place was closed and all locked up. One also called out that there was a tram due in a few minutes, and that they could go to a club that he knew would be open in the city. Did Eddie want to come with them? Eddie did not. He had other plans, but thanks for the invite and the beers, and good luck, buddy. He waved them goodbye and a few minutes later watched them disappear into a darkened tram which itself soon disappeared. Then he sat on the low wall again, looking out to sea, and again let his thoughts wander.

•

This time, his recollections were more recent. He had been drinking in some hotel with a group of young Aussie civilians, a number of hard men among them. The numbers and faces changed, but he thought he had stayed in a city apartment with a couple of them. There was talk, too, of burglaries past, present and future, of girls and money and cigarettes. Someone in a group of Aussie soldiers had said something nasty about one of Eddie's new friends, a punch was thrown, and then there was mayhem, fighting spilling out of the hotel and into the street. They were in Eddie's world now, and he went for it. He remembered dropping one soldier with just two hard punches to the heart, snapping what felt like a bone in another's arm, grabbing a third by the throat and squeezing.

But then he was dragged backwards and down, and hob-nailed boots crashed into his ribs and what felt like a small elephant dropped onto the middle of his back. He curled into a ball, which saved him from any real damage, and then the fight was over and his new friends were saying, 'Shit, mate, we've never seen anything like that.' But they patted him on the back, and they all went to another hotel to continue drinking, and then it was a couple of days later, and Captain Kauffman walked into the café . . .

•

The sound of footsteps brought Eddie back to the here and now, and he swivelled around to see who was making them. From the sound the shoes made, he knew it was a woman, and she soon appeared out of the gloom, walking on the other side of the road from the direction of Hotel Victoria. Eddie thought she might have been youngish, but it was hard to tell in the brownout and from this distance. She was of average height with medium-length darkish hair, wearing a dark coat with a lighter coloured scarf around her neck. She looked a bit like his mother, which disoriented Eddie for a minute, but he kept watching her.

She stopped at the tram terminus, looked at her watch and then looked around again as if trying to conjure up a tram out of the night. If, indeed, that was what she was trying to do, it didn't work and after a couple of minutes she gave up and walked back across to the Bleak House Hotel. She glanced at the hotel and at the two shops next door before standing still and looking all around again. Then she took a few steps towards the shops and disappeared. Eddie realised that there must be some kind of alcove or recessed entrance to the shops, and stared intently for a couple of minutes until he thought he could make out the shape of a doorway, a dark, rectangular shape.

He sat there on the sea wall and thought for another couple of moments before coming to a decision. He stood up, threw the empty beer bottle onto the sand behind him, adjusted his clothes and walked across the road towards the alcove. His resolve was strong.

•

In the end, he thought it was pretty easy. He simply brought his left arm up at the same time as he brought his right arm back from where it had rested across the woman's shoulders, all the while turning so that he was actually facing her. As his right and left thumbs met at the front of her throat, he squeezed with all his strength, putting years of rage and frustration through his shoulders and arms and wrists and into his hands.

As he squeezed, the woman's eyes rolled up and back into her head and she collapsed backwards. He had expected some resistance and was taken completely by surprise, falling forward with her rather than releasing his grip. As she fell backwards, the woman's head hit the rear wall of the alcove with a loud crack. Eddie let go, and instinctively put his hands out to break his fall. The woman hit the ground, with Eddie awkwardly astride her. He lay there for a minute, listening for something, some sound from the woman or from elsewhere.

But there was nothing beyond the sound of waves breaking on a beach.

He knew she was dead without even looking at her. She was dead because that was her destiny just as it was his destiny to kill her. The realisation dawned slowly and, as it did, Eddie thought he was getting closer to discovering some very important truths. If it was destiny which had brought about all this, maybe the truth that he shared with his mother was that his destiny involved seemingly chance encounters like this. Perhaps if there was greatness within him, it was a greatness that came from his ability to recognise the moments of destiny and act on them. If he was to kill again, and he felt strongly that he should, the act must come about when and where it was destined to occur. There was a logic to all that had happened in his life, a logic that he had sensed but never seen nor grasped. He knew, though, that he was not standing here by chance.

Time passed as he thought these things through, following a logical trail that he believed he was only now starting to see. Once or twice, or maybe more, he heard the tram come and go. Sometimes he stood and looked at the dead woman, at other times he walked and he thought he may even have returned to the sea wall to sit awhile.

Sometime in all of this, the logic became a little more obvious to Eddie. The woman he had killed – was her name Ivy? – had smiled and spoken to him although she had never before in her life seen him. She had been a bit older than he had originally thought, probably closer to forty than to thirty, yet she had spoken about seeing her boyfriend. Eddie thought he might have worked out something else, seen just who this woman was, and understood that she was no better than Mae or Pat and all the other whores who paraded around dressed up as 'gentlewomen'.

He giggled a little at this, but the thought also made him realise that others needed to know the truth about what he had just discovered. He would make it so obvious that everyone would know why he did what he did.

He knew dawn was approaching and that he would have to leave soon, but Eddie was still not satisfied. He stood back and looked down, and then leaned over. He adjusted the clothes, moved the legs apart a bit more and bent them at the knees. Whoever found her would find her lying there, completely exposed, waiting in position for her next lover. As whores do.

He thought he heard footsteps approaching, so he straightened up and walked away briskly. He didn't look back.

•

Harold Gibson was a barman. Middle-aged and single, he lived in an apartment block in Victoria Avenue, Albert Park. It was close to the beach and almost directly across the road from where he worked, the Bleak House Hotel. He was up and about early on the Sunday morning because he was off to work at the hotel. It would not be open for several hours, but Harold earned a bit of extra money by cleaning up at the hotel before it opened. It had been a big Saturday night – lots of Yanks splashing their money around – and he suspected that one of his first jobs would be to hose down the footpaths at the front and side of the hotel.

Harold would always remember the time. He knew it was a little before dawn because the sky was beginning to really lighten up in the east. It must have been around 6.47 a.m. as he crossed the tram tracks because the 6.45 a.m. tram had just left and he could still hear it clanking away in the distance. As he continued on, he paused to light a cigarette before angling across towards the Bleak House.

He suddenly noticed movement from the corner of his eye. Glancing across to his right, Harold saw a figure straightening up in the alcove between the beauty parlour and the dry cleaners. He thought it was a bit odd, as the alcove was usually inaccessible, its wrought iron door normally locked shut. He also noted that the figure he saw was an American soldier, one who adjusted his cap and then strode down Victoria Avenue to Beaconsfield Parade, where he turned left towards St Kilda. Apart from the cap he put on, Harold didn't notice much about his uniform. He seemed tall, but that was the only thing about him that struck Harold as being distinctive.

Gibson walked across to the alcove and looked inside. He could make out a shape, but it was still quite dark so he lit a match and glanced down. His first thought was that the figure he saw was a woman asleep with her head resting in a doorway. He touched her with his foot, but there was no response. He reached over to shake her knee; it was cold and clammy to the touch. He then realised that the woman was practically naked, and that she was lying in an unnatural and awkward position. She was dead.

Given the shocking discovery he had made, Harold's responses were both rational and logical. A short distance away, on the kerb of Victoria Avenue, opposite the entrance to the alcove, was a telephone box. He walked there quickly and dialled D24, the radio room of the Victoria Police Headquarters in Russell Street in the city. He told the duty officer who he was and what he had seen, and was in turn told to stay where he was as a patrol car would soon be there. As he spoke and listened, Harold kept his eyes firmly focused on the alcove.

Crossing back to it to await the arrival of the police, Harold noticed two women walking down Victoria Avenue towards him. He quickly ducked down to the Bleak House, opened the nearest door and grabbed a rug from inside. He took it back to the alcove and used it to shield the body from the public view. When the women arrived level with him, he asked them to move on and told them that the police were on the way. He then stood and waited. It was almost completely light now, and Harold thought it felt it had been a lot longer than fifteen minutes since he had shut his front door behind him on the way out.

•

Gibson did not have long to wait. A patrol car arrived within minutes and its two occupants secured the scene and spoke to Gibson about what he had seen, while they waited for the detectives from the Homicide Squad to arrive. They were there by 7.30 a.m., and the doctor they had summoned, a local man named Augustus Green, arrived soon afterwards.

Confronting though it was at times, the detectives completed a detailed examination of the crime scene. They noted that the body was that of a mature woman and that she was lying on her back with both legs bent backwards at an angle at the knees. The legs were spread wide apart with the feet turned outwards; the genital area was completely exposed. A handbag was lying on the tiled floor of the alcove between the left hand and left leg of the body where it had fallen. The detectives noted that there was a white metal wristwatch on the left forearm of the body and that the glass of that watch was cracked.

The woman was wearing a black overcoat, black dress, slip, singlet and underpants. The front of the dress was torn from the neck to the hem and also sideways at the waist. The slip and singlet had both been torn in half, while the underpants had been torn away from one leg. The body was still wearing stockings, and these were held in place by garters above the knees. Both shoes were still on the feet. There was a belt around the body's waist, and they noted that this had been cinched very tightly. They noted too that the torn clothes had been drawn back deliberately in a way intended to expose the woman's breasts and pubic area.

Dr Green was then allowed to conduct a medical examination of the body at the scene. Green noted that the woman had bled from the mouth, nose and ears and that there was heavy bruising to both her eyes and her windpipe. There was a small gash just behind the right temple, one that had not been apparent when the body was examined by the policemen. An examination of the back of her head revealed a fractured skull, which Green believed would have been serious enough to have caused lacerations to the brain but, by itself, would probably not have led to death. Green could find no signs of attempted sexual intercourse and because he could see that the woman's purse still contained money, he assumed that robbery had not been a motive either. He used a rectal thermometer to measure the body's temperature and estimated from this that the woman had been dead for between four and six hours. As he had completed his examination around 8 a.m., he gave a time of death of between 2 a.m. and 4 a.m.

Dr Green told the detectives that he believed strangulation had been the cause of death, while noting that the skull fracture had been a serious one. He also offered his opinion that the killer had left the body only to later return to rearrange it and admire his handiwork.

•

As well as a small amount of money and other valuables, there was enough material in the woman's handbag for a tentative identification to be made. That identification was confirmed later on Sunday when her father affirmed that yes, indeed, the body at the morgue was that of his daughter, Ivy Dargavel/McLeod.

The following day, a post-mortem examination of Ivy's body was undertaken by Dr Redford Wright-Smith in the City Morgue on Batman Avenue, near the city centre and overlooking the railyards of Flinders Street. His examination confirmed Dr Green's of the day before; death was the result of strangulation coincident with a severe fracture of the skull.

•

Around the time that Ivy McLeod's body was being cleaned up and placed on a viewing table for later identification, Eddie Leonski was in the public bar of the Hotel Victoria on Beaconsfield Parade, drinking beer. Around 11 a.m., he bumped into a soldier he knew, Corporal John McPhillips, also of Headquarters Company in the 52nd Signallers. The two spoke for a while, and Eddie borrowed four shillings from McPhillips before the corporal headed off elsewhere.

McPhillips returned to the Victoria around 3.30 p.m. that afternoon, around the time that Ivy McLeod's father was identifying his daughter's remains. Eddie Leonski was still there, drinking with a group of soldiers that now included Private Forrest Piercy.

Eddie was slightly drunk and had now been AWOL for thirty hours.

5.

SID MCGUFFIE, DETECTIVE

The headlines on the front pages of Melbourne's daily newspapers on Monday, 4 May spoke of Japanese advances in Asia and German retreats in the Soviet Union. There were smaller front-page stories of Australian politicians abroad drumming up support for their beleaguered nation and of Australian soldiers, sailors and airmen performing individual acts of bravery on far-flung battlefields. On another day when thousands of men and women were being killed on and off the front lines, a reader would have to go a little further to find reporting of one individual killed in an act of sheer malice.

The story was there, though, generally on page two or three, and the newspapers didn't hold back in their reporting:

Battered and naked, the body of a red-haired woman was found at 6.45 a.m. yesterday in the recessed doorway of a beauty salon in Victoria Avenue, near Beaconsfield Parade, Albert Park. Her clothes had been ripped from her body and were lying under her . . . Death was due to a fracture of the skull, apparently caused by a blow or by striking her head in a struggle with her assailant.

There was evidence that she struggled violently . . . Detectives
believe that criminal assault was the motive for the attack. The
woman's handbag contained 33/3d., cigarettes, matches, lipstick
and toilet articles . . . Late yesterday she was identified as Mrs. Ivy
McLeod, 33 [sic]*, of Victoria Street, East Melbourne.*

Most newspapers also mentioned that the murder was being invest-
igated by a team of detectives from Victoria Police's Homicide
Squad, some even identifying that team – Detective Inspector
Carey, Detective Sub-Inspector McKerral, Detective Sergeant
McGuffie, Senior Detective Hackwill and Detectives Mooney
and Page. Like many reports in the newspapers that day, the
Sun's story contained a mix of fact, fiction and filler; enough of
the first to inform and titillate and enough of the other two to
suggest that someone actually understood what had happened
and was in the process of doing something about it.

•

The Homicide Squad, and the larger Victoria Police force, had
gone through a lot of upheaval since the end of World War I,
with a police strike and ongoing problems between rank-and-
file policemen and their leaders during the 1920s. The following
decade was more stable and the force was in the process of
consolidation and professionalisation when World War II broke
out. It had set itself the goal of becoming Australia's best, and
was slowly and painfully getting there. If Victoria Police was
Australia's premier police service, within that elite force the
Homicide Squad had set itself similar goals. The outbreak of war
had an immediate impact and – unfortunately, and despite the
best efforts of the government to maintain the size and quality
of the force – a number of police resigned to volunteer for army

service. The Homicide Squad then stood out from the general force in that its membership was barely touched by the war. Homicide detectives had worked so hard to get there they were not going to give up their select status easily.

The Victoria Police Homicide Squad did not operate in the way some newspapers seemed to think it did. The senior officers – Harry Carey and his deputy Alec McKerral – provided leadership and direction while the actual investigations, the hard slog of detective work, was undertaken by small teams of two or three, generally led by a sergeant or a senior detective. The team leader reported on progress and problems with individual murder investigations. He – they were all men – would request more or different resources, recommend avenues for further investigation and identify relevant legal and jurisdictional issues. For the McLeod murder investigation, Detective Inspector Carey directed Detective Sergeant Sid McGuffie to take charge of the investigation.

Sidney Harold McGuffie was then at the peak of his profession, an experienced investigator whose name was a byword for determination and success within the police ranks. He was also a bit of a character, living with his wife in Buckley Street, Essendon, where he garaged his pride and joy – a bright red Lancia sedan which he drove to work whenever he could. McGuffie had joined the police in 1911 as a twenty-year-old, and after seven years in uniform had joined the Detectives Bureau, where he would spend most of the next twenty-five years, many of them within the Homicide Squad.

•

Sid McGuffie probably came closer than any other member of the Victoria Police to what the public expected a hard-bitten detective to be. He seemed to have a penchant for getting his name in the newspaper so that, at times, he could seem to be constantly at the forefront of crime fighting in Victoria. This public notice started early in Sid's police career. A newspaper report from early 1915 outlined how he had two teeth knocked out and sustained an ankle injury when attempting to make an arrest. Most of his reported exploits involved the stuff of the comic books which were starting to become popular: knocking out criminals who tried to escape arrest, going undercover to make an insider arrest, and firing shots in the air before arresting a notorious standover man – all these in just one year, 1920.

By then, Sid McGuffie was a detective, and his work had changed from street policing to more sophisticated criminal investigations. In the early 1920s, he often worked with a Detective Tognini, and the cases they worked on were many and varied. They included a gold theft in Ararat, complex fraud cases in Melbourne, the abduction and rape of a schoolgirl in Essendon and a number of murders. The most spectacular of the murder cases occupied the front pages of Melbourne news-papers several times in 1923 and grew out of a missing girl and a botched abortion, regrettably quite common in those days. This case also involved the recovery of a headless body from the Yarra River, careful and methodical detective work by McGuffie and the forensic skills of a pathologist named Dr Crawford Mollison.

McGuffie's work also brought him into contact with one of the Melbourne underworld's more colourful figures, Leslie 'Squizzy' Taylor. In 1921, Sid arrested a 'well-dressed young man', Squizzy, and charged him with loitering with intent after observing him intently watching a bank in Thornbury, which was subsequently robbed by associates of Taylor. A more serious confrontation occurred at the Shanghai Café in Exhibition Street,

Melbourne, in 1924. McGuffie was attached to the motor police night squad at the time and had occasion to speak to Taylor at 2 a.m. in the café. Words were exchanged, a fight started and spilled out onto the street, and Sid subsequently arrested Taylor.

Somewhere between the café and the City Watchhouse in Russell Street, Taylor offered McGuffie a 'tenner' (ten pounds) to let him go. At the Watchhouse, Squizzy was charged with using insulting words and attempting to bribe a police officer. Found guilty of the latter offence, Taylor was fined the 'tenner' that he had originally offered up. The possibility of further front-page episodes involving Sid and Squizzy ended forever when Taylor was shot dead in a gunfight with another gangster in 1927.

While there would be an occasional report about Detective McGuffie being involved in foot chases through city streets and fistfights while executing warrants, he was increasingly involved in the routine investigation work that underpins all police detectives' activities. He now worked regularly with Detective Harry Carey and the two gradually rose through the ranks of the police force. By 1941, Sid was a Detective Sergeant and Carey was a Detective Inspector; together they formed the backbone of the Homicide Squad, which had formed just a few years earlier.

By May 1942, Sid McGuffie felt that he had a lot to be thankful for. Twenty-five years earlier, as a young uniformed policeman, he had married Lillian Graham in the Victorian goldfields town of Carisbrook, where Lillian's father, Bill Graham, was the local policeman. Sid and Lillian McGuffie had one child, a daughter they named Lillian Merle who, in April 1941, married John Hortlang. One year later, in April 1942, Sid and Lillian became grandparents when their daughter gave birth to a girl, Janet Lillian Hortlang.

Three weeks after this celebrated event, Detective Sergeant Sid McGuffie was looking at the body of a woman who had been brutally murdered and then put on public display by someone whose motives – and whose very humanity – Sid could only speculate about. It was back to work for the detective.

•

McGuffie had gone to the crime scene and had been shaken by what he had seen there. The ferocity of the attack on Ivy McLeod and the careful staging of the murder scene, the almost voyeuristic arrangement of the victim's body, convinced him that this murder was different from others, just as the murderer himself – it could not possibly have been done by a woman – was different from most others. In many ways the murderer's final act had been to show off his handiwork, to put it on public display, as if he was proud of what he had done. When someone suggested that the body had been arranged so that it would not be visible from the street, McGuffie rejected it almost immediately. No, it was a carefully arranged scene, designed to both confront whoever found the body while showing a depth of hatred towards women. This aspect, more than any other, had convinced McGuffie that the murderer would strike again.

At Inspector Carey's direction, McGuffie put together a small team, with just two others to assist him, a team he believed could work the case successfully. To undertake most of the casework he chose Fred Adam. Still a relatively young man, his bright red hair meant that Adam was almost always referred to as 'Blue' or 'Bluey'. Adam had joined the Victoria Police in 1928 and, like Sid McGuffie, spent several years in uniform before transferring to the Detectives Bureau and then the Homicide Squad. He was regarded by his peers as a good detective and also as one of the force's best interrogators. To do most of the legwork, McGuffie brought a promising young detective named George Murray into the team. McGuffie also informed the rest of the Homicide Squad that he believed the murderer would strike again and warned his team that they would be on call for twenty-four hours a day.

Working through things logically on Sunday afternoon and again on Monday morning, Sid McGuffie and his team tried to narrow down what was potentially a very large field of suspects. Ivy McLeod, a single woman, had been killed early on a Sunday morning. Taking Sunday morning as an extension of Saturday night suggested that Ivy had probably met her murderer on Saturday night. She was dressed smartly. What do smartly dressed women do on a Saturday night? They go out, generally with or to see friends, and those friends usually include males. As a starting point, they would look for any males who had been with Ivy on Saturday night.

Sid was not aware that, around the time they were drawing up plans based on this logic, the very man they were seeking was talking to the police at another station. Then a phone rang in the Homicide Squad's home room.

•

John Thompson had been shocked when he read his morning paper with breakfast that Monday. He had slept in and was unaware of anything unusual happening in the neighbourhood until his landlady mentioned the 'terrible murder' that had taken place over the weekend and showed him a newspaper account of that murder. Though the name given was Ivy McLeod rather than Ivy Dargavel, there was no doubt at all that his friend Ivy had been killed shortly after she left his flat and had been killed in a particularly brutal manner. He knew that the police would be looking for him and that they may even regard him as a suspect. The decision he made was easy for the ex-soldier. After he finished breakfast, he dressed and walked to Albert Park police station where he told his story to the young policeman at the front desk. Shortly after 10 a.m., he was repeating his story in an interview room at Russell Street. Sid McGuffie and Fred Adam listened very closely.

What they heard was both positive and negative in terms of the investigation. The positive was that Thompson was able to fill in the missing details of the last few hours of Ivy McLeod's life. The times and places made sense. What they didn't tell Thompson was that the post-mortem examination of the contents of Ivy's stomach confirmed his story about beer and supper. Thompson appeared to be an honest and straightforward person who genuinely wanted to assist the police to solve a brutal crime. A quick check with the army authorities and the Commonwealth Aircraft Corporation's people revealed that Thompson not only had an impeccable service and employment history, he was held in very high regard by all who knew him. The negative aspect was that the person who, statistically, was most likely to be the killer, was not in fact that person. The murderer was still out there somewhere and they were only marginally closer to identifying him.

•

The team interviewed Harold Gibson again. His story remained consistent around the major points of his discoveries the previous morning. The timings were pretty solid, although some of the other details were a little fuzzy. One thing he could not be shaken on was his identification of the man in the alcove as being an

American soldier. That soldier was white and maybe a little taller than average. He was also wearing one of those funny little caps. While there was a real chance that the American was the killer, there was also a chance that he wasn't. The woman had been dead for several hours when Gibson found her. Perhaps the American, like Gibson, had simply stumbled upon the body, realised what it was and run away when he heard Gibson's footsteps, not wanting to become involved in whatever had happened.

Sid McGuffie discussed the various permutations of the case with Carey, who in turn spoke to his superintendent. They all agreed that, at this stage, they would not inform the US Army authorities about the possible involvement of one of their soldiers in a brutal murder.

•

McGuffie felt that the killer would probably try to follow the progress of the police investigation through the newspapers, as there seemed to be a clear element of exhibitionism in the crime. This meant that he would need to be more guarded in what information he released to the press and how he answered reporters' questions. There was always the possibility that a soldier from another country had been involved, a complication the press did not yet need to know about. But McGuffie realised that he would have to balance the needs of security with the need to generate lead information for his team to follow up. No one at the Bleak House Hotel or the homes nearby had seen or heard anything, the forensic evidence was very limited, and the only potential witness he had was Harold Gibson, and any identification Gibson made would probably be suspect.

The first newspaper reports were based broadly on what individual reporters' speculations on the crime might be: 'Police think that she may have been attacked earlier, and lain unconscious in the doorway for some time before her death . . .' By the following day, McGuffie was beginning to exert a degree of control over the direction the reporting was taking. 'Det. Sgt. McGuffie said detectives had been given good information which might help to solve the crime . . . McGuffie said that until investigations are taken further he could not advance a definite motive and he was hopeful the mystery would be cleared up soon.'

McGuffie continued the theme of giving as little as possible away while putting a positive spin on the fact that little progress was being made. 'New hope of solving the mystery surrounding the death . . . arose yesterday after intensive activities by detectives. [McGuffie], leader of an enlarged homicide squad, said that several new avenues had been opened following the long interview with the man who had been a friend . . . for the last seven months [sic]. He told police that she had been with him between 11 p.m. on Saturday night and 2 a.m. on Sunday.'

He also floated some theories about what had actually happened on Saturday night: 'Two theories receiving most attention by detectives are that Mrs McLeod had been attacked by a sexual maniac while she had been waiting for a tram or that she had been struck by someone whom she knew and had been waiting for her. A blow on her right temple, which had fractured her skull, coupled with shock, had caused her death. The sexual maniac could have ripped the clothing off her body to commit a criminal offence, but desisted when he had been disturbed, or the man waiting for her could have disarranged her clothing after she had died to divert attention.'

Sid McGuffie was offering up an interesting blend of fact and speculation, enough to interest the public and to suggest that the 'enlarged homicide squad' was pursuing two solid lines of enquiry. The real situation was, however, hinted at in the final paragraph. 'To assist these lines of inquiry police are anxious to receive information from anyone who saw a woman dressed in black with a pale blue scarf walking along Beaconsfield par. from Kerferd rd. to Victoria av. early on Sunday morning. She could have been alone, or in company with a man. Anyone knowing of her movements between 8pm and 11pm on Saturday could also give the police useful information and confirm a possibility that Mrs McLeod met with a man with whom she argued, who had followed her to Kerferd rd. and then waited until she left for the tram terminus.' And there it was; a request for public assistance coupled with an implicit admission that Ivy had been killed by a stranger, and that the police really had no idea who that stranger was.

•

McGuffie was soon leading an enlarged team – Senior Detective Mal Boyd and Detective Bill Mooney had been drafted into it. However, there was not a lot for that team to do beyond following up tips received from the public, interviewing the family and friends of Ivy McLeod in hope of something, anything, and door-knocking in the areas where Ivy was last seen alive, again in the hope of uncovering a clue to the identity of her killer. It was dull, mundane and routine work, but it had to be done.

Their enquiries revealed that Ivy preferred to use taxis rather than trams when both were available, so they undertook the thankless task of trying to identify and interview any taxi driver who may have driven Ivy from the city to Albert Park after 6 p.m. on Saturday night. They learned that there had been a party in progress at a house on the opposite side of Victoria Avenue to where Ivy had died, some distance down the road from the tram stop. Even though cars had been constantly coming and going from that party, the team were unable to find anyone who had seen a woman at or near the tram stop between 2.30 and 3.30 a.m. on the Sunday morning. They learned, too, that the telephone box from which Harold Gibson had phoned the police had no light inside, as the globe had been removed as part of the brownout. Had the globe been there, its light would have shone directly into the alcove where Ivy McLeod was murdered.

A substantial number of leads were telephoned in to the police, directly or through a suburban police station, including several from people who spoke about American soldiers in and around the Victoria and Bleak House hotels on Beaconsfield Parade on Saturday night. By mid-week, McGuffie had contacted the US Provost Corps – responsible for all military policing duties associated with the American military presence – at their Camp Pell barracks to tell them that an American soldier had been seen at the spot where Ivy McLeod's body had been found.

The Provost Corps had also been receiving plenty of tip-offs from the public and was struggling to both work through them and work out the significance of what they were hearing. An anonymous caller to their guard room at Camp Pell said that he had seen an American soldier bending over a woman he thought was asleep in the doorway of the beauty salon in Victoria Avenue next door to the Bleak House Hotel. As the caller watched him, the American straightened up, looked around, and walked away quickly.

An even more intriguing tip was received elsewhere. Two days after Ivy McLeod's murder, on Tuesday, 5 May, a private on duty at one of the US Army Headquarters offices in Melbourne answered a telephone call from a man who sounded American, but who also sounded as though he was trying to disguise his voice.

'About that dame who was murdered the other night,' the caller said, 'you should tell them to look for a man who walks on his hands.'

The private asked the caller for his name.

'Never mind about that, buddy,' was the reply. 'You just tell them to look for a guy who walks on his hands.'

The young soldier was uncertain about what to do, but he was an army private, so he simply followed the rules. He typed up the conversation as a report, which he then put into his wire outbox to be forwarded to the Provost Corps at Camp Pell.

•

By the end of the week, reporting on the murder had disappeared from the newspapers, partly because there was nothing new to report. The headlines now revealed that a major naval battle was beginning to the north-east of Australia in the Coral Sea. Japanese aircraft carriers and fleet support were in contact with American aircraft carriers with Australian fleet support. None of the papers resorted to hysteria, although one or two went perilously close. All agreed that the fate of Australia could well depend on the outcome of what they were calling the 'Battle of the Coral Sea'.

If that was not disturbing enough, Prime Minister Curtin would soon drop a bombshell of his own. At the start of the month, he had announced that the rationing of basic commodities would be introduced at some stage soon by his government; the announcement caused an immediate rush to purchase those commodities. On Friday, 8 May, Curtin issued another statement in which he announced that the government was about to introduce a quota system. Clothing, for example, would be limited to seventy-five per cent of the 1941 production figures. The real bombshell though, was that the quota system would come into force on the following Monday.

The announcement would cause panic-buying in both Melbourne and Sydney. Coupled with the major naval battle developing off Australia's north-east coast, there was plenty for people to be thinking about on that Friday night. A single death the previous weekend suddenly didn't seem so significant anymore.

6.

MRS PAULINE BUCHAN THOMPSON

Pauline Thompson was an attractive woman. Just entering her thirties, she had a glow around her that reflected her boundless energy. A little over average height with a shock of dark hair and a beautiful figure, Pauline had the looks and the poise that turned heads whenever she entered a room.

She had married a young policeman named Les Thompson in August 1934, and life had been good. They had both wanted a family, but for a while feared it was not to be, so they adopted a son, a lovely little boy they named Bruce. As is often the way, Pauline fell pregnant a short time later and subsequently gave birth to a little girl they named Caroline.

Les was posted to the old goldfields town of Bendigo, and the young family was happy. As well as being busy as only a young mother can be, Pauline pursued a number of theatrical activities. She was a talented musician and had a beautiful singing voice. Moreover, she loved the entertainment industry, and harboured a secret desire to become an entertainer herself.

Pauline threw herself into the local scene, and within twelve months of arriving had successfully set up women's and children's performing groups, even arranging regular performances for them on local radio stations. She performed whenever she could, both solo and in larger groups of entertainers, orchestras, bands and the like – in Bendigo though, the opportunities were limited. Depending on the circumstances, Pauline would often use a different name for her performances. Sometimes it was Pauline and sometimes it was Coral; sometimes it was Thompson and sometimes it was O'Brien. It was almost as if there were a number of personalities living in her body.

Both Pauline and Les were community-minded and took the opportunities that Bendigo provided to put something back into that community. They became tireless workers for charity, focusing their efforts each year – and raising large sums of money – on functions they organised in association with the annual Bendigo Easter Fair. Between times, they did a lot of work raising money for the charity they had adopted, the Bendigo Old Age and Invalid Pensioners' League.

By 1941, Bendigo was starting to feel distinctly provincial to Pauline. The war had drained the city of most of its young men and a large number of its young women. The young men had enlisted in the armed services while the young women had either enlisted as well or taken up employment in one of the relatively highly paid jobs that were available in and around Melbourne. While some were in war-related industries, many more were back-filling positions left behind by men enlisting for war service. The departure of so many young people decimated Bendigo's entertainment scene. Pauline would perform in variety shows for troops in the camps scattered around Bendigo, but they were bit parts doing things others scheduled for her. If Melbourne was where things were happening, well, then, Melbourne was where she would go.

There were heated words and there may even have been tears, but an agreement of sorts was reached. Les would remain in Bendigo; he would, however, start applying for a transfer to Melbourne. Their little son, Bruce, would remain with him. He had just started school, was enjoying it and was doing well. Pauline would go to Melbourne to seek work, accommodation and the opportunity to become involved in war-related charity work. She would use that involvement to try to develop a career as an entertainer.

Four-year-old Caroline would go with her mother to Melbourne but would stay with relatives who would be able to look after her during the day. The family would spend every weekend together, either in Bendigo or in Melbourne. When Les's transfer came through, they would rent or buy a house somewhere in Melbourne and again live together as a family.

Pauline moved to Melbourne in November 1941. She first boarded in South Melbourne, but wanted to be closer to the city centre. Six months later, on the weekend of 2–3 May 1942, Pauline moved into a room on the top floor of Morningside House, a three-storey brick, stone and plaster building located at 13 Spring Street, on the edge of the central business district. Number 13 was the first in a row of several similar buildings that extended to the north. Once the city homes for wealthy Victorians, Number 13 was, like its neighbours, raised above street level, and to get onto the verandah and into the house it was necessary to climb up stone steps.

In 1942, Number 13 was being run as a boarding house, and most of its rooms were occupied by young women who, like Pauline, had moved to Melbourne from country Victoria. The proprietors, a Mr and Mrs Phillip Hawkes, had only met

Pauline once since she moved in; she had introduced herself as
Coral Thompson.

Within a few days of arriving in Melbourne, Pauline was
working as a typist and stenographer in the main office of the
International Harvester Company, located in City Road, South
Melbourne. Within a few days more, she had picked up a second,
part-time job, working as a switchboard attendant at radio station
3AW in the evenings. She was busy but she was happy. She also
took to calling herself Coral on most occasions.

•

Friday, 8 May was always going to be a busy, busy day for
Pauline Thompson. Her efforts to become involved in war
support work and entertainment were beginning to pay off,
although not entirely in the way she'd hoped. The shows and
cabarets that most interested her were generally organised by
large organisations like the Salvation Army, and Pauline saw no
real opportunities there.

With the opening of the Pacific War and the arrival of significant numbers of Americans, new venues and new opportunities
presented themselves. There was an American Hospitality Club
that had opened in Elizabeth Street in the city, catering specifically and exclusively to American servicemen. Nearby was the
Union Club, which had opened its doors to servicemen of all
nationalities. Other cafés and clubs soon followed suit. Through
her work on the switchboard at the radio station, Pauline knew
of all of these and more, and was slowly working her way into
that scene. She was now Coral, the budding entertainer and
entrepreneur.

On that Friday night she had organised for a group of girls
from International Harvester to go to a dance at the Music

Lovers' Club in Flinders Street in the city. All funds raised at the function were to go towards the purchase of an ambulance for the army. Pauline had made certain that there would be plenty of Americans there through her contacts at the Hospitality Club. She thought that afterwards they might all like to relax a bit at the opening of the Dug Out Club, a new club debuting that night in Swanston Street.

She was also switching her work at 3AW from weekday nights to weekends, a change commencing that weekend. She would leave the weekend entertainments to the big players and, as Coral O'Brien, try to build up her profile as a welfare/entertainment entrepreneur during the week.

It was a balancing act made a little more complicated by the social life she was also beginning to build. Pauline would have bristled if she had heard anyone describe her as either 'fast' or 'loose', but those were the descriptions that others may well have used to describe her. She was a married woman with two small children, but in Melbourne she found that she enjoyed the company of other men. She also found that there were plenty of men who enjoyed her company and who actively sought her out.

The previous week, for instance, she had met a young American at the Union Club. He had told her that his name was Justin James Jones, but that everyone called him Jimmy. He had also said that he was an artilleryman with a coastal artillery regiment, that he'd only been in Australia a few weeks and that he was based at Camp Pell. In return, she told him that her name was Coral O'Brien, and that she was single. The young American – he was only twenty years old – had developed an obvious infatuation with her. When she told him that she was moving to a new flat in Spring Street, he spotted an opportunity, for he turned up at her door on Monday, Tuesday and Wednesday that week, using the pretext of helping her to move in. He was a sweet young man, and they had kissed and cuddled, but she was going to put a few boundaries on where they went from there. She had agreed to have dinner with him at the Hospitality Club at 7 p.m. Friday evening, and would raise the issue with him, gently, then.

Friday would also be busy because she would be catching up with Les. He had phoned earlier in the week to say that he was escorting a prisoner to Melbourne on Friday and hoped to be able to catch up with her. He said he might bring Bruce, who was now on school holidays. They had agreed to meet in the city at lunchtime. Pauline Buchan Thompson had well and truly left Bendigo behind.

•

Pauline caught a tram into the city from her workplace in South Melbourne at lunchtime. It was a short trip and at 12.25 p.m. she was standing outside St Paul's Cathedral, on the corner of Flinders and Swanston streets. Right on cue, her husband and son arrived. The three walked up Swanston Street to Lyons' Café, where they found a table, sat down and ordered a light lunch.

While they waited for their meals, they talked. Bruce told his mother about school and his plans for the school holidays, Les spoke about his ongoing attempts to transfer to Melbourne, while Pauline broadly described her day job and her work with the radio station. She said she was starting to have some success in war support and entertainment and outlined what she had organised for that evening. Speaking just to Les, she said that she had arranged to have dinner with an American soldier that evening. Les was surprised and asked why, obviously annoyed. Pauline spoke of organising entertainment for American audiences as well as Australian and, besides, she was meeting her girlfriends from work immediately afterwards.

It made the lunch a little frosty. Pauline left shortly after 1 p.m., saying that she had to get back to work, but also saying that she would see them at the railway station before they went back to Bendigo. Les and Bruce Thompson headed off to do some shopping and sightseeing.

And there she was again, at Platform One at Spencer Street station at 5.35 p.m. Les and Pauline spoke again about her dinner date with the American, a bit more conciliatory this time, and she was positive about how things were and how things would be. Pauline then hugged and kissed her husband and her son, and stood alone to watch them board the train, and then watched that train depart. The 5.40 p.m. to Bendigo pulled out of the station precisely on time.

•

Pauline knew the city and knew the trams and estimated that she had just enough time to get back to her room, get changed and get to the café in the Hospitality Club in time to meet Jimmy Jones there at 7 p.m. In her room, she looked at what she had to wear and decided it was Friday night, so she should dress up a bit. Tomorrow night she would be starting her weekend shifts at 3AW, so tonight would have to be her big night out this week. She had her period, and she and Les had exchanged words and looks that she already wished they hadn't; it had been a stressful day. Dressing up usually lifted her spirits, though, and besides, you never knew what might happen. She would relax and be Coral O'Brien for a few hours.

•

She was at the café at 7 p.m. on the dot. Jimmy Jones wasn't, which she found surprising, in light of the puppy love he had been so clearly displaying. She sat alone at a table in the café until 7.15 p.m. when she lit a cigarette and looked around. There were lots of people coming and going and there, at the entrance, was a tall, blond American soldier looking at her. When their eyes met, he smiled a big, broad grin that lit up his face. She smiled back, and the soldier nodded his head and weaved his way through the tables to hers, where he asked if he could sit down. She nodded. As he sat, the soldier said, 'Been stood up, eh?'

'It seems that way,' she replied.

'Boy, whoever stood you up must have had something very important to do,' he said, and added, 'I'm sorry. My name's Eddie. How are you going?'

'A lot better now,' she said, 'and, by the way, my name's Coral O'Brien.'

•

The deluge which had been threatening all day had arrived with a vengeance late in the afternoon. At times it looked like curtains of rain were sweeping from one end of the street to the other. City trams were packed – it was Friday night – and it was impossible to find a taxi. Jimmy Jones knew he was going to be late, but hoped that Coral would still be there, waiting for him. What a babe! He arrived at the café just on 7.30 p.m., looked around and couldn't see her anywhere.

Jimmy sat and thought for a while. There was a telephone outside the café and he used it to call Coral's boarding house; she wasn't there and no one had seen her. He left and walked all the way to Spring Street, to the boarding house, and upstairs to her room on the top floor. He knocked on her door and called out her name, but there was no response to either, and when he put his ear to the door, he could not hear any movement within. Disappointed, the young man returned to Camp Pell where he went to bed. He wondered what had happened to Coral.

•

'I actually came into town to have a drink,' Eddie said. 'But I guess this place only serves coffee and soda pop.'

'I think they also do a very nice tea,' Coral responded. 'But if you want something a little bit stronger than that, I do know a place up the hill a bit where you could go.'

'That's great, but would you consider joining me?' Eddie asked.

Coral thought for a moment. Jimmy was probably still on his way, but maybe Jimmy could wait a bit. It might cool him down. 'Why not?' she replied.

•

They were able to shelter beneath awnings for part of the way along Elizabeth Street, then up Collins Street over Swanston, Russell and Exhibition and then down a wide lane. Where there were no awnings for protection, they ducked into doorways to avoid the rain which still swept over the city in regular waves. It was slow going, but it was also fun to do.

'Where the hell are you taking me?' Eddie asked at one point.

'The Astoria Hotel,' Coral said back, her voice a bit louder than normal because of the noise the rain was making. 'I think you'll like it,' she added in a lower tone.

The Astoria Hotel was in Collins Place, south of Collins Street and on the corner of Flinders Lane; it was only a couple of blocks from Morningside House. Had he not been with Coral, Eddie thought he probably would have missed it. The brownout, the lowering sky and the occasional rain squall made all the buildings just dark, lumpy shapes, and he found it almost impossible to distinguish one from another. But at one corner, Coral paused and, sure enough, a door opened in a building opposite and a soldier emerged. Behind the soldier, Eddie could see a kind of lounge, people sitting and a thin haze of cigarette smoke.

'There it is,' said Coral, and they crossed the road and went into the hotel.

•

The lounge at the Astoria Hotel was quite small, and there were a dozen or so people sitting in little groups around tables when Eddie and Coral entered. A couple of them glanced up, but no one really took any notice as the new arrivals sat down at a table a little apart from the others. Eddie asked Coral what she would like to drink, and was surprised when she asked for a gin squash without ice. Eddie thought that it sounded like an interesting way to drink gin and decided to join Coral in her choice of drink. He walked to the bar and ordered two gin squashes, no ice. When they arrived, he paid the barman the exact amount.

The barman was a middle-aged man named Alfred Bliss, and he would always have a bad memory for timings. He would later recall that an American soldier and the woman arrived sometime between 10 and 11 p.m., then it became between 9 and 10 p.m., and, finally, possibly it could even have been a bit before 9 p.m. He would also have trouble with the American, being unable to remember anything but the most obvious; he was American, he was a soldier and he wore a uniform.

Other things he recalled quite clearly. The couple were drinking gin squashes without ice, they had at least half a dozen in the first hour they were there and both of them would always pay him the exact amount and not leave him a tip. And the woman was extremely attractive.

Eddie and Coral really seemed to enjoy one another's company. Eddie spoke about growing up in New York City, how his mother coped, his time in the army, and how he saw Australia and its people. Coral spoke about her war-related work in Melbourne and Bendigo, the radio station and how she hoped to forge a career in the entertainment industry, preferably as an entertainer herself but, if that was not to be, then in some kind of organisational or promotional role.

At one point Coral got up to go to the bathroom and there bumped into Esther Grunden, a girl she had gone to secretarial school with. She told Esther that she had been stood up earlier in the evening, but had met another American, and they were doing just fine.

And it went on. Eddie asked Coral to sing him something and she did. She really did have a beautiful singing voice, and he complimented her on it. At another point, Eddie realised that he had run out of money; Coral said that was all right, that she had money and that she would shout. Eddie said that he would rather listen to her singing than listen to her shouting. They laughed at that. Coral also said that while Jimmy Jones was cute, she also had other male friends and, no, she was not married.

At 10.45, Alfred Bliss called out that it was time for last drink orders, that he would be closing the doors when those drinks were finished and that it would then be goodnight to all. Coral bought them both a final gin squash. Eddie said that it still looked lousy outside, and if she didn't mind, he'd walk her home. Coral said that would be fine, she lived just a couple of blocks away.

It was probably approaching 11.30 when they eventually left the Astoria. The rain and wind had eased off, but there was still the occasional light shower. They were still able to duck into doorways to avoid getting wet. It was really just a short walk – it would have been no more than 400 metres – and they were in front of Morningside House within fifteen minutes of leaving the hotel. On the way he had again asked her to sing; she had, and he was again struck by the beauty of her voice.

They opened the gates and walked to the steps that led up to the verandah and the front door of the boarding house. The steps were undercover and they climbed the first couple to be out of the rain and then stopped. They both had a cigarette; hers, because he had run out of those at the hotel, too. Coral said that she had really enjoyed the evening, and that they should do it again. She tilted her head up for a farewell kiss, and Eddie killed her.

His arms shot out, his hands gripped her throat and as he felt the energy surge through to his fingertips he squeezed as hard as he could. This one was not going to die easily; she tried to break his grip, and she tried to kick him or at least get a better position on the steps to ease the terrible pressure she felt. While she was surprisingly strong, he was stronger, and he squeezed again, harder. Suddenly, she stopped struggling and went completely limp in his arms. He knew she was dead, and he lowered her gently back onto the steps.

Eddie stood back and looked down at her. He had of course seen through her right from the start. She was just like all the others, and everything that had happened during the evening was always going to lead to this. Did she think he was stupid? He had a pretty good idea of what she actually did with Jimmy Jones and those other 'male friends' she had spoken about.

Well, if that was what she wanted, that was what she'd get. He thought for a moment, then undid the front of his trousers and lowered himself down to the steps. He'd do her first, and then arrange her like the other one, so everyone would know exactly what she was.

•

Sometime later – it could have been minutes, it may have been an hour – Eddie was finished and was again looking down at Coral. He thought he heard footsteps in the distance. He picked up Coral's handbag and left, closing the gate behind him. He had killed Coral O'Brien and, in doing so, had also killed Pauline Thompson.

•

Henry McGowan was a contract nightwatchman and regarded himself as being pretty thorough and careful in his job. Each evening, he would catch a tram into the city from his home in Elwood for work. He had his own territory to watch over every night, a block of Melbourne's city centre bounded by Flinders Street on the south, Spring Street on the east, Collins Street on the north and Russell Street on the west. It was, he thought, a particularly interesting part of town as it held a greater variety than other, purely commercial areas. His beat contained bits of everything: residential blocks in Spring Street, upmarket shops and cafés on Collins, sweatshop tailors in Flinders Lane, plus a veritable rabbit warren of lanes and alleyways.

Henry had his own system for his work. He was required to punch a time clock in a building at 9 Spring Street every hour, so he had devised a way of covering his area, moving in an anti-clockwise route that took him precisely sixty minutes. The timings were right on that Friday night, but Henry would admit that he might not have been as thorough as he normally was. The rain was the problem. It was heavy and it came in sheets. Henry had a raincoat, so for him personally the main result of the rain was a bit of discomfort. The rain also interfered with his work though, and at times it was so thick that he couldn't see all the things that he wanted to see. At other times it forced him to make little shortcuts.

Fortunately, it had started to ease before midnight, and by the time he started his 4 a.m. circuit, there were increasingly long periods between the showers. It was this lifting of the steady rain that allowed Henry to identify something unusual in Corporation Lane, a cul de sac that ran alongside a building at 89 Flinders Lane. It was a woman's handbag which had been emptied of all its contents and thrown away. The contents were strewn around the entrance to the lane and Henry carefully collected them. There was all the usual paraphernalia that you would expect to find, cosmetics and the like, but Henry also found two small photographs of a young boy and a young girl. Henry put all the contents back into the bag and dropped it off at the office of an all-night garage in Flinders Lane. He would try to have a closer look at it in daylight.

The diversion had thrown Henry's timings off, and it was probably several minutes after 5 a.m. when he again punched the time clock in the office in Spring Street. Having done so, Henry started on his next circuit, but had only gone a few metres when he thought he saw something unusual on the front steps of Morningside House. There was a bundle of something on the steps and he shone his torch on that bundle.

Henry felt as though someone had punched him in the chest and knocked all the air out of him. For a moment he couldn't move and he couldn't breathe. In the cone of light that his torch threw was the body of a woman, sprawled back on the steps leading up to the front door of the boarding house. The woman's head was resting on one step, and her shoulders and arms were on the step below. The woman's clothes were all bunched up around her waist; those from the top had been pulled down and those below her waist pulled up. Her legs had been splayed, exposing her entire pubic area. The woman's eyes were closed.

McGowan reacted quickly. He understood that the woman was well beyond any assistance he could offer. On the footpath behind him, a few metres away, was a telephone box. He ran to it, telephoned the police on the D24 number and told the person who answered the details of what he had just found.

•

He didn't have long to wait. Within five minutes of Henry making the call, a police car pulled up in front of Morningside House and two policemen climbed out and walked across to where he stood. One of them introduced himself as Constable Des Birch of the Mobile Traffic Section; he nodded towards his partner and said, 'Constable Job.' Birch added that they had been around the corner in Flinders Street when the call came in. Leaving Constable Job at the front gate, Birch went over to the body with Henry. He leaned over and touched one of the legs; it was cold.

Birch told Job to stay where he was, and to listen for any calls on their car radio. Birch would secure the crime scene until the detectives arrived. He also asked Henry McGowan to stay with them.

Again, they didn't have long to wait. Senior Detective Mal Boyd had been the duty officer in McGuffie's team, and he was on site at Morningside House by 6 a.m. While he waited for McGuffie and the other members of the team to arrive, he undertook a preliminary examination of the crime scene.

He noted that the body was that of a young woman, lying on her back. Her legs were wide apart and her clothing had been disturbed, with the front of her body now completely exposed. He also noted that the woman's stockings and suspender belt had been pulled down to her ankles, one shoe was off and what appeared to be red and green beads from a necklace were strewn around the body. He had just finished writing down these observations in his notebook when the police doctor, Dr Alan McCutcheon, arrived, followed soon after by Sid McGuffie and the rest of the squad.

While Dr McCutcheon conducted an initial examination of the body by torchlight, Sid McGuffie directed his team to undertake a detailed inventory of the crime scene while he spoke to Henry McGowan about the circumstances surrounding his discovery of the body.

Working carefully and methodically, the team noted that Morningside House had an iron fence and an iron gate opening onto Spring Street at the front. A short path ran from that front gate to eleven stone steps which rose up to the front door and to a verandah that ran across the front of the building. They noted that the woman's body lay sprawled across several steps and was facing upwards. Her head was resting on the sixth step and was inclined slightly to the right. Her right arm was extended with her right hand touching part of an iron balustrade. Her left arm and hand were lying alongside her body. A book and a newspaper were on the ground at the base of the steps. There was also a cigarette packet and a box of matches on the ground, while two cigarette butts had been crushed out on the steps. There were some coloured glass beads under the neck of the body and others on the steps; several seemed to have been crushed underfoot.

Dr McCutcheon was joined in his examination of the body by the Government Analyst, Dr Charles Taylor. The two doctors completed their examination quite quickly, considering the circumstances, and gave McGuffie and Boyd their preliminary assessment. The woman had been dead for between four and six hours. She had been strangled; there were distinctive bruise marks on her neck and the general appearance of her facial features was consistent with strangulation. They also noted that the victim had her period at the time she died, and that it appeared that some menstrual blood had mixed with rainwater below the body.

By now, it was starting to grow light and the crime scene was becoming more noticeable. McGuffie asked Constable Birch if he had anything they could use to put over the body. Birch went to the patrol car and returned with a blanket which he and Job placed carefully over the deceased. He directed the other detectives to either conduct a careful search for clues around the crime scene or to start cataloguing and interviewing the occupants of Morningside House, beginning with those on the ground floor and asking whether they had seen or heard anything the previous night.

McGuffie himself accompanied Henry McGowan back to the all-night garage where he had left the handbag he had found a couple of hours earlier. It was still in the office there and hadn't been touched. Looking through it, McGuffie found a door key with a Morningside House tag attached to it. The pair returned to the crime scene where McGuffie was introduced to Phillip Hawkes, the proprietor, who confirmed the identity of the key, and said it belonged to a third-storey room leased recently by a woman named Coral Thompson. He added that he had only ever met the woman once.

A quick examination of the room found enough to suggest that the body outside was indeed that of a woman named Thompson, while a number of documents indicated that Pauline Thompson was the correct name. When he returned to the front of the building, McGuffie was informed that those nearest the crime scene had neither seen nor heard anything the previous evening or in the early morning. Mr and Mrs Hawkes lived on the ground floor, their bedroom was at the front and they slept with the bedroom window open. They had heard nothing.

The police photographer had been and gone, his activities overseen by Mal Boyd. A mortuary wagon was parked in Spring Street; Sid McGuffie authorised the removal of the body for a short trip to the City Morgue. A couple of detectives did a final sweep of the crime scene to ensure that they had not missed anything, and then the crowd started to drift away. McGuffie was worried because he thought he knew what all this meant, but he would sit down with his team in a little while and they would work through things. That was what good policemen did. In the meantime, it was 7.30 a.m. on what looked like being a better day than yesterday. Weather-wise anyway. McGuffie realised he was hungry.

•

It was shaping up to be a good day for Eddie Leonski too. It was approaching mid-morning and he had almost finished supervising the feeding of several hundred hungry soldiers and soon the rest of the day would be his. He thought he would probably start out at the Parkville Hotel and then see what happened. At least money wouldn't be a problem.

Eddie was also happy because he thought he may have committed the perfect crime. The woman was a stranger, there was no pre-existing relationship between them and she had not had the opportunity to tell anyone who he was. He had left nothing behind at the place where he had killed her and when he had gone through her handbag, he had made certain that he had rubbed everything he touched on his pants leg to make certain any fingerprints he left behind would be smudged beyond recognition. The bonus was that there had been more than enough money in her purse to cover the cost of the taxi he caught back to Camp Pell. He now had a bit of extra money to play around with.

There was a shadow over it all, though. Eddie knew that what he was doing was wrong and he was certain that anyone he knew would never consider what he had done as anything but a crime. And yet in the lead-up, those moments of quite delicious anticipation, and in the act of killing itself, it just felt *right*. Eddie struggled to reconcile the sentiments, and it could cause an almost physical pain when he did. But he had learned to move on. The Parkville Hotel would be open soon and he needed to change uniforms.

7.

THE BROWNOUT STRANGLER

From the beginning of May, the shorter days that presaged the onset of winter combined with the effects of Melbourne's brownout to make the nights both longer and more dangerous for the city's residents. Reduced speed limits on the roads may have been of some assistance to drivers and pedestrians alike, but the fact remained that travel in the brownout was sometimes fraught with risk. Road accidents now occurred every night. Some nights there were multiple crashes and some nights there were fatalities. To make things that little bit worse, May brought with it more rain than any of the locals could ever remember.

The accidents were between cars and cars, trucks and cars, trams and cars, and between all three types of vehicles and pedestrians. They occurred all over Melbourne, but were increasingly concentrated in the Melbourne city centre and the inner suburbs. On the evening of 4 May, a US Army private was struck and seriously injured by an army truck in the city, while two wandering horses were struck and killed in separate incidents in Port Melbourne during the first week of the month.

There were calls from a wide cross-section of society for the restrictions of the brownout to be eased if not removed altogether. The calls came from the general public and from unions representing tram and bus drivers, and from large and small business owners. They were calls that fell on deaf ears. The conservative premier of Victoria, Albert Dunstan, was adamant that the strict brownout conditions would be continued indefinitely. The problem was not with the brownout, he argued, but with the public's response to that brownout. Or rather, Dunstan suggested, the public's lack of response to the brownout.

Dunstan believed that common sense would dictate that in the prevailing conditions, people would go home when they had completed their day's tasks and then remain home until the next day. Instead, night after night and day after day people continued to crowd into the city for non-work reasons, for shopping and for the various forms of entertainment that were on offer there. If they simply stayed at home in the evening they would not be exposing themselves to any of the risks associated with the brownout and the cars and trucks and trams.

With the discovery of the body of Pauline Thompson in Spring Street, another risk could be added to the list. Somewhere in Melbourne there was at least one man who used the brownout as a cover for his own perverse and murderous purposes. He hid in the dark and the rain washed away all traces of his presence. There may be more than one man, or there may not be; it didn't really matter. The spectre out there which was killing women alone at night on the streets was given the name, 'The Brownout Strangler'.

•

Before anything could go forward in the murder investigations, there were certain formalities that had to be completed, protocols that had to be followed. A post-mortem examination of the body was undertaken by the Government Pathologist, Dr Crawford Mollison. He was able to determine that Pauline Thompson had actually died as a result of cardiac arrest, but he also found that the cardiac arrest had been caused by the victim being choked. There were three distinct bruises on the left side of Thompson's neck and one on the right side caused, said Dr Mollison, by fingers squeezing the flesh. He was unable to determine if there had been any recent sexual activity.

Later on that Saturday, Pauline Thompson's body was formally identified by her husband. Les Thompson was visibly distraught and had to be both comforted and assisted during the identification process.

In a tragic segue, the next day, Sunday, 10 May, was Mother's Day. It was a day celebrated by a Massed Bands Concert held in the upper recreational area of Royal Park, adjoining the sprawling Camp Pell. It was a concert attended by thousands of Melburnians and a large contingent of American soldiers from the camp next door. Towards the conclusion of the concert, bedsheets were carried through the crowds by uniformed Australian and American soldiers, collecting coins that would be donated to the recently established Prisoners of War Fund. It was later noted that the total raised was £294, a figure that included no fewer than 12 000 copper coins.

•

Late on the morning of Monday, 11 May, a service was held for Pauline at a funeral parlour in Sydney Road, Brunswick, after which she was buried at the Heidelberg Cemetery. The large numbers present and the grief they displayed showed how many lives Pauline Buchan Thompson had touched in her several guises and roles.

•

That day as well, newspaper headlines still detailed the Battle of the Coral Sea, with expressions of uncertainty about the outcome from most leader writers. There was a lot happening on the various war fronts, and readers would have been left with the impression that the tide was beginning to turn in the Allies' favour in the Soviet Union and North Africa at least. They would have to turn to page two or three to find the reporting on the murder of Pauline Thompson. When they found them though, the reports were a lot more detailed than anything that had been printed in Saturday's papers.

> *Strangled to death, the partly clad body of Mrs. Pauline Buchan Thompson, 31, wife of a Bendigo policeman, was found on the steps of Morningside House, where she had been living for a week, in Spring st. near Flinders st., city, shortly after 5am on Saturday.*
>
> *A post-mortem examination showed that the woman had been throttled, but the pathologist's report had not been completed suffi-ciently yesterday to indicate if she had been criminally assaulted. When the body was found there were bruises on her neck and on one side of her face, and she had probably been dead for 3 or 4 hours . . . Mrs. Thompson's handbag was found in Malthouse lane [sic], off Flinders lane, and contained no money. Detectives do not think that robbery was the reason for the crime, although it has been established that she had at least £1 in her bag.*

The same report was quite graphic in its description of the crime scene:

> *The woman was lying on her back partly up the steep stone steps with her arms and legs outstretched. Her clothing had been*

pulled down from her shoulders and pulled up from her legs to form a heap around her waist. Her top coat was ruffled up on the steps under her legs, and her hat was under her right foot. Her left shoe was on, but her right shoe was under her right foot, indicating that it had been lost in a struggle. Beads from a necklace were strewn about the steps, and the main string was beneath her neck.

Like all the major stories published on that Monday, the Melbourne *Argus* article identified the two key elements of the Thompson murder, parallel themes which continued to dominate the story as it unfolded. The first was whether this murder was related to the murder of Ivy McLeod a week earlier because, if it was, there was a serial killer loose in Melbourne. The *Argus* noted that, 'Both deaths are similar in many respects. All Mrs Thompson's clothing had been ripped off, suggesting that criminal assault had been motives [sic] in each crime.'

The second theme flowed logically from the first. Two women had been brutally murdered in Melbourne within a week. Just what were the police actually doing about this? 'Detectives began one of the most intensive hunts for 12 years. Practically every city detective was engaged on the inquiry during the weekend, and because of the similarity of the crimes, detectives investigating the McLeod death were co-opted in the second case.'

At his Monday briefing of crime reporters, Harry Carey was careful to not go any further than he believed was absolutely necessary. While conceding that there were a number of similarities between the murders of Ivy McLeod and Pauline Thompson, he was not prepared to state that they had been committed by the same person. While the police might not have been publicly prepared to make that connection, newspaper editors, the general public and at least one policeman were working on the theory that just a single killer was involved.

Sid McGuffie was that policeman, and he had no doubt that the same man was responsible for both murders. He also felt that, unless caught soon, the man would murder again. And, finally, he was convinced that the murderer was an American soldier. He had little spare time to expand on these thoughts however as the Homicide Squad had been flat out since Saturday morning. At least he now had all the assistance he needed as a further eight detectives from elsewhere in the Criminal Investigation Branch (CIB) had been reassigned to the joint-murder investigation. Carey had also decided that he would conduct all press conferences and newspaper queries. This would take a bit of the pressure off McGuffie.

Unlike the circumstances which surrounded Ivy McLeod's murder – where there were very few leads either at the murder site or in McLeod's life – Pauline Thompson's murder had generated a plethora of leads. Among the items recovered with Pauline's handbag was a small notebook containing a list of names and some contact details for several of them. Interestingly, some appeared to be American soldiers, including a number of officers. Pauline's identification as the victim also led to the identification of her employment, both day and evening jobs, and her wider interests in charity work and entertainment. In turn, interviews and follow-up enquiries generated other leads. An interview with a still-stressed Les Thompson also produced the news that Pauline had been planning to meet an American soldier for dinner at the Hospitality Club in Elizabeth Street. It was obviously the best lead they had.

It was also a lead that seemed to be strengthened by the routine enquiries the detectives were undertaking. The first of these had been those made at Morningside House, which had focused on whether anyone there had seen or heard anything unusual around the time Pauline Thompson was murdered. The answers from all those interviewed were the same, an unequivocal 'no'. Follow-up interviews revealed some more interesting detail. The proprietors, Mr and Mrs Hawkes, did not really know Pauline as she had only been there for a week. Phillip Hawkes had spoken to her several times as they negotiated over the room she would occupy, but Mrs Hawkes had only ever seen Pauline once.

Surprisingly, then, it was Mrs Hawkes who provided the most interesting information. She recalled quite clearly that an American soldier had knocked on Pauline's door around 8.30 p.m. on Friday night and asked her if she knew where Coral might be. Mrs Hawkes told the young man that she could not help him. On reflection, Mrs Hawkes recalled that there had been three telephone calls for 'Coral' during the week leading up to her death. They were all made by the same young man, who did not want to leave a message; that young man had spoken with an American accent.

Any hopes that the team had now identified the potential killer were dashed on Monday afternoon when Jimmy Jones walked into the Russell Street Police Headquarters and said that he wanted to speak to someone about the woman who was murdered on Friday night.

Jimmy Jones spoke fully and frankly about his contacts with the woman he knew as Coral O'Brien. To begin with, he stated that he was shocked when he learned of her murder and even more shocked when he realised that Mrs Pauline Thompson was the woman he had known as Coral. Jones held nothing back; he detailed all the visits to her room at the boarding house and the several telephone calls he had made the previous week. He admitted that he was the person she was going to meet for dinner at the Hospitality Club on Friday night. He explained how he was late, and that Coral hadn't been there when he eventually arrived. He took the police through his movements after that, his visit to Morningside House and his subsequent return to Camp Pell. While not precise about the exact timings, he believed he went to bed and sleep sometime after 10 p.m. His three tent mates would be able to confirm the time. Jimmy Jones was sound asleep in his bed at the time his would-be sweetheart was being murdered.

•

The detectives' palpable sense of disappointment at their best lead going nowhere was lightened somewhat by the results of routine police work. That routine involved interviewing all those who were in a position to make a meaningful comment or contribution to the question of what Pauline had been doing in the hours leading up to her death and, more importantly, who she had been doing it with.

Interviews with work colleagues quickly revealed Pauline's intentions for Friday night: meeting a group of co-workers at the Music Lovers' Club and then, possibly, on to the Dug Out Club for its opening night. Those enquiries also revealed that Pauline had not met her friends, while in the follow-up, staff at both the Music Lovers' and the Dug Out were shown photographs of Pauline; none of them could recall ever seeing her before.

Working on what they knew as well as what they suspected, the detectives set to work. The things that were known were the location of her last known sighting at the American Hospitality Club at 7 p.m., the location of her body – and probable place of murder – at Morningside House in Spring Street, and the location of her stolen handbag off Flinders Lane. The timings were all a bit flexible. Jimmy Jones said that Pauline was not at the club at 7.30 p.m., while Dr McCutcheon believed she was killed between midnight and 2 a.m., or shortly before or after.

The detectives applied a mixture of logic and experience to the problem. It was a Friday night and Pauline Thompson had dressed for a night on the town. She had been stood up by her dinner date at the Hospitality Club and had left there before his belated arrival. If she departed alone, it was most likely that she would have kept her arrangement to meet the other girls from International Harvester later at the Music Lovers' Club. She was still alive at the time she proposed to meet them, so she must have been doing something else at that time.

If she left the club with someone else, it was either someone she knew or someone she didn't know. If it was someone she knew, their name was probably on the list of people to be inter-viewed and that interview would confirm their position in the investigation. They would be regarded as either persons of no further interest or as suspects.

If Pauline left the club with someone she didn't know, it was likely that the person she left with was an American serviceman, as the club was set up for them.

Given the timings and the circumstances, it was probable that Pauline left to either have a drink or a meal.

It was raining, trams were crowded and taxis were almost impossible to find. That meant that wherever Pauline went, she probably walked there.

But that rain was heavy, and Pauline was dressed for going out, not for walking long distances. That suggested that wherever she went was within reasonable walking distance of both the Hospitality Club and Morningside House, her two known locations on that evening.

A map was produced and a walking route between those two points was drawn up on it. Down Elizabeth Street to Collins Street, up Collins Street to Spring Street, down Spring Street to Morningside House. They also noted that there were a few shortcuts through lanes and alleyways.

Sectors were allocated. Check all bars, cafés, clubs and hotels within 100 metres of that route. Show those who worked there on Friday night a photograph of Pauline Thompson and ask them whether they had seen her then. One line of enquiry had been addressed.

They started in earnest midway through Monday and had almost instant success. The barman at the Astoria Hotel, a man named Alfred Bliss, recognised Pauline's photo and said that the woman had been at the hotel on Friday night for at least two hours. He remembered her, he said, because she was a particularly attractive woman. He said, too, that she had been drinking with an American soldier. And the Astoria Hotel was in the right location, at Collins Place, a small cul de sac off Flinders Lane between Exhibition Street and Spring Street; it was in an almost straight line between the Hospitality Club and Thompson's residence on Spring Street.

•

What had been implicit but unstated was now front and centre in the investigation. Ivy McLeod and Pauline Thompson had probably been murdered by the same person and that person was an American soldier. There were thousands of potential suspects for the crimes, many of whom were living within a short distance of where the murders had been committed. While the American authorities may have harboured some suspicions, unofficially at least, they had no compelling reason to believe that there was a killer in their midst.

This changed on Tuesday, 12 May, when American consular and military authorities were informed that the prime suspect in two Melbourne murders was an American serviceman. Those authorities promised full cooperation and then followed through on those promises, although the cooperation would be tested at times. In particular, a good relationship was established at the day-to-day working level between the Homicide Squad and the US Army's Provost Corps, based at Camp Pell. Sid McGuffie would work hard to keep it so.

Always competing with other squads for resources, the Homicide Squad and its members learned just what largesse the Americans brought with them. They were able to provide the detectives with transport on request, food when it was required, and the occasional luxury item for McGuffie and his team. They also promised full access to their records, prompting Harry Carey to reveal publicly that, 'If necessary, the movements of every US soldier who was on leave or was AWL on Friday night will be checked and each one will be interviewed.' Carey felt the need to go public with this because he knew the public was starting to seek reassurance that everything was being done to catch the killer.

Both Carey and McGuffie recognised the positive impact the newspapers could have on the expanded investigation and were now prepared to share a bit more information than they had been previously. The stories the newspapers printed were therefore a lot more comprehensive, even if not completely accurate.

Before any real progress could be made yesterday by detectives inquiring into the death of Mrs Pauline Buchan Thompson . . . several new avenues had to be explored, but police are confident that a solution will be found soon.

It is now believed that Thompson was in company with a soldier for about 2½ hours before her death, which is assumed to have taken place between 1 and 2 am. The postmortem examination did not reveal that she had been criminally assaulted.

Police believe that Mrs Thompson, while waiting for the soldier, met another person whom she knew and left with him. A woman companion was left to keep the appointment but that person has yet to be interviewed. It is thought that Mrs Thompson went to a dance.

Detectives inquiring into the mysterious death of Mrs Ivy Violet McLeod . . . are assisting in the investigations, indicating that possibility of a connection between the 2 crimes has not been abandoned . . .

Police are certain that Mrs Thompson had not met her death by strangulation until after midnight, as other tenants at her apartment house had not arrived home until after 12.20am. Her body had been found at 5am and death had taken place between 3 and 4 hours previously.

So far it has not been established that she had been at [the] dance and anyone who might have seen a woman answering the published description, or during the last few weeks, should inform detectives.

The main problem McGuffie and his team faced was that they had no real idea who the American soldier they were seeking was, and would struggle to have him positively identified anyway. Neither Harold Gibson at the Bleak House nor Alfred Bliss at the Astoria had taken particular notice of the American soldier both had seen, and McGuffie suspected that neither would be able to pick the man out in an identification parade even if he were found. Convinced that there must have been many others who saw Thompson with her killer, the team released detailed descriptions of what she had been wearing on Friday night: 'Thompson was wearing a high black halo hat, black dress and black topcoat, which was undone, and with light brown fitch skins on the bottom of the sleeves. She had flesh-coloured stockings and black shoes with openings at the toe and inside of each shoe. There was a string of green and tortoise beads at the neck.'

They also released details of the names Pauline may have used: 'The murdered woman was known to friends by four different names – Pauline Thompson (her correct name), Coral Thompson, Pauline O'Brien and Coral O'Brien. Detectives are anxious to hear from anyone who knew a woman by any of those names.'

As well as issuing the usual, 'Police would like to speak to anyone . . .' statements, on Wednesday, McGuffie and his team also adopted a radical new approach in their attempts to find people who had seen Pauline with the American soldier. They arranged for a model of Pauline's height and figure to be photographed wearing clothes identical to those Pauline had been wearing on the night she was murdered. A studio head-and-shoulders photograph of Pauline taken some years earlier was then superimposed on the photograph of the model, and hundreds of copies of the composite image were prepared for distribution. Those who knew Pauline were struck by how accurate the figure was. All newspapers were given copies to print, and several dozen were given to the MPs at Camp Pell.

Police also prepared a reconstructed photograph of Ivy McLeod, but that trail had seemed to grow cold; those photographs were not distributed as widely because of the differences in the circumstances surrounding the two cases.

By Wednesday, 13 May the situation had settled into a state of stasis. McGuffie's detectives were conducting an average of twenty interviews a day, but those interviews were not generating any real leads towards the killer. All the residents of Morningside House had been interviewed as had all the patrons of the Astoria Hotel who could be identified. Pauline's friends and work associates had been interviewed, and police had again spoken to staff at the American Hospitality Club, the Union Club, the Music Lovers' Club and the Dug Out, this time showing them the composite photograph. No result. They had a fairly detailed picture of Pauline Thompson and of her movements on Friday night. They just didn't know who she'd been with.

In an effort to tempt the killer into coming forward, Harry Carey and his detectives tried a slightly different tack. From Tuesday onwards, Carey would confirm what was already known about the Thompson case, her general movements on the previous Friday evening plus the location and approximate time of her murder. He would further suggest that detectives believed she might have met her murderer when she walked home from the Astoria Hotel or that he might even have been waiting for her at the top of the stairs leading into Morningside House. They also refused to discount speculation that Pauline Thompson may have known the man who would kill her. The American soldier she had been seen with that evening may still not even know that she was the murder victim, given that her name – as the victim – and the name she sometimes used when out and about were sometimes different.

To help jog some memories, the police were preparing further composite photographs of Pauline Thompson as she most likely appeared on the night of her death. Thousands of these would be sent to every US Army camp in and around Melbourne. While the American soldier they wanted to speak to may not recognise the name, there was a fair possibility that he might recognise the woman in the photograph.

By the middle of that week, the general public was also starting to become restive. While newspaper reporters speculated about the possible connection between the Thompson and McLeod murders, the official police position was that there was no proven relationship between the two crimes. The police even let it be known that one of the theories they were pursuing was that the Thompson murder was a copycat killing, with the killer basing his entire modus operandi on what he had read about the Ivy McLeod case.

The release of the additional information misfired in some respects; the general public was able to connect the dots. Two women had been strangled to death, possibly after a fiendish sexual assault. In both cases, the police wanted to speak to an American soldier who was believed to have been the last person to see the victims alive. They wanted to speak to that soldier because they believed he could help them with their enquiries. It wasn't hard to figure out.

The public quickly developed their own theories, often with embellishments based on fears and phobias rather than facts. There was no dispute over the proposition that both women were killed by the same man and that that man was an American soldier, probably based at Camp Pell. Then the extra details were added. The victims both had their limbs dislocated and, in one case, an arm had actually been torn from the body. The sexual assaults were so vicious that the victims' genitals had been torn wide open.

As is the way, people – especially newspaper sub-editors – wanted a name or title to identify the anonymous killer. One, in far-off Brisbane, suggested that a new Jack the Ripper was operating in the southern city. Newspapers all around Australia used various combinations of 'Melbourne', 'murderer', 'soldier' and 'strangler' before coming up with one by the end of the week which was a simple combination of the when and the how of what he did. The interstate newspapers took up what the Melbourne papers and the general public were saying; the anonymous killer would be forever known as the 'Brownout Strangler'.

•

With the murder of Pauline Thompson and its attendant publicity, the Brownout Murders, as they were now being called, assumed a national rather than just a Victorian significance, especially in those towns and cities where American servicemen were based. Despite wartime restrictions and censorship, the murders and the possible murderer were written of and talked about across the length and breadth of Australia. Over in the west, newspapers were reporting that, 'Detectives are no further advanced with their enquiries into McLeod's death, nor into the murder of Mrs Pauline Thompson outside a city apartment house last Saturday.' In Brisbane, the main local newspaper was describing how, 'Pauline Thompson was well-known to radio listeners as Pauline O'Brien and was a popular announcer and conductor of children's sessions,' before advising that, 'a general warning has been issued to women to avoid dark lanes and streets unless escorted'.

That week, the activities of the Brownout Strangler began to have a ripple-on effect in Melbourne. There were noticeably fewer people on the streets after dark, and patronage at cinemas and cafés, clubs and pubs was markedly less than it had been the previous week. There were hardly any young women alone after dark in Melbourne; they travelled in pairs or threes, or in the company of one or more Australian males. Trams were noticeably empty after dark, with their passengers likely to be all males. Sales of door locks increased, and city firms that employed young women instituted a number of precautions. Some firms sent their female staff home by car – a number announced that they would be seeking extra petrol rations to cover that travel – or let them sleep at the office rather than have them walk through darkened streets, while others delegated male staff to escort female staff to the main train stations and tram stops, and there wait with them till they had safely boarded.

And for the first time the lustre had started to wear off the Americans. They were no longer seen as the exotic cousins who had travelled a long way, bringing wonderful gifts, to help us in our hour of need. Every one of them now became a potential serial killer, and the response to their presence began to change, subtly at times, severely at others. While they were rarely ostracised, a request for a dance would be declined, with thanks. A request for a light from a digger at a pub was as likely to be met with a, '*Fuck off, Yank*' as it was with a lit match.

While acts of outright aggression towards Americans seem to have been few and far between, there was a general feeling that the party was over, that the spell had been broken and that, in Melbourne at least, things would never be the same. It was like a dark cloud was hovering over the city, sitting there, threatening that there was still more bad weather to come.

•

The general public did not know what was happening behind the scenes. The Homicide Squad had shifted all available resources to the Brownout Strangler investigation: eight full-time detectives, plus a lot of part-time work undertaken by other detectives from Homicide and other squads, because they all appreciated the seriousness of what was happening. During their 'spare' time as well as during their regular working hours, the detectives frequented all the venues they had identified as being popular with US servicemen. An increased number of police patrols, uniformed and plainclothes, crisscrossed the city every night.

US Army authorities promised to tighten up leave arrangements for their servicemen and to put in place processes to monitor and enforce those arrangements. They may well have done so, but to both the police and the public, there certainly didn't seem to be any fewer Americans in the city. There was a noticeable increase in the number of American MPs though. It was reported that General MacArthur himself had taken a personal interest in the case.

The general public was not particularly reassured by what they could see. All that was important to them was that the killer was still at large, and that fact worried them. Had they known what the killer was going through, they, the police and the MPs would have been even more worried.

8.

ANTHONY 'JOEY' GALLO

Joey Gallo did not have many friends in the army; in fact, he thought he probably had just the one, and when that friend seemed to be struggling, Joey was naturally concerned. The little New Yorker had watched his friend Eddie Leonski become more and more the type of soldier and type of man who was heading for really big trouble. Back at Camp Sam Houston, Eddie had looked after Joey, protected him from the goons, and now Joey felt it was time to return the favour, except he didn't really know how. Eddie was clearly an alcoholic; every day now, he disappeared, sometimes before lunch, and usually wouldn't be seen again that day. If he was seen, more often than not he would be drunk and looking for a fight.

Joey knew that Eddie had been in the camp stockade for a month, and he also knew that Eddie continued to come and go as he pleased once he was released. That was part of the problem, too, as Joey had sought Eddie out on several occasions, only to find that he was not in his tent. This Saturday, 9 May, Joey knew where to find Eddie. He knew that Eddie had been called in to the Officers' Mess to help with the preparations for dinner there. That meant that Eddie would have been occupied until the early evening, which it now was.

And there Eddie was, sitting on the doorstep of his tent, smoking and drinking something – it looked like whiskey – from a bottle. Hearing footsteps, Eddie looked up. He was crying softly and, when he recognised who it was, said simply, 'I killed, Gallo, I killed.'

It was a comment that stopped Joey in his tracks and, for a moment, he literally could not think of anything to say. When he did gather his senses, Joey asked Eddie why he didn't go to bed; they could have a talk on Sunday. Eddie's response was to stand up and smile, then say it was Saturday night and he thought he might go into the city. Joey's response was to say that if Eddie was going into the city, well, then, Joey thought that he might go with him. He stood outside the tent while Eddie went in to change out of his work fatigues.

The pair caught a tram into the city shortly after they left Camp Pell. It was crowded and they had to stand. After a while, Eddie began to talk. He told Joey that he was pretty certain that he had killed a woman the previous evening. In fact, he was more than pretty certain; he *knew* he had killed a woman. He was just a little foggy about some of the details. As he spoke, Joey cringed. You could never be certain with Eddie. Sometimes he said things, and sometimes he did things just for effect. Take, for instance, the way he often drank, putting chilli and ketchup in beer, for Chrissake. And his stories. If they were anything to go by, Eddie had slept with most of the good-looking dames in New York City, including his own sister-in-law. He did wish, though, that Eddie would not talk that way on a crowded tram.

They exited the tram at the top of Swanston Street and walked south, down the street towards St Paul's Cathedral. On the way they stopped for Joey to buy a copy of the late edition of the Melbourne *Herald*. They walked past Lyons' Café, where the Thompsons had eaten their last meal together, and the spot where Pauline and her husband had met a little over a day and a half earlier.

The entrance to the St Paul's cafeteria, which was where Eddie said they were going, was around the corner in Flinders Street and, although the venue was relatively crowded, there were a few spare tables. Telling Joey that he was hungry and was getting something to eat, Eddie asked the smaller man to find them a table, one that offered a bit of privacy if possible. Joey found, he thought, suitable spot and opened up the newspaper after he sat down. He looked through it, searching for a story about a woman being killed. He had to look twice to find it, as it was a small story buried away between big stories about the progress of the war. He had just finished reading it when Eddie returned with a cup of tea and a plate of sandwiches.

Eddie asked Joey if he had found anything in the newspaper. Joey nodded and pushed the *Herald* across to Eddie, who hunched over the open page as he ate a sandwich. He finished the article quickly and paused for a moment, looking ahead with his eyes unfocused. After a moment, he nodded and said, 'Doorstep, doorstep, that's the one.'

Joey was gobsmacked for the second time that evening, and he really didn't know what to make of it all. Part of his brain thought that Eddie was trying to drag him into some kind of elaborate hoax; perhaps Eddie had read the newspaper earlier in the day and was now simply acting out a story he already knew.

Eddie, though, kept pushing his part of the story. From one of his pockets, he produced a packet of cigarettes; the packet was blue and Joey knew that it was an Australian brand. Eddie said that he had taken them from the woman he had killed. As he continued to eat his sandwiches and drink his tea, Eddie produced a pound note which he laid on the table. That, too, he said, had been taken from his victim's purse. Leaning across the table, he whispered that he doubted whether he would be caught because he had made certain that he had rubbed his finger-prints off everything he had touched. He added that he should have taken some kind of souvenir from the victim – something personal, something intimate – to show that he was the killer.

Expansive now, Eddie leaned back and said that one thing about the article really pissed him off. The reporter said that the victim had not been 'criminally assaulted'. They'd had sex before he killed her, or so he told Joey, and it was good. But not as good as sex with Mae, his sister-in-law. Then he added the throwaway line that he had not had sex with the woman he had killed near the beach at Albert Park the previous weekend.

Returning to the previous night's murder, Eddie said it would have been funny if he'd left his cap at the scene, as it wasn't really his cap. It was one he had 'borrowed' from a soldier in the tent next to his. It had that soldier's name written in it. That would have been a hoot, Joey, wouldn't it? He said that the woman had been beautiful and that she had also had a beautiful voice. She had called me 'Baby-face', he told Joey, and she had told me that I had a sweet baby-face, but that she also thought that there was something vicious and evil lurking underneath. Bitch.

A thoroughly shaken Gallo could only ask Eddie why he did these things. Eddie replied simply, 'I don't know.'

Joey said that it was difficult for him to believe Eddie and all that he was claiming to have done. If it was all true, he said, then why didn't Eddie seek advice or help from a priest or someone like that?

'I don't trust anyone but you,' was the reply.

'Well, then, why not give yourself up?' asked Joey, to which Eddie replied, 'Don't be silly.'

Joey said that Eddie could claim to be temporarily insane. 'I could, couldn't I?' was the reply.

•

There was silence while Eddie finished his sandwiches, swilling them down with tea. He said to Joey, 'Let's go,' and led the smaller man out of the cafeteria, along Flinders Street to Swanston Street and up Swanston Street towards the top of the town, retracing their steps of half an hour earlier. As the pair walked, Eddie continued to talk. At first he wondered aloud just how much he needed to drink to speak to Joey like this, but then proceeded to talk about the two women who had been killed. 'Did you know I strangled them both?' he asked Joey in all seriousness as they walked past the Melbourne Town Hall. All Joey could think to do was to say to anyone he thought may have overheard Eddie, 'He's drunk!' or, sometimes, 'My buddy's crazy.'

As they continued walking, Eddie mused on the fact that he only killed older women. He stopped at a milk bar, smiled at Joey and then went inside.

Head still reeling from all that he had heard that evening, Joey stood alone on the footpath, oblivious to his surroundings. He stood there for two minutes, three minutes, and then also went into the milk bar. He found Eddie at the rear of the shop, standing next to a counter stool, leaning one arm on the counter and talking to three young women whose uniforms indicated that they were waitresses. Eddie was using his lady-killer's voice, a description that for Joey had now taken on a terrible meaning. It was a voice lower and slower than his normal speaking voice, with a slightly different accent and inflections.

Eddie was pausing to sip a malted milk as he spoke, and as Joey approached he clearly heard Eddie say something about Spring Street. There was a newspaper on the counter, open to the page where the Spring Street murder had been reported. One of the waitresses looked shocked and asked Eddie what he meant. As smooth as ever, Eddie's reply was that, after all this lousy weather and all this lousy news he, for one, would be dancing in the streets when spring had sprung. He then continued as though nothing had happened.

Joey had waited quietly while Eddie finished his drink, and then the two soldiers said their goodbyes and left the milk bar. Outside, Joey said that he wanted to go back to Camp Pell. Eddie said that he thought that was a good idea, and that he'd ride along with him. And when Joey told Eddie that he'd given him a lot to think about, Eddie draped an arm across Joey's shoulder and said he shouldn't have told him so much. 'Forget everything you've heard,' he said.

It was a quiet trip home.

•

Joey Gallo did not sleep well on Saturday night and was as confused as he was tired on Sunday morning. After breakfast, he went to Eddie's tent and called out to him. Eddie was inside and came out when he heard his name called. Joey appeared serious; he asked Eddie if they could go for a walk as he wanted to ask some questions about what Eddie had said the previous evening. He noted, with some relief, that Eddie was sober, and that he had showered, shaved and dressed up.

As they walked along the path between the tents, Eddie took the lead by asking Joey if he had ever heard of *Dr Jekyll and Mr Hyde*. Joey confessed that he knew there was a film of that name currently showing in Melbourne, but he had not seen it and didn't really know what it was about. Eddie explained that it was an old story, and that it was about a good man, Dr Jekyll, who harboured an evil killer, Mr Hyde, within him. Under certain conditions, Mr Hyde would take over the body the two shared and then commit his depredations. When conditions returned to normal, Dr Jekyll was in control, and nothing untoward occurred.

The way Eddie spoke, Joey was firmly of the impression that the condition he was describing, the Jekyll and Hyde thing, was a lot more common than people understood. By the time Eddie had finished his exposition, they had walked in a circle and were almost back at Eddie's tent. Eddie said that he had to go and catch up with some Aussie guys he knew and told Joey that he was relying on him. He said goodbye and disappeared into his tent. Joey stood there for a moment or two before walking away.

•

Over the next several days, Joey and Eddie had many conversations, which Joey divided into those they had when Eddie was drunk and those they had when he was sober. There was a difference between the two, but neither sort gave Joey the real push, the hard motivation to do just what it was he thought he was supposed to do in these circumstances.

A couple of days after he had spoken about Jekyll and Hyde, a sober Eddie approached Joey and asked him if he had ever heard of werewolves. Joey again confessed his ignorance, and Eddie gave him a five-minute explanation. In certain parts of the world, he said, people accepted as the truth the proposition that some men could, in certain circumstances, change into animals – wolves – and that these animals would attack human beings and tear them apart. When these so-called werewolves changed back into their human form they became normal people living normal lives.

When Eddie was sober, they could have a decent discussion. One evening, around the middle of the following week, Joey read an article in a Melbourne paper stating that both the murdered women had last been seen in the company of an American soldier. Eddie had called in at the kitchen where Joey was working at around 6 p.m. Joey, who still had the paper, mentioned the article to Eddie, and suggested he go into the mess to read it. Eddie, who had been drinking but was not yet drunk, took the paper away and returned a few minutes later. He handed the paper back to Joey with the comment, 'There are plenty of American soldiers. There is nothing to worry about.'

At another sober time, and in all seriousness, Eddie told Joey that criminals were sometimes caught on trifling charges, but that a good detective could trick them into confessing to other, more serious offences. Joey, emboldened by this observation, again mentioned the woman who had been murdered in Albert Park, and asked Eddie if he knew anything about it. Eddie said that he had certainly been in Albert Park, but that he couldn't remember anything beyond drinking at a hotel with a group of other people.

One night, which Joey thought might be the night he gave Eddie the newspaper to read, he went to see Eddie at his tent. Eddie was preparing to go out, and Joey asked if it was all right if he went with him. Eddie grunted his approval, and the two headed off through the camp to catch a tram into the city. As they walked past the now-darkened kitchen, Joey said,

'You know, Eddie, you make me kind of afraid of the darkness.'
He then added, 'I am not going with you. You go by yourself.
Be a good boy, don't drink, and come back early.'

Eddie put his arm around Joey and smiled down at him,
saying, 'That is not true; you want me to go out and get drunk
because your conscience is bothering you and you want me to
give myself up.'

Their sober conversations were increasingly elliptical and also
increasingly oblique, with both referring to things that were left
unspoken. At midnight one night during the week after Pauline
Thompson was killed, a sober Eddie found Joey still working
in the kitchen. Joey looked up and said directly to Eddie, 'This
thing is driving me crazy and I will have to turn you in.' Eddie's
response was a simple, 'Go ahead.' Eddie said all along that he
was depending on Joey's generous nature. In their sometimes
queer and convoluted conversations, it was a theme they both
returned to.

The bottom line was that both were prisoners of each other's
personalities. Eddie told Joey that he trusted Joey and Joey alone.
Whenever Joey mentioned that he thought Eddie should speak
to one of the senior officers or even a priest, Eddie's response
was always that he could not speak to anyone else, because
Joey was the only person he could really trust. He would sometimes joke that, for both of them, all their problems would be
over if he were caught.

Then there was the drunken Eddie. *That* Eddie would usually
begin crying when he spoke to Joey, and would make statements
like, 'You wonder, but I know.' The drunken Eddie would
question Joey's trustworthiness and mix snapshot recollections
of possible murders with rambling observations about the diffi-
culties of trying to get to sleep. When sober, Eddie would joke

about his acting prowess; when drunk, it often seemed to Joey that Eddie *was* acting.

And therein lay Joey's dilemma. Eddie Leonski did not admit to committing murders when he was sober. He would tell Joey that he could remember snippets of times and places, sights and sounds, that suggested he might have been responsible for the two murders, but he did not once say, 'Joey, I strangled those two women.' It was hard to recollect a time when, even when he was drunk, Eddie had straight-out admitted to murder. Instead, he would offer thinly veiled hints and clues about his possible involvement – 'You wonder but I *know*.'

Joey could not, or would not, resolve the dilemma. He did not feel able to definitively say which were Eddie's acts and which were Eddie's fantasies or if, indeed, there was any difference between the two. Joey struggled to understand just which of the various worlds Eddie used to describe was the one he actually occupied, or whether he occupied more than one at a time. Perhaps he was Mr Hyde or even a werewolf. Eddie had struggled in the past and was struggling now. Also, Eddie had saved him in San Antonio, so he was not now inclined to desert him in Melbourne. In the end, the decision was too hard for Joey to make, and so he didn't.

•

Late in the afternoon of Tuesday, 12 May, an American serviceman followed a young woman home from a tram stop in Royal Parade, Parkville, not too far from the eastern boundary of Camp Pell. She was Kathleen Elliott, a saleswoman who worked in a city store and who resided at 186 Park Street in Parkville. Walking a little faster than Elliott, the serviceman caught up with her as she walked down Wimble Street towards Park Street. In a pleasant voice, he asked Elliott if she had any cigarettes and, when she said no to that request, asked if he could walk along with her. 'I suppose I can't stop you,' was the reply.

As the pair continued walking down Wimble Street and onto Park Street, the American explained to Elliott that he had asked her for a cigarette because they were rationed and soldiers were only given one pack a day.

By then, they had reached the front gate of Elliott's home. She opened it and then closed it behind her as she walked the two metres to her front door. As she put her key in the front-door lock, the American said from behind her, 'Aren't you going to invite me in?' Thinking quickly, the young woman smiled back and said that she certainly wouldn't be inviting the soldier inside because her husband was already there, waiting for her arrival. At this, the soldier moved quickly, placing himself between the young woman and the door, putting his hands gently on her shoulders as he did so.

He struck hard and he struck swiftly, suddenly moving his hands to her throat and squeezing with a real ferocity. As he did so, the young woman twisted her body inwards, towards him, surprising the soldier and enabling her to break free. As she did so, she loosed a piercing scream, followed by cries for help at the top of her voice. The American soldier ran off into the night.

Neither Kathleen Elliott nor her family would report the incident to the police for a long time, for reasons that were never made public. The young woman survived the attack, but not without both physical and psychological trauma. For a long time she would not be able to forget a number of little things that surrounded the assault: the soldier's broad and engaging smile and one of the little affectations he displayed. When he spoke to her, his voice was almost effeminate, and he would give a little chuckle at the end of each sentence he spoke.

•

A short time later – probably no more than twenty minutes – another young woman was returning home, again to a house in Park Street, this one a little further away from the tram stop than the first. As she opened the front door, a man jumped from the shadows and pinioned her arms to her side before grabbing her throat with both hands.

As he did so, the young woman screamed and let herself fall, breaking her attacker's grip as she did so.

That attacker also ran off into the night, but not before the young woman was able to get a clear look at him. He seemed to be a young and quite good-looking man, and he was wearing an American Army uniform. This attack was not reported to the police for many weeks either.

•

Two nights later, on Thursday, 14 May, yet another young woman was followed home after hopping off a tram in Royal Parade, Parkville. This incident followed the pattern of the previous two, with two exceptions. The first was that it took place in Gatehouse Street rather than Park Street.

The young woman knew that there was someone behind her because she could hear his footsteps. They stopped when she reached her front door. As she opened the door, there was a rush of movement and a man's body slammed into her, propelling them both through the doorway and into the passageway beyond. As they crashed through, the young woman screamed, a scream that was answered by her uncle, a retired engineer, who had been waiting for her just inside the door. The uncle called, at the top of his voice, 'Get the buggery out of here,' and picked up a chair, which he threw at the figure now running back through the doorway and off into the night.

The uncle, a Mr Jackson, and his niece both had a clear view of the attacker; he was tall and blond and he wore an American Army uniform. It was a description they passed on, with considerable detail, to the police who responded to their home after they telephoned to report the incident. And therein lay the second difference. Because they had reported it immediately, the police were able to add this latest attack to their growing database on an American soldier seemingly intent on attacking – and possibly killing – young women on their way home in the gloom of the brownout.

•

That part of Eddie that wanted to rape and kill was getting stronger now; stronger but also lazier, more reckless, and taking more risks, almost as if he wanted to get caught.

9

MISS GLADYS LILLIAN HOSKING

According to the headlines and lead stories in all of Melbourne's daily newspapers at the start of a new working week, Monday, 18 May 1942, the events of war may have started to turn in the Allies' favour. In Europe, the Red Army was trapping large numbers of Germans in strategic pockets in regions with strange-sounding names spread across the Crimea and southern Ukraine. There was talk of thousand-bomber raids on German cities and hit-and-run raids by Allied commandos up and down the coastline of Occupied Europe. There was some heavy German bombing of British cities but, increasingly, the Luftwaffe seemed to be relying on small-scale nuisance raids.

There was also positive news from a lot closer to home. The Japanese appeared to have suffered a significant defeat in the Battle of the Coral Sea, and although their aircraft were regularly bombing Australian military facilities in and around Port Moresby, those raids were matched by Allied attacks on Japanese bases among the eastern islands of the Dutch East Indies archipelago.

Australia itself was being transformed into one enormous Allied base and jumping-off point for the eventual push to take back all those areas which had been lost to the Japanese in the first few months of the Pacific War. There were increasing numbers of Australian servicemen, army and air force alike, returning to Australia from service in the United Kingdom and the Middle East – and even some from Malaya and Singapore – to help confront the Japanese threat to the north and north-west. There were also now two full US Army infantry divisions, elements of a Marine division and assorted forces from the air force and artillery corps.

This latter development was no longer being seen as an unalloyed blessing. There appeared to be at least one killer wearing an American uniform stalking women through the browned-out streets of Melbourne and the phrase, 'over-paid, over-sexed and over here', was creeping into popular usage. That morning's newspapers also carried disturbing news from Queensland.

In Brisbane, on the previous Saturday night, a nasty incident had occurred. At around 9 p.m. that evening, a 27-year-old woman was walking across a vacant allotment in Stanley Street, South Brisbane, picking her way through the weeds and general debris with the aid of a torch, when she was grabbed and dragged into an empty air-raid shelter nearby. There, as she fought her attacker, the woman was punched in the head and body, bitten and then partially stripped and raped. All the while, she called for help at the top of her voice.

Coincidentally, two Brisbane detectives were driving past the allotment and heard the woman calling for help. They stopped the car, exited and ran across to the air-raid shelter, recognising that the calls were coming from within it. As the two policemen entered one end of the shelter, the woman's assailant ran out the other end. It was night time, but it was still light enough for the detectives to make out some details. The man wore a uniform, a US Army uniform, and was an African-American.

The victim was taken to hospital, where she was treated and gave the police a detailed description of what had happened. They later learned that the assault that they interrupted was not the only one to occur in Brisbane that night. Earlier in the evening, a middle-aged woman had been walking along Cordelia Street, not all that far away from where the later assault would occur, when a man approached her and grabbed her by the throat. Nearby residents heard her screams and came to her rescue. Her attacker ran away into the gathering darkness.

He, too, wore the uniform of the US Army and he, too, was African-American. The incidents, the reports and their implications gave a number of Australians, and Americans, much to consider in regard to what each actually thought of the other.

•

Gladys Hosking would have read those newspaper reports, either that morning or later in the day, for she was a voracious reader of newspapers, poring over them from the front page and on into the culture and society pages, but generally leaving the sports pages alone. All who knew her described Gladys as a cultured and refined woman, well educated and well travelled, someone who had packed a lot of living into forty years and a tiny frame. With her short dark hair and blue-grey eyes, the 150-centimetre-tall Gladys looked a bit like a little doll and always seemed much younger than her years.

Gladys had also travelled a long way to be in Melbourne in May 1942. She had been born in Ballarat but had moved to

Perth with her family when she was a little girl. Her parents still lived there but were no longer together. They had divorced some time ago. Her father worked as a printer, and her mother had remarried and now, as Mrs Lillian Leslie, was the licensee of the Railway Hotel in the wheat-belt town of Meckering. Gladys had a younger brother, named Bill like her father, who had joined the RAAF when war broke out and was now a flight sergeant with No. 8 Operational Training Unit at Narromine in New South Wales. Her younger sister was still living in Western Australia.

Gladys completed both primary and secondary education in Perth, and in the latter years of high school her chosen area of specialisation was science. After leaving school, Gladys worked briefly as a dental nurse but work was just one of her many interests. Her passion was the theatre, and she became an active member of the Perth Concert Artists, winning a number of lead roles in their productions. This participation included an increasing role in the administrative side of theatrics. It may have been this interest which led to an involvement in the YWCA. By the early 1930s, Gladys was the acting state secretary of that organisation.

All this was in Gladys's spare time. After working for a couple of years, she enrolled at business college, where she taught typing for a period after completing her own studies. Gladys then became the bursar at the Girls College at Baldwin in Perth. After five years there, in 1932, she moved across the continent to Melbourne, where she took up a position as bursar at Fintona, a private girls school in the city's eastern suburbs. In 1937, Gladys took leave of absence for twelve months and, unaccompanied, travelled to Europe. There she visited Germany, Italy and France before staying in London for several months, undertaking a number of short-term jobs.

She had only been back at Fintona for a few months when, in 1939, she resigned to take up a position in the Department of Chemistry at the University of Melbourne, the successful candidate from among the 300 who applied for the job. The position was that of Secretary to the Head of the Department, Professor Ernst Hartung, but it actually involved a lot more than purely secretarial duties. For one, she was also the departmental librarian – hence her daily consumption of newspapers – while her background in the sciences meant that there was always other things for her to do.

As well, she had maintained her interest in the performing arts and had joined one of the university's theatre groups, appearing on stage in all of its productions as well as helping out behind the scenes. It was fortunate that she lived locally, in rooms at a boarding house at 140 Park Street, near the intersection with Gatehouse Street, in Parkville. She could walk to or from work in less than fifteen minutes.

•

Apart from her brother joining the air force, the war brought a number of other changes, opportunities really, into Gladys's life. Her background in musical entertainment was of much broader value now, and she offered her services to a number of the companies and charities established to raise funds for the armed forces. She was in considerable demand in this role, and the balancing act that was her life continued for Gladys.

Unfortunately, she was forced to take a break from all this in late 1941 when her mother fell ill in Meckering. The university year was over and she was able to return to Western Australia to help nurse her mother, who had suffered a stroke. Gladys gave serious thought to remaining in Meckering to look after her mother, but she made a gradual recovery and Gladys was able to return to Melbourne. The episode caused her to pause, however, and she thought very seriously about returning to Western Australia permanently. In the short term at least, this plan was shelved because of the difficulty of organising relocation from the eastern states to the west. The Pacific War had broken out while Gladys was away.

The outbreak of this closer war had an immediate impact on Gladys's life. Shortly after she arrived back in Melbourne, Camp Pell was established practically outside her front door. The increased number of troops in Melbourne meant an increased demand for entertainment, and Gladys was soon back into the swing of things. She joined the entertainment wing of the Red Cross, and immediately became involved in the production of plays for them and other charities, designed to raise money for war and patriotic purposes. She was even able to take part in a Sunday morning recital at Camp Pell. But in May, a pall began to descend on Melbourne with the murder of two women.

In mid-May, Gladys wrote a long letter to her father in Perth, in which she expressed both reservations and fears about what was happening in Melbourne. Reservations, because she was no longer able to move about as freely as she would have liked to: 'I hardly ever go out at night. If I am taken, I go, but never alone.' She also told her father that she had more personal concerns: 'I am terribly afraid to go out at night Dad, especially in the blackout [sic]. It is a great disappointment having to stay in, as it interferes with my war work.' Gladys also mentioned that she was 'worried' about the soldiers in the camp near her residence but gave no indications of what had caused this concern.

•

One of Gladys's good friends was her colleague in the chemistry department, a young woman named Dorothy Pettigrew. They used to say they had known each other for years, had practically grown up together and had attended the same school, and then give a little laugh. Dorothy had been an eight-year-old student at Fintona a decade earlier when Gladys commenced as bursar. Now they worked closely together and were able to share in-jokes about the old days.

On Monday, 18 May, Dorothy stayed back at work to help Gladys with one of the many tasks she had volunteered for. The half-yearly student examinations were coming up and Gladys was responsible for their preparation; it was this task that Dorothy had helped her with. The job was completed by 6.30 p.m. and the two women checked that everything was safe and secure before heading home. Gladys shut and locked the front door and dropped the key in her purse.

Weather-wise, it wasn't much of a night, and they stopped to have a final chat, and to put up the umbrellas they both carried. Dorothy had by far the longer journey home, two tram rides out to Burke Road, Balwyn, but she had a relatively short walk across campus to Swanston Street for the first of those tram rides. Gladys usually went straight across campus too, but in the opposite direction, to Royal Parade, which she then followed north to Park Street and down the short distance to her residence. Because of the threatening weather this evening, she told Dorothy she thought that she might cut through the university and go down Tin Alley to Royal Parade. Although it involved going through the 'seedier' part of the sprawling campus, it should be a little bit quicker.

The friends wished each other a good night and went their separate ways into the darkening dusk.

•

In the ten days or so since he had started drinking at the Parkville Hotel, Eddie had visited the place on so many occasions – and stayed for so long – that both staff and patrons were beginning to see him as a regular. They all knew him as 'Eddie' and saw him as a big drinker, but also as someone who could hold his drink. He did not cause trouble and could in fact be quite entertaining. His trick of walking on his hands from one end of the bar to the other was popular, but it was a trick that he would only do on request and with the approval of the barman.

Although those present would probably have neither known nor cared, when Eddie entered the public bar of the hotel shortly after midday on Monday, 18 May, he was wearing his off-duty uniform of woollen trousers, shirt and field jacket, shoes and overseas cap. The bar was relatively quiet, with just Herb Everett, the regular barman and a small group of customers sitting around a bar table. One of those sitting called out to Eddie as he entered. It turned out to be Arthur Fry, the hotel's manager, who was also one of its better patrons, although he would have considered his drinking a legitimate part of the job.

Fry called Eddie over and introduced him to the three men he was drinking with, all of whom Eddie had seen before but not met. Eddie sat down alongside the youngest of the group, a milk-cart driver named Rupert Burns, and as the afternoon wore on, the two young men decided that they had a lot in common. First and foremost among these was beer, especially Eddie's favourite, Victoria Bitter. The pair consumed them at a steady rate, too, averaging between five and six an hour during the afternoon.

Towards 5 p.m., Burns was beginning to slow down a bit. The hotel was starting to fill up, and Arthur Fry had joined Herb

Everett behind the bar. Eddie switched from beer to whisky but continued drinking at the same pace as before. He also ordered and consumed a plate of sandwiches and a can of peaches. Earlier in the afternoon, Eddie and Rupert had discussed going into the city that evening to see the new Randolph Scott film, *Western Union*, then showing at the Regent Theatre. Another interest they shared was cowboy movies, and this looked like being a good one. Rupert had also told Eddie that they could have something to eat at his house before they went into the city. They bought eight bottles of beer and left the hotel around 6.30 p.m.

Rupert lived at 'Elizabeth House', 71 Royal Parade, a short distance – perhaps fifty metres – from the hotel, and as the two walked there, Rupert explained that it was a boarding house and that it was run by his parents. Eddie expressed only a passing interest in this, but did say that he was a little tired and thought that he'd like to lie down awhile before they headed into the city. At the Burns' house, Rupert led Eddie upstairs to a large room that contained four single beds and four wardrobes. After pointing out the two beds that belonged to boarders, Rupert indicated which was his and which was his brother's; he said Eddie could take either, then said he was going downstairs to make himself something to eat. When he returned to the room twenty minutes later, there was no sign of Eddie.

•

Times and places then get a bit hazy. At around the same time as Rupert Burns was finding out that his new friend Eddie had left without so much as a goodbye, an American soldier, Private First Class Francis Hanson of the 301st Coastal Artillery, decided it was time to walk back to Camp Pell from where he had been resting, en route from the city, at a milk bar on the corner of Royal Parade and Gatehouse Street. As he exited, Hanson noted that the night had become very dark, that it had been raining and that, if he was any judge of the weather, it would be raining again soon.

Shortly after leaving the milk bar, Hanson saw another American soldier and a civilian woman sharing an umbrella as they walked slowly in the direction of Park Street from Royal Parade. The man had his arm loosely around the woman's back. Hanson was in no particular hurry, so it took him a while to catch up to and then pass the couple, who were talking quite intently to one another. He thought that the woman seemed to be doing most of the talking, while the soldier only spoke briefly in reply. Hanson also thought that he spoke with an accent or in broken English. The soldier also walked very straight and upright. He was wearing a jacket and an overseas cap with coloured piping indicating that he was a signaller.

Hanson slowed as he overtook them, and the three exchanged a few words about the night and the weather. He would always remember the woman, but would have difficulty identifying the man.

•

At a few minutes after 8 p.m., Private Malcolm Walsh, an MP from the Provost Base at Camp Pell, saw a man and a woman walking south along Gatehouse Street. Walsh was himself in Gatehouse Street because a line of army trucks had been parked there overnight and he was part of a mixed Australian–American picquet guard which would ensure that the trucks and their contents would not be interfered with. The trucks had been parked on the western side of the street, alongside a grass verge and low fence which abutted Royal Park and Camp Pell. The other, eastern side of the street was lined with terrace houses built in the late nineteenth century.

In all honesty, Walsh was uncertain about the time because he'd had a fairly big day drinking with some buddies. Other details he would remember quite clearly. The couple were sharing an umbrella in the light rain. The woman was quite short and the man was quite tall. They appeared to be talking. The woman was wearing a black coat and the tall man was an American soldier in uniform.

Shortly after he spotted the couple, they crossed Gatehouse Street to the western side and disappeared from view behind the trucks parked there. Walsh's interest was raised but only temporarily. What people did was their own business and, more importantly, he was about to go off duty.

•

Walsh's direct replacement was a young Australian Army private named Noel Seymour. Seymour had been so keen to join the AIF that he had lied about his age at the recruitment centre and now, guarding army trucks in a Parkville street on a cold and wet late autumn evening, he was probably having second thoughts about his decision to enlist. He had dreamed of going overseas to fight, and now he was walking up and down a peaceful, leafy street in suburban Melbourne, armed only with a bayonet and a torch.

At the handover with the American MP he was replacing, the Yank had mentioned something about an American soldier and an Australian woman disappearing as they walked behind the parked trucks a short time earlier. It still came as a surprise though when Seymour heard a noise in the dark beyond the trucks, walked between two of them and shone his torch at where he believed the noise had originated.

It was a good torch and its light clearly illuminated an American soldier ducking under the low fence, coming from the direction of Camp Pell. The soldier seemed to be covered in yellow mud from head to toe. He put his hands to his eyes and spoke to Seymour. 'Where do I catch a tram to Royal Park?' he asked, and Seymour replied, 'Where the hell have you been?'

The soldier's response was to giggle, and then say, 'I fell over a pool of mud crossing the park.' He giggled again, and then continued, 'My girlfriend is nice. I thought I could drink but she drank me under the table.' The soldier went on to say that he was based at Camp Pell and was simply trying to get back to his billet. Seymour suggested he simply turn around, climb the fence and walk in a straight line for a couple of hundred paces. If he avoided mud pools, he would be in the middle of Camp Pell. The soldier nodded and headed off into the night.

Seymour guessed that the time would now be approaching 9 p.m. He reported the incident when he went off duty two hours later.

•

A few minutes after this, Private Marcel Jasinski of the 52nd Signallers was finishing up his pre-retirement ablutions in the enlisted men's latrines, located near one of the camp's entry points and used almost exclusively by the 52nd. Jasinski had spent most of the afternoon in the city and was looking forward to bed. His quiet reverie was broken when a soldier walked into the latrines with what appeared to be yellow clay mud from his chest to his shoes.

Jasinski knew who the figure was, Eddie Leonski, although the two were not close. He said to Leonski, 'Where the hell have you been?' Leonski's response was to simply say that he had fallen in the mud. Jasinski advised him to wash the mud off his uniform before it went hard. Leonski mumbled something in reply, and then said that he was tired and was going to bed. He walked out of the ablution block without using any of its toilet or washing facilities. Jasinski later thought that Leonski had seemed a little dazed. He was hard to understand when he spoke and he seemed disoriented; Jasinski thought he may have hit his head when he fell over. He was not really concerned though, and finished washing and drying his hands before heading off to his own tent.

•

Private First Class Pat Forino estimated that it was probably around 9.15 p.m. when he returned to the tent he shared with Eddie Leonski and the others after he, too, had spent most of the afternoon and part of the evening in Melbourne. Leonski was already there. He was sound asleep, lying flat on his back and naked. A strong smell of alcohol seemed to be seeping from his skin pores. Forino pulled a blanket and quilt up to Eddie's shoulders, then went to bed himself.

•

Eddie slept so deeply that he was unaware of anything after he stripped off his muddy clothes and fell back onto his bunk. His was not the sleep of the just or the sleep of the weary; it was the sleep of the emotionally drained alcoholic psychopath who has murdered another woman.

Eddie had earlier thought that he had been genuine in his offer to go into town with the young milkman, Rupert, but as he sat on the edge of Rupert's bed, the idea somehow didn't seem so attractive anymore. He figured that Rupert would understand this, so he went downstairs and turned to the front door rather than back towards the kitchen. He let himself out quietly and turned left, heading north up Royal Parade.

He knew this area well now, with its wide streets and poky lanes, large mansions and cluttered guesthouses. He knew the lay of the land, where it rose and fell, where it was always dark and where it was sometimes light. He sometimes felt as if he *owned* it, as if the people who passed through this little part of Parkville only did so because he allowed them to. There were lots of young women here, drawn by the university and the city and, perhaps, by all the soldiers at Camp Pell. It was sometimes hard to tell who they were and why they were here, but Eddie was confident in his own ability to recognise each and every one of them for what they were and what they wanted.

He wandered rather than walked, aware that a light rain was falling and aware, too, that he had drunk a lot of alcohol. Strangely, that seemed to clarify some of his muddied thoughts. He was a long way from his home and his mother and – deep down – there was a weight on his heart, a weight which he knew was telling him that he would probably never see either of them again. It hurt in some ways, but in others it would not necessarily be a completely bad thing.

Had he not been engrossed in his own thoughts, Eddie would not have almost cannoned into the woman as she came out of the milk bar. As it was, he narrowly missed her, and instantly stopped to apologise. The woman was very small and petite and was wearing a black overcoat, carrying a black umbrella and trying to juggle a newspaper, a magazine and a handbag. After apologising, Eddie asked if he could help, and held the umbrella as she folded the paper and magazine over and tucked them firmly under her arm.

They introduced themselves, both commenting on the other's accent while explaining their own, and Gladys Hosking accepted Eddie Leonski's offer to walk her home as they were both heading in the same direction. As they walked, they talked. Eddie spoke of New York and the army, Gladys of Australia, Europe and the worlds of academia and entertainment. Eddie loved her voice, her accent, and didn't really even notice when another GI walked past them and said hello.

And then they were outside Gladys's boarding house in Park Street. They stopped walking but continued talking for a couple of minutes. After a pause, Eddie apologised again, said he was a bit disoriented and asked Gladys to point out the best way back to Camp Pell. I'll go one better, she said, and take you there. It's not that far, I've got an umbrella, so neither of us needs to get too wet. They crossed Park Street, went back up to Gatehouse Street, and began walking down it. As they were walking opposite a line of parked army trucks, Gladys said that the camp was a short distance beyond them. They crossed the street, passed between two trucks and stopped on the grass verge.

Gladys thanked Eddie for his earlier help, wished him well, and turned to leave.

That was when he struck, both hands shooting out, grabbing her throat and squeezing with the strength that only real rage can give. Gladys tried to struggle, but there was no hope in the uneven contest and within seconds she had collapsed. Eddie held her upright for a while, then simply let her go and watched her body drop to the ground.

Again, he was surprised by the ease and simplicity of it all. He thought it might be their voices that gave them away. Bitches and sluts. What kind of woman wandered around in the dark with an American soldier? Especially as half the world seemed to know that there was an American soldier out there murdering women like this one. She got what she deserved and he felt good. He had some more work to do now, and didn't need all the trash she was carrying as it would just get in the way. He tossed it aside.

Grabbing Gladys's body by the upper arms, he dragged her backwards to the low fence which he climbed over before dragging her underneath. He then applied a kind of inverted fireman's lift, putting his arms under her shoulders and across her chest, joining his hands and carrying her backwards until he could go no further because he had tripped over a mound of dirt and clay. It was a metre or so high and had a slope he thought he may be able to utilise. As he sat there, thinking, the dead woman started to gurgle. He simply pulled some of her clothes up over her mouth and nose and forced them down until she was both silent and still.

He thought he would have a bit more work to do on this one, so he started immediately. He remembered slipping over a couple more times, and then it was done. Afterwards, he remembered speaking to an Australian with a torch, a soldier who seemed to accept his story, as did that prick Jasinski when he bumped into him in the latrines. But mostly he just wanted to sleep. It had been a big day, and he didn't know how many more of those he had in him.

•

At around 7 a.m. on Tuesday morning, as it was beginning to grow light, a butcher named Albert Whiteway was driving his double-horse lorry north on Gatehouse Street in Parkville, taking a load of meat to a number of shops in Clifton Hill. As he came towards the northern end of the street, he spotted a woman's hat lying on the grass verge. Looking past the hat, he then saw what was obviously an umbrella next to it, with some other items scattered around. Looking beyond those and past the low rail fence which separated the verge from Royal Park – perhaps ten metres in – he also spotted what appeared to be a human body. It was resting on what looked like a pile of yellow dirt.

Whiteway stopped his cart, fixed the brake and climbed down, then walked across to where the umbrella lay on the grass. As he did so, he saw an Australian soldier walking along Gatehouse Street and called out urgently to that soldier, 'Is that a body over there?' The soldier's name was Don McLeod and he was a 24-year-old private in the Australian Army Service Corps, a driver about to collect the truck he would be driving that day. Hearing Whiteway's calls, McLeod called back, 'Where?' and walked over to where Whiteway was standing and looking at something. The two men took in the scene that lay before them.

They first glanced at the umbrella and the other items on the verge, but their eyes were inexorably drawn to what lay on the other side of the fence, and they climbed over to get a better look at what it actually was. Both knew it to be the body of a woman; it was lying face down on a muddy clay bank. The woman's buttocks and legs were bare and they, like the rest of her body, were smeared with yellow mud. McLeod said to Whiteway, 'She's been dug out of this trench!'

Whiteway responded, 'They don't dig them up with their clothes like that.'

Whiteway remained with the body while McLeod returned to Gatehouse Street and found one of the Australian soldiers guarding the trucks. The two returned to where Whiteway stood. The soldier agreed to guard the crime scene. McLeod found his truck, started it and drove directly to the Royal Park police station where he reported what he and Whiteway had found.

He said he was prepared to remain at the police station until the detectives could interview him.

Back in Gatehouse Street, Albert Whiteway told the soldier that he could not hang around forever; he had a load of meat to deliver. He wrote down his contact details, then returned to his cart, released the handbrake and clip-clopped off up the street.

•

Sid McGuffie knew that the telephone call would come, but he wasn't certain when it would be. As it turned out, it was just after 7.30 a.m. on Tuesday morning; if nothing else, the timing showed that the Brownout Strangler did not only stalk and kill at weekends. The phone call to McGuffie was from the Royal Park police station, and it reported the discovery of a body in Gatehouse Street, Royal Park, just on the border of Camp Pell. The body was that of a female; she seemed to be naked and she appeared to have been murdered.

Sid thanked the young constable and gave him a couple of instructions which he carefully dressed up as requests. He asked if the crime scene could be completely secured if it wasn't already, saying that his main concern was that it could be overrun by soldiers from the nearby camp. He also asked that Private McLeod be taken back to the site in Gatehouse Street; McGuffie would question him there.

•

McGuffie parked his Lancia in Gatehouse Street at almost exactly 8 a.m., just ahead of the arrival of Harry Carey and his own team of homicide detectives. He noted a single constable standing near the body and a cordon of uniformed officers keeping everyone else at least twenty-five metres away from the crime site. He also noticed around fifty American soldiers standing on the ground rising towards the tents of Camp Pell in the background, quietly observing the crime scene; he wondered idly if the killer was among them.

Once the whole team was all there, Sid directed a careful examination of the relatively small area in which yet another young woman appeared to have been brutally murdered. The grass verge between Gatehouse Street and the low fence bordering Royal Park was searched first. Some distance from the body, one of the team, Detective Mooney, found an open black umbrella, handle uppermost, with a copy of the previous afternoon's Melbourne *Herald* newspaper partly hidden underneath. When Mooney moved the umbrella, it disclosed a copy of the *Women's Weekly* magazine published the previous day, also. A woman's black hat, a pair of fawn-coloured gloves, a handbag and purse – which had not been interfered with – were then found separately and nearby, strewn across a small area.

While some of the team continued to examine the grass verge for clues or evidence, McGuffie led two others into the guarded area near the body. What they noted was the body was that of a woman lying face down on a sloping bank of yellow clay which appeared to have been dug out of some V-shaped slit trenches nearby. The land in this area sloped gently down towards Gatehouse Street, and the trenches and the woman's body were both located on that gentle slope and between two large gum trees. McGuffie estimated that the murder site was around 150 metres from the intersection of Gatehouse Street and Royal Parade, and perhaps fifty metres from the church at the top end of Gatehouse Street.

The detectives then looked at the area in the vicinity of the body. McGuffie noted that the ground in the immediate surrounds of that body was very wet and looked like it had, for at least a metre around, been methodically stamped down. The area looked to him as though heavy cloths had been dragged across it. What may once have been footprints were now little more than impressions in the sticky yellow clay and mud. To McGuffie, it seemed as though some kind of struggle had taken place, one that either included or ended with the woman's body being dragged to where it now lay.

Finally, the men turned to the body and, again, the devil was in the detail. The woman was lying face down on the slight bank of yellow clay overburden and the body appeared to have been deliberately arranged, with the legs bent and spread apart, so that anyone who approached it from Gatehouse Street would first see the exposed buttocks and genital area.

McGuffie noted that the deceased woman was not wearing a hat and that her top clothes had all been obviously torn and pulled up from her waist. However, her stockings and shoes were still in place. Leaning closer, he examined the body, propped up with its head down in the mud. Looking at what he could see of the face, he was able to see signs of haemorrhage from the mouth and nose and obvious bruising to the left of the woman's throat; he would leave a more detailed examination to the experts. They all noted that the woman's body and clothing were covered in yellow mud.

All the detectives took detailed case notes at the scene. The woman's blouse, slip and singlet had all been torn away from her body, with the blouse torn off completely. It and the slip, torn from the shoulders, had been bunched around the victim's waist. Likewise, her skirt and underwear had been torn away from her body and then dragged upwards where they, too, were bunched around her waist. The lower part of one of her arms was still in the sleeve of her cardigan; one of the detectives spotted her brassiere caught up in the other clothes.

Both McGuffie and Carey spent some time talking to Private McLeod, now back from the Royal Park police station. From him, they learned about the army trucks parked in Gatehouse Street, and how they were guarded overnight. New lines of enquiry opened up for the detectives as the young soldier spoke.

As the time approached 9 a.m., the area around the murder site in Gatehouse Street became a hive of activity, a mix of uniforms and suits, policemen and soldiers and civilians, all trying to make sense out of the senseless. There were a number of clear scuff marks around the body plus several indentations that could have been made by knees and feet as the woman was murdered and the body arranged for display. McGuffie had hoped to be able to use these and had sent for an Aboriginal tracker named George. George arrived shortly after 9 a.m., but took one look at the scene and said that he couldn't do anything because too many people had trampled through the area. He did note, though, that at some point an adult male had walked to or through the muddied area and had subsequently run across the park towards Camp Pell.

George's departure coincided with the arrival of a police car from Russell Street carrying Constable Arthur de la Rue, the police photographer, and a supply of gumboots for the detectives working the scene. Constable de la Rue took three photographs of the body from different angles as well as photographs of the handbag, newspaper and magazine, umbrella, purse, hat and gloves lying on the grass some twenty metres from the body.

Waiting discreetly in the background was a mortuary wagon and several attendants. When de la Rue had finished his work, McGuffie signalled to the attendants, who moved forward carrying a stretcher. They carefully lifted the woman's body onto that stretcher, turning it over as they did so. The body had left a clear imprint in the soft clay. Embarrassed at the attention being drawn to it, the attendants quickly covered the body with a sheet and carried it across to their wagon.

•

At the City Morgue, the body had to be hosed down to remove the all-encompassing mud before any form of examination could begin. While this washing down might have destroyed some evidence, it was equally clear that no real examination could be undertaken while it covered the body like some kind of yellow poultice. The formal post-mortem was again undertaken by Dr Crawford Mollison, the Government Pathologist, who spent most of what remained of the morning on the task. After the body had been cleaned, Mollison's examination quickly revealed many of the key indicators of strangulation. There was bruising around the larynx and Mollison found blood seeping from the right nostril. The victim's tongue was caught between her teeth, her face was livid and her eyes were bulging.

While Mollison found there were no signs of recent sexual activity, he found some kind of secretion which he could not identify in the woman's genital area. He also found an amount of yellow mud within the woman's vagina; he believed that it had been deliberately placed there.

•

They had known who she was almost from the time the butcher Whiteway spotted her lying in the yellow mud. Whoever had murdered her had made no real effort to interfere with her handbag which contained her purse and a number of identity documents. She was Gladys Lillian Hosking; she had lived a short distance away at a boarding house, 'Marembe', in Park Street and worked a little further away at the university. She had no known family in Melbourne. During the afternoon, Gladys's body was formally identified by another boarder from 140 Park Street, a retired grazier named John Gray; he had known her since she moved into the boarding house five years earlier.

•

Sid McGuffie felt that they were close, very close, and couldn't quite shake the feeling that the man they were chasing was just over the hill or around the corner, watching and waiting. This time though, that man was worried – or should be worried – because of the mistakes that he was beginning to make. His first two murders had not been perfect, as there were potential witnesses who could link him directly to both victims. But that was all they had on him, and it was circumstantial. This time, there was a particularly unique crime scene, one which would have left clear traces on the murderer. There were also a number of potential witnesses among the men who had been guarding the army trucks in Gatehouse Street and, hopefully, among those who shared Camp Pell with the murderer. Sid guessed that the murder scene might be crucial, and asked that it be particularly closely examined.

Detectives questioned the Camp Pell authorities and Melbourne City Council staff to learn why there was so much yellow clay mud in the exact place where the murder had been committed. The V-shaped slit trenches were for use during possible air raids and had only been dug out in recent weeks. Detectives learned that when digging at that particular part of Royal Park, the first half metre of soil was a dark, loamy material, but that below this topsoil there was a yellow clay substratum. Because this was the soil that had been excavated last, it had covered the loamy topsoil; the recent rains had made it very muddy and slippery.

The rest of the day would become a blur for McGuffie and his team and, indeed, for the American Provost Corps investigators, whose fortunes were now intertwined with theirs. MacArthur's headquarters had been apprised of the latest murder early on Tuesday morning. They were also told that an American soldier currently based at Camp Pell was almost certainly a serial killer. The response was prompt and vigorous. Full cooperation was again promised and Camp Pell was placed in full lockdown. Notionally this meant that no one was allowed to either enter or leave the facility, but the order seems to have been a bit elastic in its enforcement. Plus, there were areas of the camp where there simply was no fence to keep people either in or out. Headquarters also flagged in no uncertain terms their belief that the US Army would be ultimately responsible for the disposal of each and every one of its soldiers.

That argument was for the future. Sid McGuffie was focused on the situation at hand. He gained permission for his men to enter Camp Pell and split his detectives into two teams of four each. Those teams were instructed to work their way through the camp, at all times looking like detectives hot on the trail were expected to appear. They should also try to make eye contact with every American soldier they came across. It was a bit melodramatic, a bit Hollywood, but if the killer was falling apart, he might do something stupid when he saw the detectives.

McGuffie's men also checked the logs of the various guard posts in and around Camp Pell, and soon found the incidents reported the previous evening in Gatehouse Street by the

American private Malcolm Walsh and the Australian private Noel Seymour. Both men were ordered to report to the guard house at Camp Pell where they were given an armed escort who took them to their new quarters within the stockade. No chances were being taken; there was a killer on the loose, and these two soldiers could identify him.

Then suddenly, the morning was over, and there were a million things that still needed to be done. The Australian and American investigators had arranged to get together for a meeting before the police detectives returned to Russell Street to continue their enquiries. Sometime before the meeting was due to commence, McGuffie and Harry Carey spoke to a number of journalists who had asked to be briefed on the morning's murder and the progress of the investigations. The detectives had been matter-of-fact and had not responded to some of the wild allegations that were put to them. Not that it mattered in the long run; journalists would write what journalists wanted to write, and the public would probably accept it at face value.

The detectives simply had bigger fish to fry that Tuesday.

10.

A MUD-BESPATTERED BODY

McGuffie and his detectives were working to a timetable that they did not even know existed. As they were working to solve the cases of the deaths of three women, and to prevent the death of any more, those who were responsible for the war effort were plotting the destruction of a lot more than three people. Although the tide had yet to turn in the Pacific War, the Japanese advance was rapidly approaching its high-water mark. The Battle of the Coral Sea overlapped the Brownout Murders and represented the first real check of the Japanese thrust into the South West Pacific. They would shortly be checked again on the Kokoda Track before suffering their first real defeat, at the Battle of Midway, in the waters of the central Pacific. There would be heavy fighting on the periphery of that Japanese thrust, in Burma, New Guinea and Guadalcanal in the Solomon Islands. A lot of that fighting would be undertaken by American troops, troops who were continuing to pour into Australia. Melbourne was rapidly approaching its peak in numbers of American servicemen; by the end of June 1942, there would be 30000 of them in and around the city. But MacArthur was already planning the relocation of his headquarters, firstly to Brisbane and then – who knew where? He was also planning the movement of the southern-based troops, firstly to acclimatise and receive jungle-warfare training and then a move to – again, who knew where? The trucks in Gatehouse Street were part of the planning and would be part of the movement. In a short while, the troops who were today in Camp Pell would be somewhere else, somewhere that may perhaps be beyond the reach of the Victoria Police Homicide Squad.

•

Sid McGuffie and his detectives bought or borrowed copies of the evening edition of the Melbourne *Herald* that Tuesday, primarily to read what the general public knew and thought about the fact that somewhere in Melbourne there was believed to be an American soldier who murdered women in particularly brutal circumstances, and who appeared to have evaded all attempts to capture him.

The reporting in the *Herald*, although prominent on the front page, was almost restrained:

> *Another woman has been murdered in Melbourne. Her half-clothed body was found at dawn today inside the Royal Park boundary, in Gatehouse Street. It was the third crime of its type in Melbourne in 15 days ... She was strangled and probably criminally assaulted. A post-mortem examination is being held ... The murder site was only around 350 yards [320 metres] from the boarding house where she lived ... The clothing, as in similar mysteries in Spring Street nine days ago and Albert Park a week earlier, was disarranged.*

Other newspaper reporting was equally matter-of-fact:

The strangled and partly-clad body of the victim was found on
a clay bank beside a slit trench . . . Her clothes had been torn
from her shoulders and pulled up from her legs forming a heap
around her waist . . . The body was so bespattered with mud
that no exterior injuries could be seen . . . A post-mortem exam-
ination disclosed later that the woman had been throttled, and
that possibly she had been criminally assaulted.

What the newspapers did not report that week was the effect that the latest murder had on an already nervous city of Melbourne and its people. Shaky at best, the morale, esprit – call it what you will – dropped to very close to rock bottom. It was a situation without precedent. In parts of the city, three out of every four males were in uniform but, instead of being a reassuring presence, those uniforms – especially if they were US Army uniforms – came to increasingly represent a threat. In the late afternoons and early evenings, swarms of young men in uniform took over parts of the city, singing out loud, laughing and jostling one another and sometimes the civilians around them as well. What had been just boisterous behaviour now contained within it something dark and evil.

Even before that Tuesday morning's discovery, many young women simply stopped going to work if that work was based in the city. As winter approached and the days grew shorter, those women who continued to work in the city ended their working days in the early afternoon, to be well and truly home and safe by nightfall.

In the suburbs to which those young women travelled, doors and windows would be locked and checked before dark, and then checked again. The trams and trains that used to take those young women home were no longer packed; at best, they would be half-full and most of their passengers were male. That week, it was well-nigh impossible to see a woman alone anywhere in the city or inner suburbs.

When details of Gladys Hosking's murder were released, public reactions and public responses both increased in scope and hardened in nature. The Volunteer Defence Corps, a part-time military reserve organisation broadly based on Britain's Home Guard, proposed the formation of vigilante squads to patrol Melbourne's browned-out streets. Practical measures were also canvassed. Writing to a Melbourne newspaper, A. E. Spowers of South Yarra suggested that, 'In view of recent happenings would it not be a simple thing for any woman obliged to be alone on the streets at night to carry a good shrill whistle in her hand, attached to her wrist by a cord? In most cases there would surely be time for one good blast.'

The general warning to women issued earlier, to avoid dark lanes and streets unless escorted, was again sounded while other more fanciful suggestions were also put forward. One was for police to dress as women and walk slowly through the types of areas the murderer seemed to prefer in the hope of entrapping him; there does not seem to have been any official response to any of these suggestions.

There was a knock-on effect from all this. After dark, the streets of Melbourne were practically deserted, even though the Dunstan Government announced an easing of the brownout on the Wednesday of that week. Theatres, dance halls and the plethora of clubs that had sprung up to provide wartime entertainment sent staff home early when it became clear that there would be no patrons knocking on the door each evening.

It was a situation that was reported widely across Australia and one that gave rise to residual fears wherever large camps containing American soldiers were located. In the far north, one daily newspaper noted that:

To-day's murder gives credence to the belief that there is a maniac-killer at large in Melbourne. Girl munition workers and others who are compelled to go home in brownouts are becoming panic-stricken, and many have refused to continue working at night. Police are providing extra patrols and are being assisted by ARP [Air Raid Precautions] wardens and special constables. These have been placed on duty in various parts of the city and suburbs, especially where the brownout is severe.

Eddie's notoriety was spreading across a whole continent and, if he was aware of it, surely would have caused him to smile, just a little.

•

The newspapers were still cautious and avoided affirming what the public feared, and what Sid McGuffie and his team now knew without a shred of doubt – the murders were the work of a serial killer. The *Herald* had noted that, 'While there were many points of similarity between the murder of Miss Hosking and the deaths of Mrs Pauline Thompson and Mrs Ivy McLeod, the detectives said, it should not be taken for granted the one person committed the three crimes for there were also several points of dissimilarity.'

That statement was simply Harry Carey and Sid McGuffie talking to newspaper reporters, seeming to give them something while not really giving them anything at all, partly to keep the killer guessing about the progress of the investigation, and partly because that was the way they habitually operated when on the record with reporters. It was a game, and everyone knew and respected the rules of that game.

The simple fact was that, by the time the newspapers hit the streets that Tuesday afternoon, McGuffie and his team knew that it was a matter of days at most, hours at least, before the one man they sought was arrested. They knew there had always been just the one murderer and, apart from the three women he had killed, they were now aware of several other attacks – attempted rapes and assaults – he had also committed in recent weeks. They had a detailed physical description of him from at least two of those who had survived his attacks, and they were pretty certain that they now knew his first name and his initials. It was now a process to be worked through rather than a greenfield investigation, one they hoped to end before that one particular American soldier, whoever he was, could claim another victim.

●

Late in the morning of that Tuesday, 19 May, after the murder scene in Gatehouse Street had been cleared and local homes canvassed for possible information, Sid McGuffie and several of his detectives headed across to the Provost Marshall's complex in Camp Pell, located towards the rear of the camp and positioned behind a sports area enclosed by a little white picket fence. The Provost area itself, generally referred to as 'the stockade' by the Americans, contained several huts and a row of tents, and it was in one of those huts that McGuffie and his men met with military policemen from the Provost Corps to discuss the progress of their individual and joint investigations. Neither side was in any doubt that the killer they sought was an American serviceman and, moreover, one who was based right there at Camp Pell.

McGuffie first brought the Americans up to date on what his team had learned about the latest victim, Gladys Hosking. Enquiries at her place of residence in Park Street had revealed that she had not returned to the boarding house the previous evening. The autopsy had revealed that Hosking had eaten a meal sometime before she was killed and they learned that she had not eaten it at her boarding house. This had not caused any concern at the house because Hosking did not always have her evening meals there. The others who boarded there were aware that she sometimes dined with friends either at their homes or at cafés or restaurants in the city.

None of the residents in or around Hosking's boarding house in Park Street had seen or heard anything unusual the previous evening, and the same applied to residents who lived in Gatehouse Street within a reasonable distance of the murder site. Enquiries were continuing to identify all Australian Army personnel who may have had reason to be in Gatehouse Street the night before, while initial enquiries with Hosking's employers at the University of Melbourne suggested that she was a well-loved and much respected member of staff there.

On the American side, one of their investigators noted that they were having some success with the early telephone tip-off about the man who walked on his hands. Talking to some of their regular contacts, mostly MPs who patrolled in the city and some of their regular defaulters, they had learned of the existence of a US Army private who had developed a reputation for bizarre drinking habits and a predilection to show off his physical strength by walking along hotel bars on his hands. No one seemed to know his full identity, but he was always referred to as 'Eddie'.

McGuffie received two additional pieces of information as the meeting progressed, sent to him by Harry Carey at Russell Street. One contained the details of an attempted assault in Park Street the previous week, when only quick thinking by her uncle had saved a young woman from rape, or worse. Both the young woman and her uncle believed they could identify the attacker, an American serviceman.

The second was a report that had just been received from the New South Wales Police Criminal Investigation Branch in Sydney. There, an Inspector Matthews had interviewed a young couple who had lived in Melbourne but now resided in Sydney. Both seemed very nervous, but had come forward after reading about the murders of Ivy McLeod and Pauline Thompson in the Sydney newspapers. The young woman explained how, a little over a week before the McLeod murder, she had been on holiday in Melbourne, staying at a flat in St Kilda. There, a man had followed her to her flat where he had firstly choked and then almost raped her. She had escaped and her assailant had fled. He was a young American soldier, she said, and in his haste to get away, he had left behind his army singlet. It had his initials written on it, she continued, and they were 'E. J. L.'.

•

On the previous Thursday, 14 May, a police line-up had been held on the main parade ground at Camp Pell. Hundreds of American soldiers were lined up in company formation, at ease, until a police van and two police cars arrived at the ground, and a number of uniformed and plainclothes policemen hopped out. Those policemen formed an escort for a civilian, a woman who appeared to be in her mid-30s, brown-haired and dressed in black, with a fur stole across her shoulders.

Accompanied by her escort, the woman walked between the lines of men, looking intently at their faces and pausing every now and then. After half an hour or so, the small group returned to their cars and van and departed; shortly afterwards, the parade was dismissed without a word of explanation and the men drifted back to their own tents and their own thoughts. Try as she might, Esther Grunden had been unable to recognise the man who had murdered her old friend, Pauline Thompson, the previous Saturday night.

●

Despite the failure of the line-up the previous week, all present at the Tuesday conference felt energised by the new information, believing that they were now agonisingly close to finding their man. Agreement was quickly reached on a number of key points. The Victorian police would continue the Hosking lines of enquiry while also following up the information that had arrived from New South Wales and the details of the recent attack in Park Street. They would be particularly interested in assessing whether either or both of the young women involved in the Park Street and St Kilda attacks would be able to make a positive identification of their attacker.

The Americans would firstly try to identify the 'Eddie' and the 'E. J. L.' among the 25 000 or so American servicemen then in and around Melbourne, starting their enquiries in Camp Pell. That camp was now locked down. The previous week, when the first line-up had been attempted, there had been no lockdown and no one seemed to know exactly how many servicemen were present or absent anyway. They now had two witnesses – the American private Malcolm Walsh and the Australian private Noel Seymour – safely holed away elsewhere in the stockade, and both of them had seen the American soldier near the murder site the previous evening. They agreed to hold another line-up at Camp Pell later in the afternoon, and they were reasonably confident that all the men they wanted to be there would actually be there this time.

It was still early in the afternoon, and they all now had tasks they wanted and needed to be doing. They stood up, shook hands and headed off to work.

•

Like most of the other Americans in Camp Pell, Joey Gallo learned that another woman had been murdered – and this one on the very doorstep of Camp Pell – shortly after breakfast on that Tuesday morning. He decided to confront his friend Eddie Leonski with this, and again attempt to get a straight answer from him about what he really knew about the series of murders that had occurred. When he arrived at Leonski's tent, he found his friend outside, looking pale and dishevelled, trying to light a cigarette. When their eyes met, Gallo's courage failed him, and he simply nodded a greeting and continued walking.

He saw Eddie again later that morning in the building which served as the combination canteen and mess hall. This time, Joey's courage did not fail him and he asked Eddie point blank whether he knew anything about the murder of a woman the previous night in Gatehouse Street. This time, Eddie seemed to be taken aback by the directness of Gallo's question, and he hesitated before answering it. No, he told his little friend, he knew nothing about that or either of the other murders. He then tried to reassure Joey by saying that robbery was the worst thing that he had ever done.

The two met again in more unusual circumstances later that day. All those at Camp Pell knew that something was afoot, and most of them were smart enough to realise that it had something to do with the previous night's murder and perhaps even to the recent series of murders. They had been told that the camp was in lockdown until further notice and then, around the middle of the afternoon, they were told they would be assembled, unit by unit, outside the mess hall where, again unit by unit, they would file through as part of a police line-up; no further details had or would be given.

Eddie and Joey were together when it was the turn of the Headquarters Company of the 52nd Signallers to pass through the line-up parade. As they walked into the hall, Leonski quipped to Joey, 'This looks like the end of the trail for me.' Despite this, both of them entered the hall, marched past a group of men seated behind a trestle table, stopping briefly to attention in front of them, and exited again without any form of challenge. A clearly relieved Joey Gallo said to Leonski when they were again outside and alone, 'You had me worried for a long time, but everything is all right now.' The two men then separated, heading in different directions back to their own tents.

Despite all that had happened that day, Joey Gallo continued to harbour deep-seated doubts about Eddie and remained unconvinced by his denials and semi-denials about his knowledge of the murders. Gallo spent a very fitful night, but at some stage during that night decided that the following day he would report his suspicions about Eddie. After breakfast on Wednesday, 20 May, Joey Gallo approached one of his regimental officers and asked to speak to that officer in private.

When they were alone, Joey Gallo poured his heart out to the officer, explaining all his doubts and concerns about his friend Eddie Leonski, his belief that it might have been Eddie who had murdered the three Melbourne women, and continued by recounting several of the quite bizarre conversations the two had shared in recent weeks. The officer was so concerned about what he had heard that he escorted Gallo across to Camp Pell Headquarters where, later in the day, Joey repeated everything that he had earlier said to the officer. This time, what he said was taken down by a stenographer and then typed up to become a formal statement, which Joey signed and which was witnessed. By then, however, Joey's statement had been largely superseded by events elsewhere in the camp.

•

The failure of the Tuesday afternoon line-up was a disappointment rather than a major setback. The detectives, both Australian and American, thought that the witnesses might struggle to make an immediate identification because of the circumstances in which they had seen the suspected murderer – poor visibility, suspect covered in mud, etc. They were also aware that there were probably a significant number of US soldiers who had missed being in the line-up that had, after all, been organised in a bit of a rush. It was therefore decided to hold another, more organised line-up on the next afternoon, Wednesday, 20 May.

This second line-up was held on the Camp Pell parade ground, and the Victoria Police and US Army Provost Corps detectives believed they had a much stronger group of witnesses this time. The main witness was the young woman who had been attacked while entering her home in Park Street the previous week, and who had been saved by the intervention of her uncle. That uncle, Mr Jackson, would also be present, as would Private Francis Hanson, the US soldier who had seen and spoken to Gladys Hosking and another American soldier in Gatehouse Street shortly before Hosking was murdered.

This second parade ground line-up was not a success either. To begin with, it was another cold, wet and windy afternoon. There was a small group of police and witnesses, huddled beneath umbrellas for the most part, and there were hundreds, thousands, of American soldiers lined up in formations in the persistent drizzle. On command, those formations would march to the front, walk past the little group with the umbrellas in single file, before returning to their original positions on the parade ground.

It felt like hours before the last of the soldiers completed their march past the witnesses, and in that time not one of the soldiers was either called out or challenged. When the entire parade was called to attention and then dismissed, it was to a chorus of hoots, catcalls and Bronx cheers.

As the soldiers, policemen and witnesses started to disperse, Mr Jackson stood talking to a group of Victorian detectives and American military police, as the latter were attempting to organise transport to take all the civilians and police officers home from the camp. A loose group of chattering soldiers walked past them and, as they did, Jackson suddenly stiffened, pointed to one of the soldiers in the group and said, 'There. That's the man who attacked my niece!'

Private Eddie Leonski was then arrested without any cer-emony and without any drama. One of the MPs called him over and informed him that he was being taken into custody, then called the other MPs over to guard the prisoner, ready to physically restrain him if necessary; it wasn't. Provost Sergeant Samuel Trager, in charge of the detachment of MPs, formed them into an escort around Leonski and led them all to the stockade. With the agreement of the Camp Pell Headquarters, they were accompanied by Detective Sergeant Sid McGuffie and Detectives Fred Adam and George Murray of the Victoria Police Homicide Squad.

Sergeant Trager led the group to one of the tents used to accommodate detainees in the stockade. He was aware that Leonski had walked out of the area without any real difficulty some weeks earlier and decided that no chances would be taken with the prisoner this time. When he ordered that one of Leonski's hands be handcuffed to the iron bedstead of the tent's single bed, a kind of struggle ensued. The handcuffs were of the one-size-fits-all variety, while Leonski's wrists and forearms weren't; Trager thought they might well have been the thickest wrists he had ever seen.

The handcuffs were eventually successfully attached to wrist and bed, and Leonski made himself as comfortable as he could on the bed. He then looked up at the policemen, American and Australian, service and civilian, who were sitting on chairs in a half-circle, all staring intently at him.

•

At around the same time as the American soldiers were being herded into their formations on the Camp Pell parade ground, a little over a kilometre away, another sort of coming together was taking place. At 2.30 p.m. in the Trinity College Chapel at the University of Melbourne, a funeral service for the late Gladys Lillian Hosking commenced. Gladys's parents were unable to attend; her mother went into shock when told of her daughter's death and her father's health was also starting to break down. A number of more distant relatives, first and second cousins, were in attendance, as were a large number of fellow staff from the university, staff from Fintona Girls' School, and numerous friends that Gladys had made through either her artistic and patriotic endeavours, or simply through being the good person that she was.

The service was not a long one – a brief summary of a rich life cut too short – and was conducted by the chaplain of Trinity College. The lesson was read by John Medley, Vice-Chancellor of the University of Melbourne. Afterwards, a small procession followed the hearse up Royal Parade, past Gatehouse Street and along Sydney Road to Fawkner Cemetery, where the remains of Gladys Hosking were interred.

Once the service there had concluded, the mourners headed off, most hurrying to get home. The weather was threatening, it would soon be dark, and Melbourne after dark was no longer a safe place to be.

11.

THE RIGHT TO REMAIN SILENT

Sid McGuffie was anxious to conclude the process of collecting evidence to bolster a case that was already taking shape in his head. He did not yet know whether Eddie Leonski had killed three Melbourne women in a spree that had lasted just over two weeks or whether he was innocent of everything, including the Park Street assault of the week past. Leonski was the only suspect they had, though, and everything about him – his name, his initials, his appearance and his demeanour – said that, to Sid at least, they had their man. What McGuffie and his team now had to do was build an airtight case to support that belief.

US Army Headquarters had promised full cooperation and were as good as their word. Sid wanted to examine Leonski's tent; he and Detective George Murray were given an escort of seven military policemen who led them straight there. While a couple of those MPs kept onlookers away, others spoke to Leonski's tent mates, telling them about what was going on, telling them that they should be prepared to make formal statements and warning them not to discuss anything with anyone who wasn't either a member of the Provost Corps or a Victorian detective, and then only if there was a US Army officer present.

The first thing both McGuffie and Murray noticed when they entered Leonski's tent were a number of yellow mud stains on his bed and bedding and, indeed, on the tent itself. Each of these was examined closely, with both men taking notes and drawing sketches of what they found. Although it appeared that some effort had been made to wash away the marks, they remained quite obvious to the naked eye. The detectives also looked at some yellow clay smudge marks on the inside surface of both the roof and one wall of the tent alongside Leonski's bed. Acting in roles, they found that the marks were in the exact positions you would expect to find them if they were the hand-prints of someone trying to keep their balance as they dressed or undressed while unsteady on their feet.

They were able to draw similar conclusions about the other smudges and stains. The yellow mud marks on the bed's iron bedstead approximated the position a person would place their hands if they were having problems either getting into or out of the bed. The stain on the bed's bedspread was where the left hand of a person sleeping on their back would have rested.

The Victorian detectives then examined all of Leonski's clothing and personal effects, some of which were in a cupboard and some of which were in his footlocker. In the hanging space, they found an army field jacket with a faint yellow stain on its front; the stain and the area around it were damp from what appeared to be efforts to scrub it away. Hanging alongside the jacket was a pair of army field pants. They, too, were quite wet and seemed to have been recently washed. Despite this, McGuffie believed he could clearly see where there had been a yellow stain on the left knee. Both these items were placed in one of the large brown paper bags the men had with them.

The two detectives also seized a pair of shoes with yellow clay spots obvious in several places on them. One of the military policemen entered the tent while they were doing this to state that one of Leonski's tent mates had told them that Leonski's shoes had been completely covered in yellow mud the previous day and that he had seen Leonski attempting to clean them up with a scrubbing brush. That scrubbing brush was found underneath Leonski's bed, alongside a small tin box. When opened, that box was found to contain newspaper clippings about the murders of Ivy McLeod and Pauline Thompson. The box had also been sitting on top of a copy of the Melbourne *Herald* of 5 May, the edition that contained all the details about the murder of Ivy McLeod.

Three other items went into the brown paper bags. One was a bath towel, also still damp, which seemed to have a number of yellow stains on it. The second was another pair of army field pants with 'Edward, 52nd Signallers' written inside the waistband and what appeared to be bloodstains on the bottom of both legs. Finally, they also took away a pair of men's underpants which seemed to have a number of bloodstains around the crotch area.

McGuffie and Murray then collected their several paper bags and, again escorted by the MPs, returned to the stockade where they had left Eddie Leonski. In the detention tent, they found that Leonski's original guards had been replaced by Sam Trager and another Provost sergeant, both of whom stood up when the detectives entered. Item by item, McGuffie removed from the paper bags the evidence they had taken from Leonski's tent and, item by item, Leonski admitted ownership of them all. The scrubbing brush, he explained, was not actually his but was one that he had taken from the kitchen area of the mess hall, and several items were wet because they had been dirty and he had washed them. It was very hard, he added, to get things dry in this goddamn weather.

When asked if he had anything to say, Leonski shook his head. McGuffie and Murray picked up their bags and turned to head off into what had now become night time. At the tent door, McGuffie turned back to Leonski and said, 'I'll be back tomorrow, Private Leonski,' he said, 'and I'll have some colleagues with me.' Raising one of the bags, he added, 'And we'll have some questions for you.'

●

The items collected in Eddie Leonski's tent were taken directly back to Russell Street Police Headquarters, where they were then carried up to the offices of the Police Scientific Bureau for analysis by Dr Charles Taylor. In the Bureau's laboratory, the damp items were first dried in front of an electric radiator and, when dry, rubbed together to release the soil particles onto sheets of thick white paper spread across a table top. These soil particles would then be compared, microscopically and chemically, with samples of the yellow clay soil taken from the spot where Gladys Hosking's body had been found.

●

The arrest of Eddie Leonski had also prompted a flurry of behind-the-scenes legal manoeuvring, much of which involved compromises. From the time both the Australian and American investigators realised that the murderer was most likely a serving soldier in the US Army, a number of legal issues were brought into clear focus. If the murderer was indeed an American soldier and the case was allowed to proceed to trial, the first question to be answered was what exact court proceedings would that soldier face? The offences that had been committed in Melbourne had taken place within the jurisdiction of Victoria and were offences against the laws of that state. However, the United States military authorities had made it quite clear from the time they had arrived in Melbourne that they expected to have the final say in any legal proceedings involving their troops.

Fortunately, common sense and goodwill prevailed. This was helped in no inconsiderable way by General MacArthur, who, when told of the Hosking murder, personally contacted the Provost Corps Headquarters at Camp Pell and told them to make certain every effort was made to, firstly apprehend, and then try, convict and mete out the appropriate punishment to the murderer. The cause was also helped by the fact that, in May 1939, the Australian Parliament had passed the *Defence (Visiting Forces) Act* which would allow, subject to a formal request to the Australian government, for the accused if that accused was an American soldier, for instance, to be handed over to the American government and tried in Australia under US law. The current circumstances were probably not what were envisaged when the Act was passed, but all believed it would be robust enough to cover those circumstances.

To strengthen their claims against possible legal challenges, US Army lawyers filed legal opinions claiming that because Gladys Hosking had been murdered within the gazetted boundaries of the Camp Pell military base, her murder had technically been committed on the equivalent of American soil, a claim neither the Australian nor the Victorian governments would challenge. The Camp Pell authorities quickly opened and closed a court martial to confirm that responsibility and that authority.

The Victorian government also indicated its willingness to assist in any legal processes that would help to prosecute and punish the offender. Under Victorian law, a coroner's inquest was required to be conducted into every death that occurred in unusual circumstances or if the coroner considered one necessary. What the state government was prepared to do was to allow the coroner to open an inquest for the purpose of the formal identification of the killer's victims, and then adjourn that inquest pending the result of a general court martial conducted under US military law. US Army authorities agreed to this proposal.

At the working level, the Americans firstly removed Leonski from the official strength of his regiment, placing him into the administrative responsibility of the Provost Corps. That corps then gave official permission to the Victoria Police for Leonski to be formally interviewed by detectives from the Homicide Squad. It was agreed that if those detectives wanted to take Leonski away from Camp Pell for an interview, there would need to be two American officers present at each interview held in those circumstances. Plus, the Americans insisted that Leonski could not be charged with any criminal offences unless US Army Headquarters issued the appropriate authorisations. Through Harry Carey, the Victoria Police agreed to these conditions, indicating that they were prepared to have the investigation based at Camp Pell and that they were happy to conduct their interviews there.

If Eddie Leonski was to face a court martial trial for the murders of three women in Melbourne, he would become the first citizen of a foreign country to be tried in Australia under his home country's laws for crimes committed against Australian laws. Before that could happen, however, a prosecution case had to be built from the ground up.

•

Sid McGuffie was a good detective, which meant that Sid McGuffie was a thorough detective. He did not yet know whether or not Eddie Leonski was going to be difficult or easy to break down, to gain confession to the three murders Sid believed the soldier had committed; he didn't even have a good feel for whether or not the man could even be broken. But Sid was going to give it his best shot and that meant a carefully thought out plan and enough patience to let that plan come into effect. The first full day of detention would offer the best opportunity to put the plan into place, even if the results might be a long time in coming. The key to it all, Sid knew, was to maintain control, even when it looked as though someone else – even Leonski himself – was running things. Everything that happened that Thursday needed to have Sid McGuffie's imprimatur somewhere on it.

•

The first formal interview of Eddie Leonski commenced at 8 a.m. on the morning of Thursday, 21 May in a hut in the stockade, the Provost Marshall's area within Camp Pell. Armed American MPs escorted Leonski from his detention tent to the hut, and took him inside to where two men in dark suits sat behind a trestle table and two US Army officers sat in their chairs along one side wall. The MPs led Leonski to a chair placed in front of the table. Before he could sit down, the older of the two men – both of whom had spoken to him in his tent the previous evening – stood up, extended his hand and said in a serious voice, 'Private Leonski, I am Detective Sergeant McGuffie and this', indicating his partner, 'is Detective Adam.'

The three exchanged handshakes, and McGuffie indicated that Leonski could now sit, doing so himself at the same time. Fred Adam remained standing and, looking down at the prisoner, went through the legal caution given to all persons before a formal police interview was commenced. Leonski did not have to answer their questions, he was told, and he had the right to remain silent. He was then reminded that if he did provide answers, those things he said would be taken down and might be used in a court as evidence against him. Leonski nodded his understanding, and Fred Adam sat down.

Sid McGuffie then took over. He did not usually shake hands with people suspected of several murders, but he had wanted to be able to gauge the man's strength himself and had chosen the most natural way possible. It had worked, and he had been impressed by the man's grip. He also wanted to keep Leonski slightly off-balance, so when the prisoner asked him if he would be able to smoke, McGuffie told him that, no, he couldn't – just to ratchet the pressure Leonski was feeling up that little bit more. He softened the atmosphere a bit as well, by asking Leonski about his upbringing, and how he came to join the army and finish up in Australia.

This was all part of another of McGuffie's ploys; he knew you could learn a lot about a person by asking such a question and then listening carefully to the answer. Again, Sid was not disappointed. From his rambling recollections, it was obvious that his mother was the central figure in Leonski's stories about growing up in New York City. The detectives also learned that Leonski was inordinately proud of what he saw as an exceptional capacity to drink alcohol, exceptional strength in the upper body and an exceptional ability to attract women.

Almost by stealth, McGuffie then proceeded to introduce the concept of murder by saying that he and Detective Adam had spent a lot of time the previous evening and again early that morning reading an extremely interesting statement about Eddie by his good friend, Private Anthony Gallo. The statement, said McGuffie, seemed to suggest that Eddie may have murdered the three women in Melbourne and, in fact, had partly bragged and partly confessed to Gallo that he had done so.

Eddie Leonski took all this in his stride, and responded quite affably to what was put to him. His little friend, Joey, said Leonski, probably had no other friends in the world, and Eddie said he had taken his fellow New Yorker under his wing way back in San Antonio because the others were always picking on him. They did so, Eddie suggested, because Joey was, well, a little bit simple. He was likeable, but simple and even a little bit gullible. Eddie had used this in a way that may have been a bit cruel, by saying things that he knew would lead Joey to think that he was a killer, and then stringing him along with it. Eddie said that he had even taken to collecting newspaper articles on the Melbourne murders, and reading them carefully so that he could add authenticity to some of the stories he told Joey.

By the end of all this, the interview had been going for almost two hours and it was approaching 10 a.m. McGuffie said that there were some other things that needed to happen and that they would therefore suspend the interview for an hour and recommence it at 11 a.m. While they were gone, Eddie might be able to go outside with the guards and have a cigarette.

•

At almost precisely ten o'clock, Leonski was given a complete and detailed medical examination by Captain Clyde Servis, a doctor in the Medical Administrative Corps who was currently attached to the 4th General Hospital. That hospital was itself located near Camp Pell at the Royal Melbourne Hospital. While that examination was taking place, McGuffie and Adam returned to Russell Street to collect some of the items they had taken from Leonski's tent the previous evening and to see what Charles Taylor and his team had found.

That team, and Taylor himself, had done an excellent job in the limited time available to them. Taylor had started on Leonski's shoes, finding a small quantity of mustard yellow clay in the eyelet holes of both shoes, on the stitching on one side, and on the upper part of the sole. They, and the separate samples taken from Leonski's clothes, tent, bed frame and bedding, were described by Taylor as 'most probably' coming from the place where Gladys Hosking's body had been found. That was good enough for McGuffie, who took Taylor's professional assessment, and several of Leonski's possessions, with him when he and Fred Adam returned to Camp Pell to continue the interview.

•

McGuffie got straight down to work when the interview recommenced. He and Fred Adam removed a number of items from large brown paper bags and placed them on the table in front of Leonski. When asked, the American freely admitted that they all belonged to him. Picking up one of the shoes, McGuffie pointed to the small specks of yellow clay still clearly visible in the eyelets and in some of the stitching. He then asked Leonski where that yellow clay mud had come from. 'Around the kitchen,' was Leonski's reply.

In this manner, McGuffie and Adam worked their way through all of Leonski's possessions laid out on the table. Pointing to the trousers, one would ask, 'What about this yellow stain here?' while the other would do the same with discolouration on an army jacket or a pair of socks. Always, the answer was the same, 'I fell over in this part of the camp,' or, 'I slipped and fell when walking through that part of the camp.'

It only started to change when McGuffie started to ask Leonski about the yellow mud marks they had found on his tent and bedding.

Leonski may have sensed that his short and repetitive answers must have started to sound like a stock reply, one that may have been predetermined, for his answers now became more expansive. His clothes had been wet the previous day, he explained, because he had done a lot of washing that morning, and they simply had not had enough time to dry because of the weather. He had done a big load of washing because he had noticed that a lot of his clothes had been dirty. While some had simply been soiled with everyday dirt and grime, others had been splashed with mud as he made his way around the camp.

There were equally simple explanations for the other mud stains as well, he continued. Some of the yellow marks were probably from a couple of nights earlier when he had fallen over near the kitchen. The stains clearly evident on the towel the detectives produced were from another soldier, who had borrowed it; he had no idea where they came from. The mud on his bedstead and bedclothes were from yet another soldier's boots. That soldier, drunk, had passed out on Leonski's bed. The marks on the inside of the tent were probably from the same man.

At this, Sid McGuffie seemed to change tack. He conferred briefly with Fred Adam and then with the American officers seated in the background, before telling Leonski that they were all going for a walk to the places that he had spoken about, to examine just where he had suggested that he might have got the yellow mud on his shoes and clothes. For ease of movement, they were going to remove Leonski's handcuffs, but they would be accompanied by three armed MPs who had been instructed to shoot Leonski if he made any attempt to escape.

The group went firstly to the kitchen area where Leonski pointed out a couple of areas that were indeed very muddy and slippery, but the mud there was black. From the kitchen they went to several other sites around the camp, mainly high-use areas like the ablutions block and the canteen/mess hall areas. There were several muddy patches near each but, again, the mud they found was always black. When they returned to the interview hut and were again seated, McGuffie asked Leonski about this, questioning how slipping on or falling in black mud patches could leave yellow mud on his shoes, clothes and tent. Leonski was prepared to argue the point, with an argument that suggested that the yellow mud was 'old' mud that had only become apparent when the newer, black mud was removed. At this point, they broke for lunch – eaten separately – and agreed to continue the walk around and interview in half an hour.

●

McGuffie opened the afternoon session by asking Leonski where he had been during the afternoon and evening of 18 May, the Monday just passed. Without any real hesitation, Leonski replied that he had spent the afternoon drinking at a hotel near the camp, and then had gone to a nearby house with one of the men he'd been drinking with. At the house, he lay down on a bed for a while, probably no more than a few minutes, before getting up and leaving because the man hadn't come back.

McGuffie followed up by asking Leonski if he had been in Gatehouse Street at any time on Monday evening. Leonski hesitated for a moment before asking the detective how far Gatehouse Street was from the hotel. He asked this, he said, because sometimes when he was drinking he went to places but could not remember those places afterwards. On occasion, friends would tell him that they'd seen him in places that he was certain he'd never visited.

Now adopting a more official tone, McGuffie told Leonski that a woman had been murdered in Gatehouse Street on the night of Monday, 18 May, and that the interview they had started that morning was part of the police investigation into that murder. McGuffie then cautioned Leonski for a second time, explaining again his right to remain silent before asking Leonski if he wanted to make a statement; Leonski said he didn't. Finally, in response to a direct question from McGuffie, Eddie Leonski formally denied that he had walked with a woman in and around the intersection of Gatehouse Street and Royal Parade on the night in question.

McGuffie next suggested that it was time to repeat the morning's exercise, as there were a number of sites that he wanted Leonski to see. Again, he would have Leonski's handcuffs removed and, again, they would be accompanied by armed MPs who had instructions to shoot Leonski if he made the wrong move.

The detective then led the same small group through Camp Pell and directly to the area along Gatehouse Street where the trenches had been dug and where Gladys Hosking's body had been found. As McGuffie explained the significance of the site, he also pointed out the yellow clay mud, indicating that this was the one and only area from which the yellow mud on Leonski's possessions could have come. When questioned on this by McGuffie, Leonski conceded that he may have passed through the area and may, indeed, even have fallen over in that mud. But, he added, when he had a load of liquor aboard, he sometimes had difficulty remembering where he had been and what he had done.

Leonski did not recognise – or did not admit to recognising – a couple of notable sites in nearby Park Street. One was the boarding house where Gladys Hosking had resided, and the second was the house where a young woman had been attacked the previous week. Nor did he think that he had been to the milk bar on the corner of Gatehouse Street and Royal Parade before. He had no hesitation, however, when it came to identifying the Parkville Hotel and the nearby boarding house where his erstwhile drinking buddy, Rupert Burns, had lived and where he, himself, had laid down for a few minutes in one of the four beds in there, that upstairs front bedroom.

As they walked around, the two men talked in an almost collegiate manner. Sid McGuffie pointed out the various sites of interest in the Gladys Hosking murder case, explaining how the killer may have walked here and there, and probably stopped there and there. Eddie Leonski nodded to some, denied ever seeing others and remained mute at many more. At one point, Sid asked him directly if he felt responsible for all his actions since he arrived in Australia; Eddie replied that, yes, of course he did.

McGuffie had asked the question because of the patterns that were starting to emerge from Leonski's behaviour and answers to the various questions they had put to him. He seemed to be mentally preparing some kind of defence in case he was ever put on trial. He was a big drinker, sure, but that drinking left some blank spots in his recall. He may have gone to places and done things that he was not aware of. In fact, he probably did, because friends would remind him of them afterwards. Sure, he also accepted responsibility for his actions, but only those actions that he consciously took. How could he be held responsible for things that he wasn't even aware had happened?

It was similar on the walk around. Leonski freely admitted to being in places where he knew many others had seen him and could testify to that effect. The hotel and boarding house, and certain spots around Camp Pell, for instance. If he said that he hadn't been there and a parade of witnesses testified to the fact that he had been, he would be branded a liar. But if he denied being at places where no witnesses could place him – the yellow clay slit trenches – then it simply became a matter of supposition and not disputed fact.

Their walk had taken the group in a broad circle that both started and ended in the stockade in Camp Pell, and they had walked in a counter-clockwise direction. It was mid-afternoon by the time they arrived back at the interview hut, and there McGuffie informed Leonski that the interview was now over for the day and that he and Detective Adam had to leave because some other people wanted to speak to them about the case. Eddie again said that he had no wish to make a statement; McGuffie said they would be back to continue the interview sometime on Friday and with that, the detectives left without another word, or another handshake.

•

Discussing the day later on, McGuffie and Adam were both happy with what they thought had been achieved. Both believed that Eddie Leonski was the killer – he certainly had the strength to be a strangler – and by giving him a guided tour of the places they believed the killer had been, they let him know they were well aware of the sequence of events on that Monday night. In doing so, they were also telling Leonski that if they had a witness to link him to the killer's known movements with Gladys Hosking, their case was complete and Eddie would be charged with her murder. They also let him know, although somewhat more subtly, that they were not looking at anyone else and that they still had a number of potential witnesses to interview. The detectives felt they had ratcheted up the pressure today; they would increase it even further tomorrow.

●

Like the war, of which it had become a very small part, the investigation into the murders committed by the Brownout Strangler proceeded on several different fronts. During that Thursday afternoon, while McGuffie, Leonski and their entourage were walking and talking their way around Parkville, Constable Arthur de la Rue, the police photographer, returned to Camp Pell, this time to take a series of photographs inside the camp. These included photographs of the location of Eddie Leonski's tent, the interior and exterior of that tent, and close-up photographs of Leonski's bedstead.

After leaving Leonski in the interview hut, McGuffie and Adam had separated. Fred Adam returned to Russell Street to start preparing for the next day, in which he would have the leading role. Sid McGuffie went to the Camp Pell Headquarters where he met another detective, Bill Mooney. The two policemen were taken to a room where they met Private Joey Gallo accompanied by a Provost officer. For the next hour, they grilled Gallo extensively, testing some of Leonski's responses to the claims that Gallo had made.

It was dark before McGuffie, his team and Harry Carey again assembled in the Homicide Squad rooms at Russell Street. It had been a long and hard day, but they all felt they had made some progress. They would do the same tomorrow and the day after that and the day after that, however long it took.

Ivy Violet McLeod, aged thirty-nine, was the first of Eddie Leonski's victims. Better known as Ivy Dargavel, she was on her way home from visiting her beau, John, close to Albert Park Beach when she was approached and brutally murdered by the American soldier. (State Library Victoria, Newspapers Collection)

A composite image of Pauline Buchan Thompson, thirty-one, prepared by Victoria Police. A studio headshot of Pauline was superimposed on a model the same size as her and dressed as she had been on the night she was killed. Thousands of copies of the image were distributed around Melbourne. The second of Leonski's victims, Pauline had spent the night drinking with him before he murdered her and defiled her corpse outside her boarding house. (State Library Victoria, Newspapers Collection)

Gladys Lillian Hosking, forty, was Leonski's final victim. She had met Leonski at dusk while walking home in the rain, and accompanied him to Royal Park where she was strangled. As with Leonski's other victims, she was deliberately left exposed for passers-by to see. (State Library Victoria, Newspapers Collection)

The original gates of Camp Pell. Located in Royal Park, it was the main US Army base n Melbourne and home to thousands of soldiers, including Private Eddie Leonski. Author's collection)

Tent 16, Row 4 (second from left) at Camp Pell was part of a group of tents belonging to the 52nd Signal Battalion. Eddie Leonski shared it with three other New Yorkers, none of whom had much time for him. (National Archives of Australia/A472, W7493/Arthur de la Rue)

Hotel Victoria on Beaconsfield Parade, Albert Park. This was where Eddie Leonski had spent the evening drinking heavily, after the legislated 6 p.m. closing time, before the murder of Ivy McLeod. (State Library Victoria/H32492 5871)

A contemporary photo of Victoria Avenue, Albert Park, where it meets Beaconsfield Parade at the beach. In the centre is the terminus where Ivy McLeod fatefully missed her 1.45 a.m. tram. Between the trees on the left was the alcove where she huddled from the cold before she encountered Eddie Leonski, the same alcove where her body was found. The brick building on the right is the apartment block where barman Harold Gibson lived. As Gibson walked across to his workplace, the Bleak House Hotel on the left corner, he saw Eddie Leonski walking away from the crime scene. He then discovered Ivy McLeod's near-naked corpse. (Author's collection)

Detective Sergeant Sidney Harold McGuffie had a long history of working high-profile cases and was the lead investigator in the Brownout Murders. He was seconded to the prosecution team for the duration of Eddie Leonski's court martial. (Victoria Police Museum)

The Parkville Hotel, close by to Camp Pell, was a favourite drinking hole of Leonski's. He had become well known to the regulars, entertaining them with feats of strength such as walking along the bar on his hands. He drank there not long before or after all three of the murders. (Author's collection)

'Elizabeth House', Parkville, where Eddie rested before he murdered Gladys Hosking. (Author's collection)

A contemporary photo of Gladys Hosking's residence in Parkville, a short walk to her workplace at the University of Melbourne. (Author's collection)

The crime scene set up around where Gladys Hosking was murdered, just off Gatehouse Street in Royal Park, on the outskirts of Camp Pell. Next to the army truck on the left, the victim's hat, gloves and umbrella lie where Leonski had discarded them. In the centre, between two trees, a screen is erected around Gladys Hosking's body. (National Archives of Australia/A472, W7493/Arthur de la Rue)

An Aboriginal tracker, George, and Senior Constable Haygarth examine footprints in the distinctive yellow mud near where Gladys Hosking's body was discovered in Royal Park. (News Ltd/NP1258706)

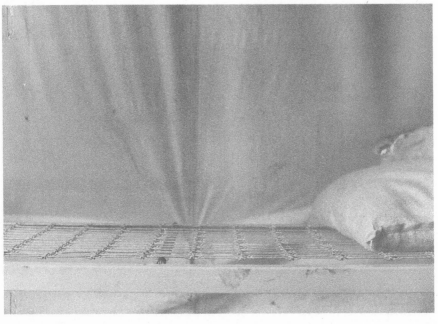

Eddie Leonski's bed frame at Camp Pell. The yellow mud stains along the side would serve as evidence to secure his conviction.

(National Archives of Australia/A472, W7493/Arthur de la Rue)

Private Eddie Leonski (centre) is led to his court martial in Russell Street, Melbourne.
(News Ltd/NPX286766)

Detective Fred Adam (right) and Government Analyst Dr Charles Taylor (centre) have their passes checked by a US Army guard before entering the court martial building.
(State Library Victoria, Newspapers Collection)

Barman Harold Gibson, who discovered Ivy McLeod's body and saw Eddie Leonski leaving the murder scene, arrives at the court martial.
(State Library Victoria, Newspapers Collection)

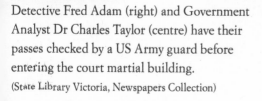

A 1944 photo of the then Colonel Hayford Enwall (left), the prosecuting Trial Judge Advocate in the United States General Court Martial convened to try Private Eddie Leonski for the murder of three Australian women. With him is Colonel John Stagg, who conducted the first review of Leonski's court martial.
(Australian National Maritime Museum/ ANMS0148[021])

Eddie Leonski in the exercise yard at the City Watchhouse shortly before his hanging. Constantly cracking jokes, his nonchalant attitude towards his own fate reflected his attitude towards the lives of others, particularly women.
(Herald and Weekly Times Library)

12

WITHOUT FEAR OF PUNISHMENT OR HOPE OF REWARD

Towards the end of that week, the Melbourne newspapers became aware that something was happening and whatever it was, Camp Pell was at the centre of it. Harry Carey was still, officially at least, expressing the police view that there were multiple lines of enquiry, that there were similarities between the three recent murders, but there were also differences. The newspapers were not buying into it: 'Detectives carried on with inquiries in different parts of the metropolis but senior officers spent the greater part of the day at a military camp, where it was reported last night investigations led to some definite conclusions and hope of an early solution to the mysteries surrounding the crimes, or at least one of them.'

•

McGuffie knew that if Thursday had been a physically draining day for him and his team of detectives, it would have been even more so for Eddie Leonski, who was now being very much left alone with his demons. On Friday, then, they would take advantage of this, and let Eddie and those demons do much of their work for them. The detectives' plan was to leave him alone to begin with that day, and then to introduce incremental pressure by increasing uncertainty about two things: what they were actually doing, and what they actually knew. They let Eddie relax in the stockade tent until mid-morning before they put the plan into action.

Sometime around 10 a.m., Eddie was taken from his cell tent and led across to the interview hut. Outside that hut were six other American soldiers, all dressed in fatigues, and all similar to Eddie in height, build or general appearance. Eddie's handcuffs had been removed before he left his tent, and he was now placed among those other six soldiers. They were formed into a single line which, with MPs at the front and rear, entered the interview hut where Eddie had spent a large part of the previous day.

The interior of the hut was very much as it had been the previous day, with a trestle table, chairs along one side wall, and several people already present and seated. The American officers were in their chairs along the wall, and there were three people seated behind the table. Leonski would have recognised Fred Adam from the previous day, but he was not certain about the other civilian in a dark suit. Between them sat another American soldier who may or may not have seemed vaguely familiar to Eddie.

The soldiers from outside were stopped and brought to attention facing the table and the men behind it. Each of those soldiers was then, in turn, asked to say something – probably name, rank, unit and where they were from – before all stood to attention for another couple of minutes. They were then led outside the hut again, where six of them were temporarily dismissed and the seventh, Eddie Leonski, was taken back to his cell tent and handcuffed to his bed.

Back in the hut, Fred Adam was questioning the soldier who had been sitting alongside him. That soldier was Private Francis Hanson, the man who had spoken to Gladys Hosking and her killer on Monday night and who had later identified Hosking's body at the City Morgue. Hanson, though, had not been able to recognise the soldier he had seen in the line-up held in the mess hall on Tuesday afternoon, and he was struggling again now. He thought that one of the seven who had just paraded before him looked a bit like the soldier he had seen with Gladys Hosking, but he could not state categorically that it was him. That soldier (it was Eddie Leonski) had a similar build and a similar face to the man he had seen on Monday night, but Hanson felt that the man's complexion and accent were definitely different. Hanson would not be moved to give a more positive identification. Fred Adam thanked him for his cooperation, and he was escorted from the hut and back to his own area of Camp Pell.

The process was repeated an hour later. Leonski was again led across to the interview hut, where he joined the six other soldiers in a line-up. The only difference this time was that the soldier seated between the two detectives was an Australian private who also may or may not have seemed familiar to Leonski. After going through their lines in the interview room, the line-up was dispersed and Eddie taken back to his tent. Those inside the interview hut had an animated conversation as soon as they left. The Australian soldier was Private Noel Seymour, who on Monday night had shone his torch on a mud-covered figure scrambling away from the Camp Pell slit trenches. Seymour, too, had been unable to identify the man he had seen at the Tuesday afternoon line-up, but seemed to have no such doubt today. One of the men in the line-up, he said, certainly looked a lot like the man he had seen on Monday night. Actually, he said, I'm certain he was the man I saw.

When asked which of the men in the line-up it had been, Seymour replied that it was the man who said his name was Eddie Leonski.

·

They decided to let Eddie wait a little bit longer. Lunchtime came and went – Eddie ate alone and under guard in his tent – and it wasn't until mid-afternoon that the MPs came to take him back across to the interview hut. This time, there were no surprises waiting for him. Apart from the MPs who were always there, the only others present were Fred Adam, Clyde Servis and Lieutenant William Johnston, one of the senior MPs who had been monitoring the Leonski interviews.

After everyone had settled into their seats and before anything formal was started, Leonski leaned forward and in a calm voice asked Fred Adam if the civilian police had anything on him. Equally calmly, Adam responded by saying that yes, they did have several things. Since that morning's line-ups, they had a solid and reliable witness who could place him at the scene of Gladys Hosking's murder at the time that the murder had occurred. As well as this, they had a witness to another similar attack Leonski had made earlier. Forensically, they had expert opinion on the yellow mud samples they had taken from his clothes and other belongings that conclusively linked him to the murder site.

'As well . . .' Adam started to say, when Leonski turned to Clyde Servis and William Johnston. There is no definitive account of what happened in the next few minutes, but it started with Leonski asking what would happen if he was tried for murder under Victorian civil law. The response, probably from Fred Adam, was that if he were tried and found guilty under Victorian law, he could expect to be hanged. He then asked what would happen if he were tried for the same offence under US military law. Someone, probably Johnston, said that he would face a court martial, and that he would be provided good counsel to assist his case. Johnston may or may not have also said that the military trial was contingent upon a confession and that, should such a confession not be forthcoming, Leonski would be handed over to the civil authorities.

Whatever the prompt, and whatever the incentive Eddie Leonski thought he may have been offered, he decided to confess and – leaning forward – he began to speak slowly and in a low voice. 'I killed her . . .'

•

Eddie Leonski then went on to describe how he murdered Gladys Hosking, very sparely and almost like he was describing a number of still photographs which, when put together in the correct sequence, would create a moving picture. 'On the corner, I met a girl. It was a small girl . . .' he said. 'We went to the girl's house and then went down the street towards the camp . . .' Probably because of her build, Leonski was convinced that Hosking was quite a young woman.

'I grabbed her by the throat. I choked her,' he said, not once but several times over.

Realising that the woman was dead, Leonski decided to move her body from where the attack had taken place. 'I then got her to a fence. I pushed her underneath. I got over and pulled her by the armpits underneath it. I carried her a short distance and fell in the mud.' Then he got a sudden shock.

'She made funny noises, a sort of gurgling sound, so I tried to pull her dress over her face. I became frightened and started to run away.'

Leonski said that he recalled meeting a soldier nearby and asking him for directions back to his area within Camp Pell. He could also remember meeting another soldier in the latrines at Camp Pell, and that soldier asking him what the hell had happened. I just told him that I'd fallen in the mud, he said.

Looking straight at Fred Adam, Leonski said that he then went back to his own hut, where he went to bed. When he woke up the next morning, he straightaway noticed the mess he had made, and he thought, 'My God! Where have I been? What have I done?'

Then, while many of his fellow soldiers drifted over to the perimeter where a woman was believed to have been murdered, Eddie Leonski took all his soiled clothes to the camp laundry where he attempted to scrub them clean.

•

As soon as Leonski indicated that he was prepared to confess, Johnston sent one of the MPs out of the room to contact the key people involved in the case. Sid McGuffie arrived later in the afternoon, as did Captain Wayne Bailey, the adjutant at Camp Pell, and therefore the camp's senior administrative officer. Others would arrive, and depart, as that afternoon became evening. Decisions were made at senior levels in army headquarters, police stations and government departments.

•

At times, Leonski seemed to be unaware that he had an audience. When he started speaking, he slumped forward on his chair and rested his head on his hands. He spoke softly, almost as if he was reciting a tale to someone else, someone that only he could see. He would, at times, speak almost in a whisper, and the others in the room would have to lean forward to catch his words. At other times, he would seem to struggle to recall specific details about the murder, and he would stop talking as he searched through his jumbled memories. To those watching him, Leonski seemed to have gone very pale. He also appeared to be somehow disassociated from the reality of the situation in which he found himself. He was somewhere else inside his head, acting out a little play in which he brutally murdered an innocent woman, a 'little girl' who had died because Eddie Leonski had learned to enjoy killing.

●

Everything that Eddie Leonski said was written down in longhand by Clyde Servis, whose notes were to be typed up by Fred Adam. While those two were discussing how best to proceed, William Johnston, who was the senior MP present, asked Leonski if he would be prepared to help them clear up some 'other things'. When Leonski asked him what kind of things he meant, Johnston replied simply, 'The murder of Pauline Thompson.' When Leonski said that he could certainly help them with that, Servis suggested that they have a short break first.

As they all gave orders for coffee and sandwiches to one of the MPs, Servis, Johnston and Adam briefly discussed the legalities of hearing another confession. The consensus was that they had nothing to lose, and so Leonski was asked to continue, which he did. As he talked, the MP returned with coffee and an assortment of sandwiches, which they sat and ate and drank as they listened to Eddie continue his story.

Without any further prompting, Leonski went on to describe the murder of Pauline Thompson in much the same way as he had described that of Gladys Hosking.

'I remember a woman singing in my ears as she was looking into my eyes . . .'

He spoke softly again, with pauses and gaps in the story, some of which he returned to and some of which he didn't.

When he had finished, Clyde Servis again handed his hand-written notes to Fred Adam, who proceeded to type them up. There were more people in the room now: Sid McGuffie and Bill Mooney had both arrived during the afternoon, while there continued to be a steady stream of MPs entering and leaving the hut. Some were empty-handed, but most carried written messages or envelopes; sometimes both. After the end of the Thompson confession, more sandwiches and coffee were ordered, and, for twenty minutes or so, the men in the hut sat around, eating, drinking, or just thinking.

●

One of the first to be informed of Leonski's confession was Camp Pell's commanding officer, Colonel C. S. Meyers. Meyers went straightaway to MacArthur's headquarters at Victoria Barracks in St Kilda Road to inform MacArthur's staff of what had taken place. After brief discussions with those staff, Meyers then travelled to the Police Headquarters in Russell Street where he met with Inspector Harry Carey. He told Carey that the Americans were determined that Leonski would be subject to US military justice and that he would not there-fore be handed over to the custody of the Victoria Police. As there had been previous discussions and agreements around this, Carey said that he – and the police – had no objection to this occurring. There was just one complication, Meyers suggested. Leonski had already escaped once from the Camp Pell stockade, and it would therefore be inappropriate for him to remain there under the current circumstances. Meyers asked if the Victoria Police had a secure facility where Leonski could be lodged pending his trial and its outcome. We certainly do, said Carey . . .

•

Fred Adam finished typing up both confessions, and Captain Bailey took them away. As the conversation in the room flagged, someone – possibly William Johnston or Bill Mooney – asked Leonski if he knew anything about the murder of Ivy McLeod. Eddie thought for a minute, and then said that he seemed to remember choking someone near a beach, but that he would need a photograph, an article of clothing or something to jog his memory.

At this point, the decision was made to suspend the interview for the day. It was now after 9 p.m. and people were visibly tiring. McGuffie was supportive of the decision because there was still quite a bit to do that night and he thought, too, that the break would allow Leonski a night of reflection, which might help him recall all the circumstances of the McLeod murder and some of the features of the other two that he had yet to mention. The Americans, too, were happy to break as they also had a lot of things in front of them.

Wayne Bailey returned from the Camp Pell Headquarters building where he had organised covering notes for Leonski's confessions to the murders of Gladys Hosking and Pauline Thompson. Each of them now began with the words, 'I, Edward Joseph Leonski, after being made aware of my rights, without fear of punishment or hope of reward, make the following statement . . .'

Bailey handed each of the confessions to Leonski, asking him to read them and sign each at the marked spot if he believed the typewritten statements to be true and accurate accounts of what he had said. Eddie seemed to scan rather than read the documents, barely glancing at each page before turning it over to look at the next. When he had finished with them, he took the pen Bailey offered and signed both confessions where Bailey indicated he should, before handing both back to the captain with the quip, 'That is my life.' He then sat back in his chair and looked around, as if to say, 'What's next?'

•

It had been a long Friday afternoon. Eddie Leonski had first asked Fred Adam what the Victoria Police had on him at around 3.30 p.m. and it was now 9.30 p.m., and there had been few breaks in those six hours. In that time, Leonski had confessed to two murders and indicated that he was probably responsible for a third. He had described those murders in some detail, signed full confessions and had generally given every indication that he was now prepared to cooperate fully with the civilian and military authorities who were investigating the killings. He had even suggested that he would do so in the full knowledge that his cooperation may well cost him his life.

It had not been a continuous session of confession, questions and answers. There were little breaks, as coffee and sandwiches were ordered and consumed, as messages were sent and received, and as the various components of a complex legal issue were examined by policemen and lawyers, some inside Camp Pell, some at Russell Street, and still others at Victoria Barracks on the southern edge of the city. Decisions were made and agreed, and a number of legal processes either commenced or accelerated.

Thus it was that shortly after 9.30 p.m., William Johnston informed Eddie Leonski that he was being removed from the stockade at Camp Pell and taken to permanent civilian prison accommodation. An escort of military policemen was quickly formed and, without further ado, Leonski was led to the camp road outside the stockade where a number of dark-coloured cars were parked. Leonski sat in the back seat of one of the middle cars – helped in because he was again handcuffed – between William Johnston and Sid McGuffie. A mix of MPs and homicide detectives climbed into the other cars and the small convoy headed off.

It was not a long trip, ten minutes, no more. The fleet drove across the top of the Melbourne city centre and into Russell Street where they passed through guarded gates and into the bluestone police garage, opposite Russell Street Police Headquarters and abutting the City Watchhouse. Eddie Leonski was then taken, via an internal door and short passage, to the Watchkeeper's Desk, where he was officially admitted to the Watchhouse. From there, he was taken to a cell, Number 6, in the middle of a long, brightly lit corridor, and told to sit on the edge of the bed. The MPs stood back after removing Leonski's handcuffs, but kept him covered with their automatic weapons. McGuffie and Johnston, too, remained in the cell and were soon joined by a third person, a well-dressed US Army major, who spoke directly to Leonski, telling him that he would be charged with two counts of wilful murder. He would be tried on those charges, the major continued, under US military law and according to the Uniform Code of Military Justice.

The major asked if Eddie had any questions and, when the answer was only a shake of the head, turned on his heel and left.

Johnston, too, asked Eddie if he had any questions, and received the same response. As the two men, Johnston and McGuffie also turned to leave, Leonski caught the Victorian detective's eye, and said, 'Fancy, me a murderer! I guess the girl Thompson was the hardest; she was strong and – oh, boy! – could she drink gin squashes. She told me I had a baby-face, but I was wicked underneath.' And he smiled at the recollection.

•

Shortly after the arrival of substantial numbers of US troops in Melbourne in February 1942, a Judge Advocate General's unit was established to handle the legal issues that were likely to arise. It was established in quarters separate from US Army Headquarters at Victoria Barracks in St Kilda Road, but not too far away. The headmaster's residence at the Melbourne Grammar School, a short way down St Kilda Road, became the unit's new quarters. One of the officers posted there was Major Harold Balff, and it was he who addressed Leonski in his cell that Friday night. He had been, and would continue to be, very busy organising the legal processes that, he believed, would only end with the death of Eddie Leonski.

•

All the Melbourne newspapers, and a number of the major inter-state dailies, were aware of the overnight developments in the Brownout Strangler case, and the story featured prominently on their front pages. Under the heading, 'American Soldier Held', one reported:

About 10.30 p.m. last night, an American soldier was taken to the City Watchhouse and held there under armed guard from US military forces.

Detective Inspector H. J. Carey, who had been in charge of investigations, accompanied by Detective Sergeant S. H. McGuffie and other members of the Homicide Squad, handed over the man to the military guard after arrival at the Watchhouse, and thereafter declined to make any statement on the subject of their long and arduous manhunt, except to say that the matter was now in the hands of the military authorities.

It was learned yesterday afternoon that the detectives, who had been working in close cooperation with military police, had narrowed their investigations to a point where they felt justified in taking definite action.

The general public, in Melbourne in particular, were mightily relieved that the Brownout Strangler's reign of fear was over, but would not be celebrating the fact just yet. The past few weeks had been a brutal time to be living in Melbourne, and it would take more than one reported arrest to lift the sense of foreboding which had descended on the city since the discovery of Ivy McLeod's body twenty-one days earlier.

•

The military and civilian investigators also knew that their work was not quite over as well. There were elements in the confessions that needed to be teased out, and the Friday night discussion about Ivy McLeod needed to be brought to some kind of conclusion. On Saturday morning, Eddie Leonski's cell became quite crowded as the Americans Clyde Servis and William Johnston and the Australians Sid McGuffie and Fred

Adam all took their notebooks and their folding chairs into it. They found an Eddie Leonski who was in an expansive mood.

He, too, started where he had finished the previous evening. Pauline Thompson had, he said, been by far the hardest to kill and she was also the only woman he had met who could outdrink him. He recalled that she had told him about being stood up by Jimmy Jones earlier in the evening, and repeated her quip about something evil in him hiding behind his baby-face. McGuffie took up the conversation now, firstly giving Eddie a few ready-made cigarettes and then saying that he had taken the opportunity the day before to look at some material provided by a young woman whom they believed Eddie had attempted to rape a month earlier at her flat in St Kilda.

McGuffie said that the information provided included details of an army singlet he had left behind and a description of the birthmark she had seen on her attacker's penis. Leonski seemed quite pleased by the woman's powers of observation under stress, and laughed at her description. He backed up her observation by dropping his pants, removing his penis from his underpants and comparing the woman's description of the birthmark with the real thing. It was a performance that Eddie seemed proud of.

Leonski then spoke about the day, three weeks previously, when he had been drinking at the Hotel Victoria in Albert Park. This time, in a very matter-of-fact way, he described how he murdered Ivy McLeod near a tram stop opposite the beach. His voice and manner sometimes became distant again, and he was quite animated when he specifically remembered tearing at the woman's clothes and his frustration at not being able to tear her belt off.

When Eddie finished his story, Fred Adam took the notes they had all taken across the road to the offices of the Homicide

Squad. He would spend the afternoon putting them together and then typing them up into the formal statement that would represent Eddie Leonski's confession to the murder of Ivy McLeod. While Fred Adam was banging away at his typewriter, Sid McGuffie and William Johnston were saying their farewells to Eddie, and Clyde Servis was making his way back to Camp Pell. Before the two policemen left, Leonski asked Sid McGuffie if he could arrange for a priest to visit him in his cell.

McGuffie and Johnston took an unmarked police car from the police garage next to the Watchhouse and drove down to Beaconsfield Parade in Albert Park. There, the two policemen walked the route that Leonski said he had taken three weeks earlier, confirming for themselves the times and places and lines of sight, verifying, where they could, the story they had heard just hours earlier.

They both had photographs of Eddie, which they took into the Victoria and Bleak House Hotels and showed to both the staff and patrons. They were particularly interested in anyone who had been in either place three weeks earlier and who could remember a group of American soldiers who stayed there, drinking heavily, well into the night.

•

Sunday was also a busy day for the key figures in the investigation and arraignment of Eddie Leonski. Fred Adam had finished his typing and taken Leonski's typed confession to the murder of Ivy McLeod to Harold Balff at Melbourne Grammar. On Sunday morning, Balff convened a summary court martial with two other officers to establish the preliminary military processes of trying Leonski. From there he went to the City Watchhouse where he met William Johnston; the two were escorted to Leonski's cell by MPs. There, Johnston asked Eddie a couple of questions about points that he had spoken about on Saturday morning, before handing him the typed confession and asking him to read it. Leonski skimmed through it, as he had the other two, and signed it at the end; his signature was witnessed by Harold Balff. The two American officers then departed, Johnston to Camp Pell and Balff back to the Judge Advocate's offices at Melbourne Grammar.

That afternoon, Major Balff reconvened the court martial he had opened that morning. The members of the court decided that Private Edward Joseph Leonski should be charged with the murders of Ivy McLeod, Pauline Thompson and Gladys Hosking; it also noted for the record that there appeared to be indications of 'mental lapses' in Leonski and, because of this, recommended that a medical board be established to determine Leonski's mental condition.

On Sunday evening, Harold Balff and Clyde Servis visited Russell Street Police Headquarters to inform Victoria Police that the United States Army and government had determined to prosecute Leonski for the three murders. On Monday morning, Balff returned to the City Watchhouse and was again escorted to Leonski's cell where the senior MP called Leonski to attention. Balff entered the cell and, reading from a prepared document, formally charged Leonski with those murders, and then left.

Somewhere in the system, a clock started ticking away the seconds of Eddie Leonski's life. The investigators and detectives had finished their work. From here on, it would be up to the lawyers to finish things, one way or another.

13.

THE UNIFORM CODE OF MILITARY JUSTICE

In Melbourne and beyond, the morning papers on Monday, 25 May 1942 trumpeted the news that not only had an American soldier been taken into custody over the Brownout Murders, but that the soldier would also be tried for his crimes by a military court. The relief at the first was almost matched by the curiosity at the second. Much of the reporting that week would focus on what lay ahead for the American soldier – he would be named as Eddie Leonski for the first time that day – in terms of the administration of justice, for that was what the readers all wanted. The Australians wanted justice for three women brutally murdered on the streets of Melbourne and for a city that had been held to ransom. The Americans wanted justice for the stain that one man had put on the reputation of an entire army and, by extension, an entire nation.

•

'At the Watchhouse, Leonski was turned over to the custody of the United States Army, who directed that he be held in close confinement . . .' began one of the Melbourne news reports, and it was like a signal to what was probably the most efficient unit in General MacArthur's entire headquarters structure, the Public Relations Unit. Under direct instructions from the general himself, that unit flooded the newspaper market with details of what was most likely to occur in the coming weeks and months as the United States Army judged one of its own for a series of crimes which had shocked the army and the country that hosted it. When the public relations blitz was over, the newspaper-reading people of Australia probably knew more about US military law than many American soldiers and most American civilians.

Well-briefed and well-presented US Army public relations officers walked Australian journalists through the complexities of their legal system, the Uniform Code of Military Justice (UCMJ). It was customary, those journalists were told – and they in turn told others – for the United States Army to handle all criminal procedures involving its own men. Outside the United States, this had to be done by arrangement with the local authorities; there seemed to be every indication that the details of such an agreement had, or would soon, be reached between the US military and Australian civil authorities.

The preparation of a case for trial involved the sorting out of the charges, which were thoroughly explained with the accused person present. According to the evidence presented to the Investigating Authority, the person delegated to consider whether or not a crime had been committed, that Investigating Authority could recommend a trial by a summary, a special or a general court martial. Summary trials were for minor offences, special court martials for more serious matters. But in a general court martial penalties could include lengthy prison sentences and even, in extreme cases, the death penalty.

In the case of Eddie Leonski, the alleged offences were of such a serious nature that they had been referred directly to a general court martial. The general court martial, it was explained, was similar to a Supreme Court trial in any one of the Australian states. The court martial itself comprised a minimum of five officers – US soldiers could not be tried by other soldiers of lower rank – but usually more than five officers would sit in judgement.

Members of the court were appointed by the commanding officer of the military zone in which the trial was to be conducted. In that trial, the prosecutor would be known as the Judge Advocate, while a senior officer would be appointed as President of the Court. As President, that officer had a number of specific rights and obligations. A 'Law Member' was also usually appointed by the Judge Advocate's Department, the legal unit responsible for organising and oversighting all courts martial. The role of the Law Member was to advise the court on points of law, things like the admissibility of evidence and other legal strictures. Like the court's President, the Law Member had certain rights and obligations under the UCMJ.

The Defense Counsel was always an army officer, and one of the customary practices had been to assign officers from combat units to the Defense Counsel role in general courts martial. Legal experience in civilian life was not a prerequisite for the role. The defendant also had the right to brief a civilian lawyer and could call any civilian witnesses they desired.

The basic procedures under which the trial would be conducted were set out in the 1928 *Manual for Courts Martial*. If the accused offered a 'Guilty' plea, taking of testimony was at the discretion of the court. A 'Not Guilty' plea would be followed by what would seem to be a normal criminal trial. At the end of that trial, all members of the court would vote on the accused's guilt or innocence. All votes were equal. The ballot was secret and a three-quarters majority was required for all verdicts. A unanimous vote was required for the imposition of a death sentence. The newspapers explained that, because Leonski had been charged with violation of Article 92 of the US Articles of War, murder, he would face the death penalty.

There had apparently been a number of questions on that exact point. Under the uniform code, the penalties for murder included death and a general court martial could designate whether that sentence was carried out by firing squad or by hanging. By tradition, however, if Leonski was found guilty and then sentenced to death, he would be executed by hanging. Execution by firing squad was reserved for soldiers found guilty of purely military offences like desertion in the face of the enemy. Hanging was the method of execution in cases of crimes by soldiers against civil law.

•

Despite confident assertions that the 1939 *Defence Act* covered all eventualities, the Australian government was not prepared to take any chances in the case of Eddie Leonski. Sir George Knowles, the Commonwealth Solicitor-General, handled the legal processes at the federal level. Knowles said that, if necessary, a regulation would be gazetted to cover the American court martial in Melbourne. That regulation must have been deemed necessary, because, on 28 May, Prime Minister John Curtin announced in Parliament that just such an action had been taken, and the appropriate regulation was now gazetted. That regulation 'conformed to common agreement between the countries'.

Such concerns did not extend down to the state level. The Victorian Attorney-General, Henry Bailey, noted that the Commonwealth regulation had primacy over state laws, and that Victoria was comfortable with the outcome.

•

The recommendations from Major Balff's summary court martial on the Sunday after Leonski's arrest were passed up the chain of command to Major General Julian Barnes, the officer commanding all US Army forces in Australia. Barnes accepted those recommendations and ordered the convening of a general court martial to consider the charges against Leonski. The Adjutant General's Department had been awaiting such instructions and sprang into action.

For the legal protocols attached to the court martial, the Accusing Officer was deemed to be First Lieutenant Walter Blandin, Headquarters Company, 52nd Signal Battalion, while the Investigating Officer was Lieutenant Colonel Nels Soderholm. The officers of the court were also selected, with a Colonel named Simon Woodward nominated as President of the Court. Woodward was then commanding officer of one of the US Army camps in Melbourne. Prior to his enlistment, Woodward had been a high-school principal.

The Trial Judge Advocate, the man who would prosecute the case against Eddie Leonski, would be Major Hayford Enwall. Enwall's father had been a Methodist minister before doctrinal doubts led him to take up more secular responsibilities. He would eventually become a professor of philosophy at the University of Florida. Hayford Enwall graduated in law from the same university, which he had also represented in basketball. At the time he volunteered for military service, Hayford Enwall was

the Assistant Attorney-General in the Miami Division of the
Southern District of Florida. Attached to the Adjutant General's
Department by the army, Enwall had travelled to Australia on
the same transport as Leonski, although the two had never met.
In May 1942, Hayford Enwall was arguably the best-qualified
and most experienced American prosecutor in Australia.

The Law Member was Colonel John Welch, sixty years of
age, with decades of both legal and military experience. Prior
to the war, he had been a partner in a large firm of solicitors.

Eddie Leonski would be defended by Lieutenant Colonel
Spencer Eddy, another experienced military and civil lawyer. A
New Yorker like Leonski, Spencer Eddy's father was a wealthy
socialite and diplomat who had been a close personal friend of
President Theodore Roosevelt. A short and personable man, and
one with considerable combat experience from the First World
War, Spencer Eddy had been recalled to the army while serving
as a county judge in upstate New York.

Assisting Eddy would be a young army captain and attorney
from Colorado named Ira Rothgerber, Junior. Rothgerber had
been born in Denver in 1913, and after graduating in law from
the University of Colorado in 1935 he had joined the law firm
his father had established there thirty years earlier.

To round out the personnel of the court, some supporting
appointments were also made. Another American soldier was
sworn in as Court Reporter, and US authorities also allowed the
Australian government to nominate their own court reporter
for the trial.

Finally, in recognition of the peculiarities of the case, and
as a nod to public opinion in Melbourne, Detective Sergeant
Sid McGuffie was seconded to the prosecution team for the
duration of the trial.

•

Early on, the US Army briefing officers had made it plain that US courts martial were open, and the public were admitted to them except in instances where the testimony could be considered 'scandalous' or where military secrets were involved. This statement led to considerable newspaper speculation about the most appropriate venue for a trial that was open and which had already attracted enormous public attention.

That speculation was fuelled when an official inspection was made of the Third Civil Court in the Law Courts Building in Melbourne at the end of May. That court was considered large enough to accommodate all of those who would be involved in the trial, and it had previously been used by the five Justices and Chief Justice who comprised the High Court of Australia. Official approval to use the building would need to be obtained, but no one foresaw any problems with this.

No one, that is, except MacArthur's headquarters, who had no intention of letting an army court martial come to resemble anything like a public circus. In early June, US headquarters made a number of public announcements. They had firstly determined that the general public would not be admitted to the trial. Instead, a limited number of newspaper representatives and war correspondents would be allowed to report the proceedings. An initial figure of fifteen reporters and correspondents was mooted, although this was raised to twenty by the time the trial commenced.

MacArthur's headquarters then announced that fifteen 'observers' would be allowed to attend the trial, a figure that was also subsequently raised to twenty. MacArthur asked Prime Minister Curtin to nominate those observers, and eventually a mix of senior legal, military and political figures were granted official observer status. Official passes were produced for all those who were to be allowed into the courtroom to observe the trial. Pass holders were told that the passes were not trans-ferable and that no one – *no one!* – would be admitted to the courtroom without one.

The only other stipulation that the American authorities made was that the press not report the names of any of the American servicemen involved in the trial with the exception of Leonski himself. This would lead to some interesting reporting of the principals in the case, like, 'A well-known American criminal lawyer, at present serving in the US forces, will defend Leonski … The lawyer has a big criminal practice in America and has figured in a number of sensational American trials.'

Finally, the headquarters announced that the venue for the trial would be kept secret to prevent a general crush by the public when the trial was underway. It was a secret that was pretty well kept for the duration of the trial.

The venue selected for that trial was a large upstairs room, almost a hall, in an old office building in Russell Street, right at the northern end and just before that street becomes Lygon Street and Melbourne city becomes Carlton. The building had originally been owned by a fraternal benevolent society and the court martial would be held in what had been a large function or meeting room known as the Victoria Hall. It was within easy walking distance of the City Watchhouse – really nothing more than a short stroll across Russell Street – and Eddie Leonski would remain incarcerated in that Watchhouse during the trial, being driven to and from the court each day. The building itself would be cordoned off by armed American MPs during the trial;

it had a limited number of entry and exit points, so access could be quite easily controlled.

The court room, the Victoria Hall, would be sparsely furnished for the trial. All involved, participants and spectators alike, would be sitting on folding wooden chairs, and the court officials would have to write and rest their books on wooden trestle tables. Behind the main table where the officers who would deliver the verdict sat, a large American flag was nailed to the wall.

Finally, the working details of the court martial were announced. When formally constituted, the court martial would be held in two sessions every day, the first from 10 a.m. until 12.30 p.m. and the second from 2.30 p.m. until 5.30 p.m. Once officers were sworn in to the court, Leonski would be arraigned before them to submit his plea. If that plea was 'Guilty', the court would decide whether or not to take evidence before sentencing. If, however, the plea was 'Not Guilty', the court martial would proceed from that point. It had been estimated that there were around sixty potential witnesses and, if all were heard, the trial would take up to seven sitting days.

The eleven officers who would make up the court martial would be sworn in on Monday, 8 June 1942; Eddie Leonski's trial would commence two days later, on the morning of 10 June.

•

Until that trial had been completed, Eddie Leonski would be held in close confinement in one of the inner cells in the City Watchhouse. It was a basic cell, the middle one in a line of several. It was also the largest in that line, sometimes used to hold up to a dozen Saturday night drunks. Now it would contain just a single prisoner while all the other cells in the wing would also remain vacant. It was a cell that measured around five by four metres, but for Eddie it would remain very basic, containing a bed, a barred window overlooking an inner courtyard and a toilet. He was given only blankets and a pillow; there were neither sheets nor bedspreads for Eddie. That cell was his only home; he was not permitted to exercise outside it, and all his actions within it were subject to normal Watchhouse regulations.

For the first few days of his imprisonment, all of Eddie's meals were brought by jeep from the kitchen at Camp Pell. After that, they were prepared in the kitchen at the Russell Street Police Headquarters and simply brought across the road. Whatever the source of the meal, its service was always the same. Eddie would be ordered to stand at attention well back from the cell door and an unarmed MP would carry the meal in on a tray. A second MP would stand in the doorway with his carbine trained on Eddie as the first MP placed the meal tray on the end of Eddie's bed. At the end of the meal, the process would be repeated, this time to remove the empty tray.

Not that Eddie would have got very far had he attempted to escape. At all times of the day and night he was guarded by six armed MPs from William Johnston's 813th Military Police Company. Two were stationed in the corridor outside his cell door, there were another two at either end of the corridor the cell was in, and a final two were located on the other side of the locked doors that enclosed the corridor.

In some ways, incarceration seemed to be good for Leonski, and he quickly settled into a routine or, rather, a number of routines. He proved to be a very good sleeper and, unless awakened earlier, he would consistently sleep through until 9.30 a.m. He was also a very good eater, devouring everything he was served and regularly asking for a second helping of the main meat dish in the evening. He could be fastidious as well, once sending sausages back to the kitchen and asking for his preferred steak instead.

While fastidious in some things, Leonski was close to compulsive in others, particularly physical fitness and cleanliness. Every morning he would rise, dress, fold his blankets neatly and place them in a corner of his cell, with his pillow on top. He would then fold his bed back up against the wall. This done, he would ask for a broom and thoroughly sweep the cell before performing his morning exercises. For Eddie, exercising meant walking on his hands, and for a minimum of fifteen minutes he would walk around and around his cell on his hands. On some days, he would repeat this exercise several times, but mostly it was just once a day before breakfast. He was doing it, he would say, to keep fit and to prepare himself for whatever lay ahead.

Eddie always seemed to have something to do, and most days one activity would segue seamlessly into another. He was a voracious reader, with his favourite books being either love stories or thrillers. Early on, one of his visitors – most probably a Homicide Squad detective – told Eddie the story of Ned Kelly and the Kelly Gang. Eddie became firstly interested, then fascinated and, finally, obsessed by the Kelly story, especially after that same visitor gave him a book on the history of the gang. Eddie soon knew the story off by heart. He was also interested in Captain Starlight, the fictional bushranger in the classic Australian story *Robbery Under Arms*, who was based on a number of real-life bushrangers.

Eddie loved magazines as well, and would read them during the day and even in bed at night. He seemed to prefer those with a focus on women and fashion. He would often use the photographs of the women in them as models for the sketches he drew, because he also grew to spend a lot of time drawing and sketching. He had been given a selection of lead pencils and paper in his first few days of confinement and he could occupy himself for hours with his drawings. Most were of nude or semi-nude young women. In some, the women would be singing, and Eddie would draw little speech balloons coming from their mouths, in which he would put the words of the songs they were singing. In other sketches, his models would be wearing an assortment of bizarre hats and headwear.

Eddie also used those pencils to decorate his cell. On the walls, he wrote the words of the popular songs of the day, and he would hold little sing-alongs all by himself. When drunks were brought into the Watchhouse on most weekends they would sometimes be singing and, if he heard them, Eddie would sing right along with them at the top of his voice. At the end of the songs, he would quip to his guards that he thought he would probably die from a sore throat. He also used the pencils to write on one of the cell walls in large letters, 'It's a lovely day today', and adding two large question marks to the end.

Eddie spent quite a bit of his cell time writing and reading letters. Most of those he wrote were either to friends or to his family in New York, and most of those he read were from those same two sources. Strangely, within a few days of his arrest, Eddie also started to receive letters from strangers, including a number from young women. There were also persistent but unfounded rumours about several young women who tried to visit him in the Watchhouse.

If all else either failed or paled, Eddie would fall back on his games and puzzles. He enjoyed both draughts and Chinese chequers, and could amuse himself for hours by playing long games against imagined opponents. His favourite pastime, though, was solving crossword puzzles. Most of the magazines he read contained at least one, and others would be torn out of newspapers and given to him by the guards. If he struggled with a word, he would call out to one of those guards or a Watchhouse warder to ask for assistance; this would continue until he had completed the particular puzzle.

He would occasionally ask how the war was going, but his questions were almost perfunctory and he didn't seem to be particularly interested in the answers. Eddie appeared quite content to live in his own little self-contained world.

•

Others would come into Eddie's world. He was visited on a regular basis by a priest, while the Homicide Squad detectives who had hunted for him would occasionally call in to see how he was going. To a man, they abhorred what he had done, but they were somehow able to separate the man from the act, and thus were able to speak to him as they would to anyone else. Besides, they all felt they knew what was most likely to happen to him in the not-too-distant future and had some sympathy for him. Eddie's most regular visitors, though, were his defence team of Spencer Eddy and Ira Rothgerber.

When they first met in Eddie's cell in the City Watchhouse, he had seemed very pleased that someone of Spencer Eddy's background and experience had accepted the brief to defend him. If one Eddie was impressed, the second Eddy wasn't. Spencer Eddy found Leonski to be an essentially weak character, one who seemed to crave attention and who wanted to be seen as being in the very centre of a lot of important things and people who were swirling around him. Eddy also found Leonski to be quite sycophantic in his present situation, and suspected that in other circumstances he was quite capable of being a bully. He believed him to be a narcissist and thought that he probably always had been. But Spencer Eddy also knew that sometimes you just had to work with what you were given.

Ira Rothgerber was less critical of Leonski than Spencer Eddy. He saw their defendant as being both well educated and reasonably well mannered. He recognised that Leonski had a range of personality and character flaws, but thought these related in large part to his obsession with voices and his desire to collect and keep those voices.

Eddy and Rothgerber started their preparations for Leonski's trial by having their client given a comprehensive medical examination to see if there were any indications that Leonski's three confessions had been beaten out of him. There weren't. The two lawyers then went through Leonski's life story with him, focusing on his recent army experiences, and taking copious notes as they went. Eddie was always pleasant and cooperative when they did this, and genuinely seemed to enjoy being in the company of the two officers.

It was a feeling that was not always reciprocated. Spencer Eddy, in particular, disliked the way Leonski always saw himself as the most important person in any situation, even when he clearly wasn't. Eddy always considered several aspects of Leonski's personality as deficient at best, and some of his behaviours had the potential to seriously damage his case. Leonski was forever looking for the cheap gag, and he seemed to think that gallows humour was an appropriate vehicle for this.

More than once, Eddy had to warn Leonski about his general attitude towards his situation, and about the way he interacted with others. He would say to Leonski that it was entirely inappropriate for a man accused of strangling three women to point to photographs of young women in a magazine with the comment, 'What a lovely neck.' Nor did it help when Leonski discussed various defence strategies with the guards and warders, asking them which ones they thought would generate the biggest headlines.

As they sought to put together some kind of credible defence, Eddy and Rothgerber interviewed dozens of soldiers who knew Leonski at Camp Pell, and were quite depressed by the results. Few people who knew Eddie Leonski were able to find anything positive to say about him. Most found his attitude and his behaviour – especially when he had been drinking – to be not only offensive, but to be completely unacceptable in an American soldier on active service overseas.

In the end, both Eddy and Rothgerber concluded that the only way they were going to save Eddie Leonski's life was through being able to prove to the court that their client was insane.

•

On the other side of town, in their rooms at Melbourne Grammar School, Hayford Enwall and his prosecution team were also feeling pressure. They had been left in absolutely no doubt that the highest command levels, up to and including General Douglas MacArthur himself, wanted the Leonski matter dealt with quickly and efficiently and with an outcome that would satisfy both army authorities as well as the Australian public. Again, they were left in no doubt as to what that outcome should be.

With Eddie Leonski's three comprehensive confessions in hand, Enwall considered that there was only one possible outcome to the case, but he was an extremely competent District Attorney and was not a person to cut corners or take chances.

He and his team felt that, apart from the confessions, the keys to the case would be the Government Analyst Charles Taylor's evidence concerning the provenance of the yellow clay mud on Leonski's belongings and in his tent, and Joey Gallo's recollections concerning Leonski's confessions to him, including the subsequent denials and general demeanour when talking about the murdered women. Enwall, highly regarded for the meticulousness of his case planning, was noted for his introduction of evidence into the cases he prosecuted and for his use of expert witnesses. He felt that both could be crucial in determining the outcome of the court martial.

Sid McGuffie spent time with Charles Taylor going over his likely testimony, and also joined Enwall and Joey Gallo going over everything Leonski had ever said to his friend that might have some bearing on the case. When that process was complete, they felt they were ready for anything Leonski's defence could possibly bring to the trial.

14.

THE MEDICAL BOARD

At 10 a.m. on the morning of Wednesday, 10 June 1942, the General Court Martial established to try Private Edward Joseph Leonski for murder opened with the President of the Court, Colonel Simon Woodward, reading the Army Regulations which established the court martial. The charges against Leonski were then read out, and he was asked to plead to the three specifications – each of murder – and one charge, the generic one of breaching the US Army's Articles of War. To each of these, Leonski spoke out loud and in a firm voice, 'Not Guilty.' As Leonski resumed his seat, his Defense Counsel, Lieutenant Colonel Spencer Eddy, stood at the defence table and asked for leave to address the court. When this was granted, Eddy said that the accused's mental state would undoubtedly be considered by the court during its deliberations and had, in fact, already been touched upon by those who had interviewed him since his arrest. Eddy quoted a military investigator, probably Major Balff, who had written a report about the preliminary examination of Leonski. Included in that report was an assessment that:

there is evidence of distinct mental lapses on the part of the accused
and the process of obtaining a confession from him was not a
process of reducing any resistance but consisted of aiding him to
remember facts and circumstances . . . [There is] reasonable doubt
as to the sanity of the accused and [we] recommend that a board
of medical officers be appointed to determine his mental status.

Eddy then moved for Leonski to be examined by a medical board
and for the court martial to be adjourned until that board had
reported. The court, having no objection to the request, directed
that a medical board be formed to undertake that task. At 11.20
a.m., Woodward adjourned the court until the report on Leonski's
mental state had been completed and was ready to be presented.
At that, the court rose. Eddie Leonski smiled and gave a little
wave to the spectators as he was escorted from the courtroom.

•

For many of the thirty-five reporters, war correspondents and
invited observers who were there, the adjournment was an anti-
climax, and meant they would not return to the court whenever
it resumed. There were two Victorian Supreme Court judges
whose schedules would not allow them the opportunity to
witness the unique court martial. And there was Constable Leslie
Thompson, who had hoped to see justice delivered to the man
who had murdered his wife and now had to return to his duties
and responsibilities as a policeman and as a father. About the
only persons genuinely happy with the outcome were the two
Victoria Police photographers who had been required to appear
to give evidence that day. Neither had the correct official pass
and both had been refused entry to the courtroom.

•

The Medical Board formed to assess Eddie Leonski's mental state comprised three doctors, two of whom were nominated by the prosecution, with the third to be nominated by the defence. The two nominated by Trial Judge Advocate Hayford Enwall were the Board's nominated chairman, Major Edward O'Neil Harper, and Lieutenant Hugh McHugh. As well as being medical doctors, both were psychiatrists with considerable experience to go along with their professional qualifications. At the time of their appointment to the Board, both were also attached to the US Army's 4th General Hospital, then based at the Royal Melbourne Hospital complex.

Spencer Eddy and Ira Rothgerber took extensive advice on who would be the most appropriate person for their defence nominee and, based on the discussions they held with both legal and medical specialists, they chose to nominate an Australian Army doctor and psychiatrist, Major Harry Maudsley, to the Board; it was an inspired choice.

Henry Fitzgerald Maudsley was always called Harry, to distinguish him from his father, Sir Henry Carr Maudsley, a prominent Melbourne neurologist and psychiatrist. Harry Maudsley had an excellent professional reputation which extended beyond Melbourne, and he had two other qualities which Spencer Eddy valued almost just as much. The first was that Maudsley was an Australian, as were the murder victims, and would therefore not be expected to make any decisions to suit a purely American legal process. The second was that Harry Maudsley had been an infantryman during the First World War. He had seen extensive combat on the Western Front and had also been awarded the Military Cross for bravery. The combat veterans on the court martial would appreciate that.

Leonski would come to know all three doctors very well over the next few weeks. Once constituted, the Medical Board met with him on at least ten occasions, sometimes as a full board, but more often individually. Edward Harper met with Leonski at least twice a week between 10 June and 7 July, Hugh McHugh saw him by himself on five occasions, while Harry Maudsley had six private sessions with Leonski.

All of the meetings between the three doctors and the accused took place in Leonski's cell in the City Watchhouse. The original plan had been for Leonski to be taken under guard to the 4th General Hospital for examination there, but the gravity of the charges he was facing and the security considerations attached to the case dictated that all the meetings and medical/psychiatric examinations be held under conditions of maximum security. These meetings and examinations always lasted for well over an hour and, as Eddie answered their questions and took their little tests, the psychiatrists looked and listened and took notes for the report they all knew would determine whether Eddie lived or died.

•

As could be expected, the doctors all asked Eddie about his childhood and upbringing. He spoke quite freely about both, and said that he had always regarded himself as being perfectly normal as he grew up. He recalled that at one point, during adolescence, he had thought himself to be overweight, but that was about all he could remember about himself that wasn't positive. Eddie spoke quite openly and frankly about the problems and issues that had arisen within his family. He detailed the history of alcohol abuse that had surrounded them all, with both his father and his stepfather being alcoholics, and physically abusive alcoholics to boot.

Nor did he shy away from the issue of mental illness, admitting that his mother had been hospitalised with mental problems when Eddie was a child, while his brother, Walter, had been in a mental hospital since 1940 and was unlikely to ever be released. Eddie said that he, himself, had never had mental issues. It does appear though, that Eddie failed to mention that he and other family members had experienced problems with the law in New York City and, for Eddie, in San Antonio, Texas.

Leonski was also prepared to talk openly about the murders, although he did try to put them into some kind of context. He said that after he was released from the Camp Pell stockade in late April, he went on a drinking spree and pretty much stayed drunk for eighteen days. It was during that time that he murdered the women and generally behaved in a way that he had never even thought of doing before. Afterwards, when he thought about the murders, he felt as if he had almost dreamed them.

Eddie said that he had not attacked the women to either rape them or rob them, and the only thought he really had on the matter was that the alcohol made him think things and do things that he would not have otherwise thought or done. While he could clearly recall elements of all three murders, his memory of the second, the murder of Pauline Thompson on the steps of her boarding house, remained the most vivid.

While he seemed to struggle to understand why he had done the things that he had, Leonski never tried to deny or deflect his own responsibility for the murders. Early on in the examination process, he said that he wished that he had been caught after the first murder because that would have saved everyone a lot of future trouble. He said that he would also pay whatever penalty the court martial handed down, even if that were to mean that he would lose his life. In many ways, Leonski suggested, a death sentence could well be the best outcome for everyone.

It was a theme Eddie explored often with the doctors, with his belief that either of the alternatives to execution were quite unpalatable to him. If he were convicted of the crimes but not sentenced to death, he would be incarcerated for the rest of his life, and every day of that life he would be reminded that he was a murderer. If he were to be found not guilty by way of insanity, he would spend the rest of his life in an institution for the criminally insane. In many ways, Eddie believed that this would be the worst outcome of all possible outcomes. When talking about his future he once remarked, 'I don't want to live because this will all be thrown up against me, and what is the use of living under those conditions?' Harper and McHugh, in particular, believed that Leonski simply wanted the whole thing over and done with.

All three doctors did agree on a number of things. One was that Eddie's reference to his love of women's voices and his desire to somehow capture and keep them was not normal. It was a delusional belief that had no known factual basis, but while it was an interesting delusion, it was not insanity. Seemingly normal people often had little delusions they lived by: avoiding standing on cracks in pavements, throwing spilt salt over one shoulder and even taking folk medicines for ailments even when medical science had shown that the folk medicine had no true medicinal qualities.

Another thing they agreed on was that Eddie was consistently and openly upbeat and good-humoured in what would normally have been very depressing circumstances. All three members of the Board had previous experience dealing with others in similar circumstances, and the more usual responses to those circumstances had included long periods of both introspection and depression. None of the three had noted any of these in Eddie; at least, not when he was with them.

The only exception to this generally happy disposition came when one of the doctors brought Eddie's mother into the conversation. Whenever that occurred, Eddie would seem to physically shrink into himself. He would drop his head, break eye contact and mumble rather than speak aloud. He said straight out that he resented the fact that the army had forcibly separated him from his mother, who depended on him in so many ways, while expressing genuine concerns about how she would be coping with the news about his own problems.

All three doctors agreed that Eddie's interpersonal skills were marginal and that his emotional relationships were stunted. While he appeared to be outwardly sociable and claimed to have a lot of drinking buddies, he had only ever made one friend in the army, and that was Joey Gallo. An examination of their friendship suggested that it revolved around Leonski's ability to protect the smaller man from bullying.

It seemed to the psychiatrists that the only time Leonski was genuinely sociable was when he was drinking alcohol. Even then, his interactions with others usually involved elements of both bullying and exhibitionism. The mixing of sauces and ice-cream with alcohol and feats of strength, like walking around a bar on his hands, seemed to be inextricably linked to those social interactions. As well, when he drank, Leonski always drank to excess, but saw such behaviour as being acceptable. He would drink to the point where normal social interactions were difficult, if not impossible. Again, he saw little wrong with this.

Each of the doctors was able to establish their own separate relationship with Leonski, and they all had their own individual opinion of him. Hugh McHugh, for instance, found Eddie to be a 'charming, intelligent, handsome individual, and a man of great physical strength who had the rest of his company terrorised because of his prowess'. McHugh and Harper also agreed almost completely on a general psychiatric assessment of Leonski.

Doctors Harper and McHugh concluded that Eddie Leonski was not insane, although they had identified a number of psychiatric problems. They described Leonski as having a psychopathic personality, although they were unable to find any identifiable psychosis. The doctors all described him as being very egotistical and as someone who consistently used his physical strength to intimidate others.

All three Medical Board members believed that Leonski's memory was more or less intact, although they also believed that it had been affected by the excessive consumption of alcohol. They pointed out that he remembered key elements of the first and third murders, like trying to tear Ivy McLeod's belt off and falling in the Camp Pell mud after killing Gladys Hosking, but other details were rather sketchy. He did, though, remember quite a lot about the murder of Pauline Thompson and the sequence of events leading up to that murder.

Considering their different backgrounds, experiences and appointments, it would not have been surprising had there been differences of opinion among the three members of the Medical Board. However, if there were any, they were minor and well hidden, for when it came time to write their final report, it reflected a large degree of unanimity. In formal language, the Medical Board appointed by the General Court Martial concluded that Private Edward Joseph Leonski was sane at the time when he was examined by the Board members, both individually and as a group. The question of Leonski's sanity at the time of the murders he was accused of committing was a separate issue that could be explored during the court martial proper. As a preliminary conclusion, however, the Medical Board asserted that Leonski was sane but under the influence of alcohol at the time of the murders.

Eddie Leonski was not then, and had never been, insane.

•

The adjournment to allow the Medical Board to do its work lasted for a little over a month and the court was scheduled to reconvene on Monday, 13 July. Any thoughts of additional preparation by either the prosecution or the defence teams were frustrated by health issues. On the prosecution side, Hayford Enwall became quite ill with jaundice and needed medical assistance to fully recover. On the defence side, Spencer Eddy suffered a severe reaction to a series of yellow fever inoculations he was given and he, too, was bedridden for several days.

The ongoing legal processes and formalities were not disrupted, and during the adjournment all Australian witnesses were served with subpoenas to appear, the documents being hand-delivered to them by US Army motorcycle despatch riders.

•

The court martial reopened in Victoria Hall at 9.30 a.m. on that Monday morning and would sit each day until the trial was completed. Apart from withholding the names of all the American participants – excepting Leonski – US Army public relations officers told the war correspondents and newspaper reporters that there would be no restrictions placed upon what they reported, provided that it was accurate and did not libel anyone. The early reporting therefore set the scene for what was to come.

As Leonski was the centrepiece of the trial, the usual pen pictures were painted of him, with 'youthful', 'strong', 'clean-cut' even 'handsome' being among the most popular adjectives for the reporters. Those who had seen him at the original opening of the court in June noted that his hair had been cut very short and no longer hung down on one side of his forehead.

The security precautions surrounding the trial also drew a lot of comment. It was noted that special arrangements had been made to transport Leonski to and from the Watchhouse, just a short distance away, and that the accused both entered and left the building by a side entrance. Whenever the court rose for recesses and adjournments, no one in the courtroom would be allowed to leave until Leonski had been escorted from the building.

By the end of the trial, those reporters would also be commenting on their photographers' inability to get a clear photograph of the accused. Photography was not permitted within the courtroom, or elsewhere in the building for that matter, so Leonski's arrival and departure each day represented the only opportunity for the photographers to snap a shot of him. At both the gates to the City Watchhouse garage and at the street end of the lane that led to the court's guarded and off-limits side entrance, the photographers stood and waited, morning and evening, every day. It was all to no avail. Those photographers only ever saw the back of Leonski's neck; as his car passed them, he would lean forward and tuck his head well down between his knees.

There also seemed to be armed guards everywhere, tall American military policemen in impeccable uniforms and with impeccable manners, but also with steely eyes and a clear set of orders. Two stood at the main entrance to the building in which the court sat; they were relieved regularly, but every one of those guards seemed to meet a minimum height require- ment of 188 centimetres. Two more armed guards stood at the foot of the stairs that led up to the courtroom, while another two stood at the doors that led into the courtroom itself.

Those doors would be locked, and would remain locked, whenever the court was sitting. They would only be opened to allow witnesses and reporters to enter or leave. All those who approached the front door of the building had their special passes scrutinised by the guards there, a process repeated inside the building and at the entrance to the courtroom. If there were any doubts about those passes, any deviation from what had been specified, admission was refused. There were no avenues to appeal the decision. Within the courtroom and within the building, the military policemen ruled, and ruled absolutely. Anyone who wanted to use the toilets located outside the courtroom would be given an armed escort while they did so; there were no exceptions.

Inside the courtroom itself, a long trestle table extended almost the complete width of the room, situated at the rear of the hall if one entered from the main doors. Behind that table sat the four colonels, two lieutenant colonels, one major, one captain and two lieutenants who made up the court itself – the original eleven officers now reduced to ten. Two other trestle tables faced the main table. At one sat the accused, Eddie Leonski, flanked by his Defense Counsel, Spencer Eddy and Ira Rothgerber. Two armed MPs sat behind them at all times.

Two metres away was the prosecutor's table. There, Sid McGuffie sat alongside Hayford Enwall, described by one reporter as 'a good-looking young major with an attractive southern accent'. Along one side wall, behind a trestle table, the American and Australian court reporters sat; opposite them was the lone chair which would act as the witness box. Behind the prosecution and defence tables, at the rear of the courtroom, were several rows of folding chairs for the war correspondents, reporters and official observers. All seats were taken on the Monday morning of 13 July. A number of MPs stood at the back of the room watching those who sat there.

•

The first item of evidence offered that day would determine whether or not the trial would actually go ahead. Colonel Woodward opened the proceedings by calling for evidence as to the fitness of the accused to stand trial, and Major Harper was sworn in to respond. Harper identified himself as a doctor and psychiatrist who was attached to the 4th General Hospital of the United States Army's Medical Corps. He also stated that he was the chairman of the Medical Board that had been appointed to examine the accused, Private Edward Leonski.

Harper then continued to testify stating that he had seen and examined Leonski twice a week since the trial had been adjourned on 10 June, and that those examinations had all been conducted in the accused man's cell at the City Watchhouse. Some of the examinations he had conducted by himself, others in the company of Lieutenant Hugh McHugh and a few with McHugh and Major Harry Maudsley. On the basis of his own, and the joint, examinations, the Medical Board believed that the accused was sane and therefore fit to stand trial.

The next witness called identified himself as Lieutenant Hugh McHugh, also a medical doctor and psychiatrist who was currently attached to the 4th General Hospital as a medical officer. McHugh's evidence mirrored Harper's and concluded on the same note; Leonski was both sane and mentally fit enough to stand trial.

A tipping point had been reached. As Trial Judge Advocate Enwall moved that the report of the Medical Board be accepted by the court, Spencer Eddy was on his feet objecting almost before Enwall had finished speaking. Eddy said that the Medical Board report was a comprehensive report – which was as it should be – but, if the court accepted the report, it would be giving that report a legal status which not only did it not deserve, but would also be in direct conflict with long-established legal principles.

The report, Eddy argued, contained significant amounts of material about whether or not the accused had committed the crimes for which he had been charged. In the form in which this material had been included in the Medical Board report, the material represented the second-hand reporting of the doctors, 'Leonski said that he then . . .' As such, it was hearsay, and therefore not admissible to the court. Because of that, the document was tainted and could not be either admitted or accepted by the court.

Eddy had made a good point, and one that the court was happy to hand over to John Welch, the Law Member, for consideration and decision. Perhaps forewarned, Welch responded quite rapidly. Rather than admitting or accepting the report, Welch said, the report could be received by the court, for identification purposes only, that is the court acknowledged the existence of the report. Furthermore, the court only recognised within the report the findings as to the accused's fitness to stand trial. At this point, everything else was irrelevant until and unless it was subjected to the court processes of examination and cross-examination.

The court accepted all this, and adopted a minimalist approach. Eddie Leonski was sane; the trial would therefore continue.

15.

EVIDENCE-IN-CHIEF

The trial of Eddie Leonski would hear from fifty-seven witnesses, with forty-six of these appearing for the prosecution and just eleven for the defence. It was a trial with few moments of real drama and few attempts at theatricality. A trial marked by polite exchanges between lawyers whose task was to take away a man's life and those committed to saving his life. It was also a trial followed by millions of people who lived well away from the city where the crimes that led to the trial had been committed. Finally, it was a closely stage-managed trial by a foreign power in a sovereign country, and was therefore unique in Australian legal history. The weight of this sat squarely on the shoulders of the main protagonists: the lawyers and officers who were the working members of the court, and it is to their credit that they all rose to the task in a way that in turn brought well-deserved credit to their army and their professions.

The reconvened General Court Martial opened with Hayford Enwall, as Trial Judge Advocate, moving directly into the prosecution's case. The planning sessions with his team at Melbourne Grammar had devised a strategy based around the perceived strong points the investigators had uncovered with the strongest of all, apart from Leonski's confessions, being the evidence which linked Leonski directly to the murder of Gladys Hosking. Enwall proceeded to open the prosecution case with what happened after the near-naked and mud-caked body of a woman was found on the outskirts of Camp Pell early one morning in the middle of May, almost two months to the day earlier.

Enwall called, as his first witness, Detective Sergeant Sidney McGuffie of the Victoria Police Homicide Squad, and proceeded to lead McGuffie through the events of that Tuesday morning. The experienced policeman was both strong and confident in delivering his evidence, although he did make one or two uncharacteristic stumbles, one when he mistakenly labelled some scuff marks in the mud at the murder scene as coming from the wrong person's shoes, and a second when he admitted that he was unable to positively identify Leonski's tent in a police photograph of Camp Pell.

McGuffie then went on to describe the circumstances which led to the identification and arrest of Edward Leonski for the murder of Gladys Hosking, the subsequent discovery of the yellow mud clay on Leonski's clothing and tent, and what this had meant for the investigation. The only artfulness during the process concerned Gladys Hosking's clothing, torn and mud-covered. Enwall introduced it into evidence by holding each item aloft for McGuffie to identify, before theatrically carrying it to the front table and parading it past the officers seated there.

Spencer Eddy, for Leonski, objected strongly to what he believed was an unnecessary act of grandstanding. He said that, while he would not object to the items being offered as a composite exhibit, the prosecution's introduction of them individually – and holding them up for all in the courtroom to see while doing so – was a somewhat obvious effort to prejudice the court. While Eddy's various objections were not sustained, Enwall did offer an apology of sorts. He would not parade further items of victim's apparel under the noses of the judges, but would insist on introducing individual items into evidence, consistently detailing the damage wrought to that clothing by the savagery of the murderer's attack.

When McGuffie had completed his evidence, Hayford Enwall introduced the supporting cast to his star witness, the players whose evidence, though limited, was important to buttress the details of the brutal murder, and murderer, he was presenting to the court. The police photographers came and went with their photographs of the crime scene and of Leonski's tent and personal possessions. A number of Australian loungers – regular drinkers at the Parkville Hotel – recalled Leonski's antics on the afternoon and evening of Hosking's death, as did his drinking buddy and putative companion to the cinema that evening, Rupert Burns.

Two soldiers, one Australian and one American, testified about their encounters with a mud-spattered and seemingly disoriented Eddie Leonski around the time and near the place where Gladys Hosking was killed, and Dr Crawford Mollison, the Government Pathologist, gave the cold, hard medical details about how life was taken away from the victim.

Dr Charles Taylor gave his expert opinion that the yellow mud stains in question could only have come from the murder site in Gatehouse Street, and Taylor was followed by another expert, a geologist from the University of Melbourne. That geologist testified that the Camp Pell slit trenches had been dug into an ancient fossil zone, a layer of clay that contained ironstone gravel, which gave the clay a distinctive yellow colouring. The only place where that particular clay – unique to that part of Melbourne – had been exposed was where the slit trenches had been dug. Excavations elsewhere at Camp Pell had not been deep enough to expose the clay layer.

After he had completed the dissection of the murder of Gladys Hosking, Enwall continued in the same detached vein when looking into the other two murders. He introduced a succession of witnesses – some experts and others merely observers of events – to talk about the horrible deaths of Pauline Thompson and Ivy McLeod. As Monday segued into Tuesday, and Tuesday became Wednesday, the court heard of Pauline Thompson missing a prearranged meeting with one American soldier only to have a chance encounter with another. That encounter would lead to several hours drinking on a rainy Melbourne night and ultimately to Thompson's death, brutally strangled and then put on display on the doorsteps of her own apartment building.

The court also heard of the lonely death of Ivy McLeod, a woman who had remained living a dignified life in what were sometimes trying circumstances. Ivy McLeod may well have suffered less than the others, because the initial strike by her killer had fractured her skull and rendered Ivy unconscious. Like the other two victims, Ivy's body was subjected to a number of post-mortem indignities, some of which may have been inflicted because of her killer's inability to remove her belt.

When the circumstances of these other two deaths had been laid out in clinical detail for the court, Enwall turned his attention to the details of Leonski's identification, arrest and subsequent confessions to the three murders. He led the court through the unsuccessful line-ups at Camp Pell and to the final, successful line-up with Mr Jackson again identifying Eddie Leonski as the American soldier who had attacked his niece as she arrived home from work one evening.

The Trial Judge Advocate then described how Detective Sergeant McGuffie and Leonski had walked around Camp Pell and Parkville after Leonski's arrest, and then had McGuffie recalled to the witness stand to bring out the conversations and discussions the two had shared as they walked around.

All of this was leading, with a kind of obvious inevitability, to the Friday afternoon confessions of Eddie Leonski. Hayford Enwall had Captain Clyde Servis called to the witness box, where the American testified that when Detective Fred Adam informed Leonski that he had been identified by an Australian soldier, who had thereby linked him to the site where Gladys Hosking had been murdered, Leonski's only response had been to ask what that meant for his position. Servis said that he had then told Leonski that what was to happen would be a matter for the military authorities but that, in Servis's opinion, the matter would be dealt with through a military court martial.

Detective Fred Adam was then recalled; he, too, had testified to the course of the murder investigations. Enwall now asked the policeman to describe what had happened when Leonski asked if the civil authorities had anything on him. Adam stated that he had then informed Leonski that he had been identified in a line-up and that the police also had scientific information about the yellow clay mud found in Leonski's tent and on his clothes and other possessions. It was at this point, Adam said, that Eddie Leonski confessed to the murder of Gladys Hosking.

Under cross-examination by Spencer Eddy, Fred Adam told the Defense Counsel that Leonski had spoken slowly but spontaneously about the murder of Hosking. He did not seem to have been distressed about it, and seemed to have no trouble recalling the key elements of the crime. To Adam at least, Leonski appeared to be telling the truth.

Lieutenant William Johnston followed Adam into the witness box to tell the court that when Leonski had finished his confession to the Hosking murder, Johnston had told him that a woman named Pauline Thompson had also been murdered a short time earlier, and that her body had been found on the front steps of her apartment house in the city. Without any prompting, Leonski had then given quite a detailed account of what had happened the evening of Thompson's murder, describing events in much the same way as he had described the killing of Gladys Hosking.

By the time Johnston finished his testimony, it was four o'clock on Wednesday afternoon. Court President Woodward proposed to close proceedings early that day. He had seen a list of the next day's witnesses, he said, and he thought that Thursday would be a very big day for them all.

•

The defence team of Spencer Eddy and Ira Rothgerber had quite deliberately kept a low profile during the first three days of the trial. Where they felt it was appropriate, they challenged on points of law and court process, but they had chosen to selectively cross-examine the witnesses called by the prosecution. They would, for instance, ask Sid McGuffie if any one of the many witnesses who had seen Pauline Thompson drinking with an American soldier at the Astoria Hotel on the night she was murdered was able to say *definitively* that Eddie Leonski was the American soldier who was with her. Not that Leonski *looked like* or *could have been* the man, but that he positively was the man.

Similarly, they would ask other witnesses not whether there were yellow mud stains on Leonski's bedstead and bedspread and on the inside of the tent above where he slept, but whether they or anyone else had actually *seen* Leonski leave the stains there.

It wasn't much, but the defence lawyers hoped that it was enough to give the court some food for thought about the actual thoroughness of the prosecution's case, to drop a little hint that Enwall and his team had placed all their eggs in the confession basket and that – for the prosecution – in other things, near enough seemed to have been good enough. Their argument would not rely on circumstance and statement. Everyone seemed to agree who the killer was, so Eddy and Rothgerber would not argue the who. Their defence would rest on the why.

●

Private Anthony 'Joey' Gallo was the first witness called by Enwall on Thursday, 16 July, and from the moment he was sworn in, it was obvious that Gallo was very nervous. At times, he stumbled over answers, and he occasionally contradicted himself, but he came across to his audience as an honest young man who was doing his best to tell a story as he remembered it. By way of introducing that story, Gallo said that he had known Eddie Leonski since the middle of 1941 and that the two men were friends.

Gallo then told his stories of Leonski's boasts about what he had done, boasts that he would repeat whether drunk or sober. He spoke of Leonski's discussions with him about the nature of good and evil, and about the existence of Mr Hyde within the body of Dr Jekyll. He said that Leonski had spoken of werewolves and of killing women on stairs, only to recant the next day, saying that he had made the whole thing up to try to impress – no, *scare* – his friend.

Joey Gallo spoke at length about the night, shortly after Pauline Thompson's murder, when he and Eddie Leonski caught a tram into the heart of Melbourne and had dinner in the cafeteria attached to St Paul's Cathedral. He detailed Leonski's aberrant behaviour on the tram, at the cafeteria and in the Swanston Street milk bar later. He described how his friend's voice would change completely when he was talking to and trying to impress women, of how he would speak slowly and in a way that was itself almost feminine.

As an unmoving and seemingly unmoved Eddie Leonski sat and watched his friend, Joey Gallo concluded by describing how his fears gradually overcame his doubts and how, after Leonski successfully passed a line-up at Camp Pell, those fears all coalesced and he could no longer keep them to himself. He took his concerns to one of his regimental officers, and afterwards repeated them to other officers at Camp Pell Headquarters. Shortly after signing off on the statement he had made, Joey Gallo learned that Eddie Leonski had been arrested in connection with the latest murder.

For all his nervousness and struggles with complex language, it was a gallant performance by the little New Yorker and one that potentially did a lot of damage to Eddie Leonski's case, showing him – as it did – to be a conniving and manipulative figure who played with his friend's innermost fears just because he could. It was an assessment Spencer Eddy could not allow to go unchallenged, and nor did he.

When he rose to cross-examine Gallo, Spencer Eddy did not pull any punches in his attempts to discredit Gallo's testimony. He had some success in this, but it was very limited. Gallo conceded that Leonski had been much more voluble on the murder of Pauline Thompson after he had read the newspaper article on it than he had been before, but would not be shaken on his insistence that Leonski had told him about leaving a body on some steps long before he had even read the newspaper article.

Likewise, when pushed hard by Eddy, Gallo conceded that he and Leonski could be regarded primarily as 'camp buddies' and that they had only ever been out twice socially since they had arrived in Australia. Leonski had regularly sought him out for talks on a wide range of subjects, just as Gallo regularly sought out Leonski. They did not have to always be somewhere, doing something, to enjoy being in each other's company. That, to Joey Gallo, was friendship, and that was something they had shared up until a couple of months earlier when his friend, Eddie Leonski, had started to change. Spencer Eddy had no further questions.

●

Joey Gallo was followed into the witness box by Fred Adam, Clyde Servis and William Johnston, each of whom testified to the circumstances and content of Eddie Leonski's three confessions, going through them and verifying exactly what it was he had confessed to.

The investigators in turn were followed by Hayford Enwall himself, who read into evidence the final report of the Medical Board. He did not offer any comment on that report but, when he had finished reading, he called the chairman of the Board, Major Edward Harper, as a witness. After being sworn in, Harper took the court through the medical dimensions of both sanity and insanity.

Harper commenced by identifying and commenting on the important role that heredity played in the likelihood of anyone suffering from a mental illness. He said heredity had been found to play a significant role in a cluster of conditions that existed around what was referred to as manic-depressive psychosis. In answer to questions from Enwall, Harper said that, yes, he had read a detailed report on the Leonski family's mental history but, no, he did not consider it to be a factor in Eddie Leonski's case.

Harper said that Leonski had a psychopathic personality, which made it difficult for him to adjust to the changed circumstances that army service entailed. These issues were, for Leonski, complicated by an excessive use of alcohol. The closest Harper would come to defining Leonski's illness was to state, 'I would say that the psychopathic personality was a very maladjusted or unadjusted individual, and that maladjustment keeps him from falling in the group of so-called normal individuals or mentally well people; in other words, it does represent a terrific amount of emotional instability, which does not imply insanity.'

Spencer Eddy was again aggressive in his cross-examination. He opened by closely questioning Harper on the nature of insanity and followed a specific line of questioning about whether or not it was possible for someone who was insane to mask that insanity for much of their daily life. Harper's response was that while such a condition was theoretically possible, it would be highly unlikely to occur in real life.

And then Eddy might have pushed a bit too hard with his questioning. Harper repeated what he had said earlier, about Leonski being a psychopathic personality, unable to adjust himself satisfactorily to his environment but not necessarily insane. Harper then suggested that similar crimes would be committed by Leonski if he were free and alone with a woman while under the influence of alcohol.

It was a point immediately seized upon by Enwall who, as soon as Eddy indicated that he had no further questions of the witness, rose to ask one final question of Harper himself. 'Assume that the defendant walked out of this courtroom and was permitted to go about his business in the normal way of life, without any control, and he again engaged in the excessive use of alcohol and the opportunity appeared at night, with him alone with a woman; would you anticipate that he might again commit the same crime?' Harper's answer was a chilling, 'Yes, sir.'

When called to the witness box, Lieutenant Hugh McHugh supported almost completely what Harper had said in his initial testimony, including the likelihood of Leonski reoffending and, when he finished, Eddy indicated that he had no questions for McHugh at that time. With the two prosecution nominees to the Medical Board having completed their evidence, the court had heard, twice over, that both doctors believed that, if earlier circumstances were repeated, Eddie Leonski was more than likely to kill again. As well, both doctors seemed unshakeable in their belief that Leonski was sane at the time he committed the murders to which he had confessed.

The defence team's only real hope of redeeming something from what was shaping up as a disastrous day lay in the chance that their medical expert, Dr Harry Maudsley, would be able to offer such a significantly different diagnosis and prognosis that the judges would have some doubts about Leonski's sanity both then and now, thereby giving them something they could exploit.

Those hopes were stillborn. In his opening statement to the court, Maudsley said that he was initially surprised by the fact that Leonski seemed to him to be a lot more cheerful than could rightfully be expected of a man in his position. During the time Maudsley spent with Leonski, the accused had displayed no real despondency and, in fact, had only ever shown signs of tension when his mother's name was brought into the conversation. Leonski's only concern was that, if he was found to be insane, he would be locked up in a mental asylum, and he certainly didn't want that. He was, however, more concerned about the possible effect that the revelation of his crimes would have on his mother.

Cross-examined by Spencer Eddy, Major Maudsley said he concurred with the other Board Members' diagnosis of Leonski as having a psychopathic personality, one that prevented him from adapting to his environment. This did not mean though, that he was insane. He had no psychosis underlying this, so he was a sane person who was capable of committing insane acts. Maudsley felt that, when Leonski drank the amounts of alcohol attributed to him on the night of the Thompson murder, he might act in an insane manner. Any comfort the defence team may have taken from this was lost immediately when, prodded by one of Enwall's questions, Maudsley said he believed that, under similar circumstances to those previously described, he would expect Eddie Leonski to kill again.

After Maudsley had completed his examination and cross-examination, Hayford Enwall said that he would like to recall Lieutenant McHugh to clear up a minor point he had missed. When he was seated, Enwall asked McHugh to again define Leonski's mental health. 'I thought that he was a psychopathic personality,' McHugh responded, 'and that under the influence of alcohol as he claimed he was for, I believe, eighteen days, many of the emotional conflicts that one finds in a psychopath come to the surface. That often happens with psychopathic personalities.'

There were no further questions and Hugh McHugh was dismissed. At this, Hayford Enwall rose to announce that the prosecution now rested its case.

●

It was getting late, but the day was not yet over. After Enwall's announcement, Spencer Eddy stood up and moved that the trial be ended because there was insufficient evidence to support the charges against the accused. Eddy said he believed that all three confessions were flawed, the products of a mind that was clearly troubled to a considerable extent, and should therefore be put aside. If they were put aside, it became quite clear that the prosecution had offered far too little to realistically connect Eddie Leonski to any of the murders.

As soon as Eddy had finished, Hayford Enwall was on his feet. Arguing vigorously against Eddy's motion, he said that the very details of each of the three murders – the times, the places and the actual method of killing and displaying the victim in each case – went far beyond the possibility of mere coincidence, and that the same person had committed all three murders. That person had confessed to the murders, that person was in court and that person's name was Edward Joseph Leonski. The court dismissed the Defense Counsel's motion.

Spencer Eddy then asked the court's forbearance for his sometimes uneven performance, saying that he was visiting legal areas that he hadn't visited for a long time, and that his personal law library was a long, long way away. He did, however, look forward to opening the defence case the following morning. Woodward thanked him and adjourned the court for the day.

●

The general public avidly followed the case that week through the considerable newspaper space devoted to it in both capital city and provincial newspapers right across Australia. The readers were probably only marginally interested in the finer points of US military law, but were captivated by the ebb and flow of the evidence presented, especially that which spoke of the lives of real human beings. 'Doctors told a poignant story of Leonski's unhappy home life, in which his parents were chronic drunkards, one brother served time in a penitentiary and another is in a mental hospital,' allowed readers a glimpse into the life of a murderer, and numbers of those readers found it all slightly titillating.

There was not a lot more they could glean about Leonski the person rather than Leonski the killer. Apart from the official head-and-shoulders photograph of a smiling and boyish Eddie Leonski, the only photographs available for publication were distant shots of an American soldier's back as he ducked into the side entrance of the court building, manacled hands clearly visible. The physical descriptions of him sitting in court added very little to this.

Leonski's behaviour in the courtroom was almost as closely scrutinised by the reporters there as the evidence that was being presented, perhaps as a way of understanding the man who could become the monster. At times, his youthful appearance and behaviour suggested a schoolboy on an excursion, talking about and pointing to things he found interesting. At other times, he seemed anxious to join in the proceedings, to rise to his feet and direct a series of questions to one or other of the witnesses.

He frequently took notes and sketched members of the court and the witnesses that were called. Several reporters observed that Leonski's notes were taken in the shorthand he had learned at a business college in New York City. He was always neat with his pens and notebooks and smiled pleasantly at the witnesses as they were sworn in.

But to the reporters and those who read what those reporters recorded and wrote, Eddie Leonski remained an enigma. He may have been a narcissist, now basking in the fact that he was at the centre of a national, even international, story. Or he may have been a tormented soul, driven to commit terrible deeds by inner demons that others could only imagine. The reporters, and their readers, hoped that Spencer Eddy and Ira Rothgerber would reveal the real Eddie Leonski to the world on Friday, 17 July 1942.

16.

FOR THE DEFENCE

On Friday morning, following the conclusion of the case for the prosecution, Spencer Eddy and Ira Rothgerber were no closer to having any hope of saving Leonski's life than they had been on the day they had accepted their appointments as his Defense Counsel. The evidence, and the odds, were simply stacked too high against them. Their initial hope – that the Medical Board would find Eddie insane, at least at the time the murders were committed – had been systematically and comprehensively shredded on Thursday, and they were now left with little more than fragments of a defence and a modicum of a small mixture of hope and wishful thinking.

While they may have lacked a comprehensive strategy, they did have a series of little tactics. If they could suggest that Eddie Leonski had not been a murderous monster before he was drafted into the army, but had become one while serving as a soldier in a time of war, they could then argue that there must have been something somewhere in that service which had made him what he had become. The army had therefore created a problem and so had a moral, if not a legal, responsibility to do something about it. A long term of imprisonment – even a life sentence – with access to professional psychiatric assistance, could form the major part of that responsibility. As a defence, it felt weak, even as they tossed the ideas around but, really, were there any other alternatives?

Eddy announced to the court on Friday morning that there would be a number of witnesses called for the defence, and that those witnesses would help the court to understand how the accused came to be in the position he now occupied. Unfortunately, said Eddy, he himself had suffered a minor recurrence of a recent illness and so would not be conducting the examination of the witnesses; he would leave that task to Captain Rothgerber, but he did reserve the right to examine or cross-examine as and when appropriate.

The first witness called for the defence was Private Julian Tiller, who was a member of the 52nd Signal Battalion's Medical Detachment. Tiller had, at times, been a drinking partner of Leonski's, and had taken part in several prolonged drinking sessions in and around Leonski's tent at Camp Pell. At one of those sessions, which Tiller thought had taken place sometime around 15 May, another soldier who had been drinking with them lay down on Leonski's bed. That soldier had been wearing muddy boots, and those boots had soiled Leonski's bedding. Tiller was not able to recall anything further about that incident, but did give a good description of Leonski's binge-drinking habits. To some, it seemed a curious opening.

The next witness was Private Lewis Bartell, like Leonski, a member of the Headquarters Company of the 52nd Signallers. Bartell described to the court how he and Leonski had gone into the city for a drink at a hotel a short time after they had arrived in Australia. Afterwards, as they walked along Swanston

Street, Leonski had several times snuck up behind young women and yelled out 'Boo!', causing both consternation and fright. The two soldiers had then parted company. Bartell also testified that Leonski had not wanted to come to Australia and had cried about it in San Antonio and San Francisco. But, he added, Leonski had also told him that he was an actor.

Cross-examined by Hayford Enwall, Bartell admitted that he had only been out drinking with Leonski that one time in Melbourne, although he said that he believed Leonski's drinking had increased substantially after that incident.

Captain Christian Kauffman, now of the US Army Air Forces, followed Bartell into the witness box. Kauffman stated that he had been Leonski's company commander both in the United States and, for a time, at Camp Pell. Kauffman described Leonski as a soldier who was continually in trouble over minor offences and also as a young man who was inordinately proud of his physical strength.

Kauffman expanded his comments by describing how he had to discipline Leonski for being absent without leave from Camp Pell. He gave detailed evidence about finding an AWOL Leonski in a Melbourne café after a tip-off, and of taking him back to Camp Pell in a taxi. In that taxi, Leonski started to cry – 'like a baby' – and was very apologetic about the trouble he had caused. When they arrived back at Camp Pell, Leonski had smiled and said that he would now like to go back to the city. Kauffman said he responded to this by having Leonski placed under arrest, later sentencing him to thirty days in the stockade.

Kauffman concluded his testimony by saying that he had believed Leonski had the potential to become a first-class soldier, but that he also doubted that Leonski ever would do so because he did not consider him to be 'normal', a fact he attributed to Leonski's excessive consumption of alcohol.

There were several more witnesses called for the defence, but they were bit players who were able to testify to having seen Eddie Leonski sometimes drinking, sometimes crying, and sometimes doing both together in any one of a number of locations: San Antonio, San Francisco and Melbourne. The overall picture they painted was that of a potentially good soldier who had gone horribly bad.

As the last of these witnesses was escorted from the courtroom, Spencer Eddy rose at his table to announce to the court that the defence now rested its case. There was a moment's silence as those in the courtroom absorbed the significance of this. Several among the journalists had apparently expected Leonski to testify in his own defence but, realistically, that was never going to happen. Once the question of his sanity had been addressed by the Medical Board, there were no positives in having Eddie Leonski testify. If he either behaved irrationally or gave irrational answers, and both were equally likely, the court would think that he was putting it on for effect. There was an even greater chance that Eddie would welcome his moment in the spotlight, and his natural arrogance and egotism would do even more damage to his case than had already been done.

And so the defence rested and the court adjourned until the afternoon, when the closing arguments of both sides would be heard.

•

Hayford Enwall addressed the court first, and opened with a summary that went straight to the heart of the case. Three women had been brutally murdered. The accused had confessed to the murders. He was sane when he committed the murders. He was sane now.

Enwall then proceeded to expand on these opening remarks. The prosecution of Edward Leonski for murder was reliant in part on three clear and unequivocal confessions made by the accused, confessions that were backed up by the evidence – credible evidence – offered by a reliable witness, Leonski's friend, Anthony 'Joey' Gallo.

Enwall then chose to directly address the question of whether alcohol was either an excuse for or a mitigating factor in a series of acts that were otherwise inexplicable. An interesting question, he said, because Eddie Leonski would often boast of his capacity to drink large quantities of alcohol, with little apparent effect. The alcohol consumption did not produce insanity. When he murdered Pauline Thompson, Leonski had been sane enough to go through her handbag to find money to take a taxi back to Camp Pell. He had also been sane enough to rub his fingerprints off the purse from which he had taken that money.

Enwall also mentioned, almost in passing, that Eddie Leonski had probably raped Thompson, either before or after her death, but that the evidence, blood on Leonski's trousers' fly and underpants, was not amenable to scientific analysis because of the passage of time.

Leonski was a big, strong man and his victims were all small, almost powerless women. When his hands clamped on their necks, there was only ever going to be one outcome, he suggested. If Leonski was insane, he should be acquitted, said the Trial Judge Advocate. But he wasn't insane, and three eminent medical experts had all testified to his sanity at the time of the murders and at the present time as well.

Enwall then moved on to place the trial in a broader national and international context:

> *For five days this court has heard a story of human tragedy and depravity unparalleled in the administration of criminal justice in the United States Army. The trial . . . created more public interest than probably any other held in Australia.*
>
> *The people of Australia and the United States have the same basic concepts of justice. They share the same value of human life, they have the same fundamental beliefs in human order and decency. We have the same abhorrence of crime, particularly crimes of violence.*
>
> *Every citizen of either country who has heard the details of this case has felt complete revulsion and horror, and it is not only the fiendish character of the crimes that makes us recoil. This youth has placed a foul blot on the service in which we are engaged.*
>
> *The preservation of the basic concepts of human decency, justice and order was one reason why Americans were in this country. Resistance to international plundering, murdering and wreaking of violence on the defenceless and weak was only an enlargement of our concept of international justice and order.*

Enwall stated plainly to the court that his sole concern was to see that justice was done, 'even to this poor unfortunate youth . . . I believe that in the eyes of the people of this nation, these proceedings here have a meaning which is more than solely the issues in this tragic case. The American system of justice is also on trial.'

Enwall then quoted one of Leonski's victims: 'I think Mrs Thompson labelled the accused pretty well when she said, "You have a baby-face, but you are vicious underneath."' Hayford

Enwall concluded that, by the ferocity of his attacks, undertaken without any thought for his victims, Edward Joseph Leonski had forfeited his right to live, and asked for the court to so find.

•

Enwall's had been a bravura performance which Spencer Eddy did not even attempt to match. Instead, he would offer an alternative view of the circumstances that the Trial Judge Advocate had so graphically portrayed. He, too, traced the course of the crimes that Eddie Leonski was accused of committing but, where Enwall saw the emergence of clear patterns, Spencer Eddy saw nothing but anarchy and chaos.

Eddy pointed out to the court that Leonski's confessions revealed nothing more than flashes of recollections about his presence at the sites where Ivy McLeod and Gladys Hosking had been murdered. Even the Pauline Thompson murder – the only one which he could actually recall in any detail – was committed because he liked her voice so much that he wanted to keep it with him forever. One view of the confessions that Leonski had made was that he was so eager to please the investigators, so keen to cooperate and remain the central character in what he saw as some kind of play that he simply told them what it was that he thought they wanted to hear. Apart from those confessions, all the prosecution's case was based on circumstantial evidence; no one had actually seen Eddie Leonski commit any of the crimes of which he was accused.

Spencer Eddy then turned to the Leonski family, where mental disorders had seemed to be the norm rather than the exception. Eddie Leonski had been able to cope with the issues attached to his family until, ironically, he was separated from it. The army might have given him a new home and a new family, but it was not the one that he wanted and it existed in a new and alien environment.

In turn, this inability to cope led to excessive drinking which eventually – and inevitably – led to homicidal violence. It was a spiral which logically led to the circumstances in which they now all found themselves. Eddy did not and would not link Leonski directly to the murders – 'That duty is yours' – but said that while Leonski's actions certainly did merit many things, the death penalty was not one of them.

•

At that, Spencer Eddy thanked the court and sat down. Simon Woodward, as President of the Court, asked Eddy if he had anything further to say on behalf of the accused. The Defense Counsel said that he did not. Hayford Enwall then stood and asked, for the record, whether Leonski had been told his rights and whether he understood what those rights were. Eddy answered in the affirmative to both questions and then, for all intents and purposes, the body of the trial was over.

•

Woodward then ordered that the courtroom be cleared, and after Leonski had been escorted to a small room on the same level as the courtroom, where he was placed under guard, all others left the main room and went downstairs to the lobby, where they stood around in small groups, some talking quietly, others just standing around and smoking. Exactly twenty-two minutes after they had left the courtroom, they were asked to return and the trial continued.

When the court reassembled, Woodward asked if there were any previous court-martial convictions in Leonski's service record.

Hayford Enwall stood and read out sections of that service record, confirming that there were no previous convictions and outlining Leonski's service experience. Enwall finished, and Woodward again ordered that the courtroom be cleared.

When all the others had left the room and the doors had been locked, Woodward led the other officers in a brief discussion on legal issues before calling on all members of the court martial to vote on the verdict and, if necessary, the sentence, in a secret ballot. Elsewhere in the building, Eddie Leonski again sat and waited under armed guard while all the others – reporters, observers, guards and legal counsel – once more gathered in their small groups in the lobby. They did not have to wait much longer than before and were called back to the courtroom some thirty-five minutes after the doors had been locked behind them.

When all had returned, and the doors were again secured, Colonel Woodward called the court to order and directed the accused to stand before him. Reading from a piece of paper he held in his hands, Woodward spoke aloud:

> *Private Leonski, it is my duty as President of this court to inform you that the court, in closed session, and upon secret written ballot – three-fourths of the members present at the time the vote was taken concurring in each finding of guilty – finds you, of all the Specifications and of the Charge, Guilty.*
>
> *And again in closed session and upon secret written ballot – all of the members present at the time the vote was taken concurring – sentences you to be hanged by the neck until dead.*

The sentence was passed to absolute silence in the courtroom. It was a silence that was not broken until it threatened to become embarrassing. Leonski then snapped a copybook salute and returned to his chair behind the trestle table. He looked subdued, even glum, before regaining his normal jaunty pose. As he did so, Woodward ordered the removal of the prisoner. At that, Leonski again stood, swivelled, and was escorted out of the courtroom, and out of the lives of many of those who had sat in the makeshift courthouse that week. As he did so, one of the newsmen swore that he smiled broadly at the reporters and observers, giggled, rubbed his hands together in a gesture that suggested some kind of satisfied amusement and said, 'Well, I guess that's that.' To most of those reporters, Leonski simply seemed to be monstrously disinterested in his fate.

•

For a trial that had lasted just five days, the court martial of Eddie Leonski had certainly packed a lot into a short period. In the end, fifty-six witnesses had been sworn to give evidence, forty-five for the prosecution and eleven for the defence. The prosecution had submitted ninety-eight exhibits to the court; the defence had submitted only one. When the court reporters had finished their work, the transcript of the trial proceedings came to almost 450 pages. That transcript was completed by early August, with several complete copies being made. Most were to remain in Australia, but one was flown to the United States immediately once it was available.

In both countries, military law experts would ponder over the transcripts, examining everything that had been submitted and argued. Only when they were satisfied that there were no errors of either omission or commission would they pass the court martial's findings further up the line for final approval, or rejection. No one in either country knew how long the process would take, because they were still all working on unfamiliar territory. The consensus, though, was that it would be months rather than weeks or years.

•

It was dark when Eddie was led downstairs and into the waiting car for the short trip back to the Watchhouse, but the dark had never worried Eddie, who sometimes wore it like a cloak. As he exited the car in the police garage, Eddie and his guards engaged in one of their little rituals, smoking a cigarette together before Eddie was escorted back to his cell. As they stood there smoking their cigarettes, a Victoria Police officer who knew Eddie walked past and called out a greeting. Eddie waved back, and held up his cigarette. 'I'll have to give up smoking,' he said. 'It's bad for my throat,' and he gave his funny little laugh.

For Eddie Leonski, everything had changed; for Eddie Leonski, nothing had changed.

17.

KILLING TIME

The findings and sentence of the court martial – guilty of all counts and death by hanging – marked the end of one process, but also the beginning of several others. One of the perceived strengths of an army court martial was that, in many respects, all members of the court were peers of the accused, hence the preference for combat veterans who had experienced soldiering at its hardest and most extreme. This could, however, be a double-edged sword, as combat experience was not always a good substitute for legal experience or training. There was also no appeal mechanism once a verdict had been reached, so all decisions and findings from courts martial were subject to legal review before any penalties were applied.

In the Leonski case, there were additional layers of interest and complication. Australian legal precedent had already been set, and the actual implementation of the death sentence would probably create another set of precedents. The Australian government and the Australian public also had their own sets of expectations, which sometimes clashed with each other and with those of the US Army and even the US government. There were a lot of bridges to be crossed before substance could be given to the will of the court.

●

One of those processes would take place overseas. When the transcripts of the court martial were completed in early August, one complete copy was given to Major General Julian Barnes, still commanding all American forces in Australia. Barnes was to briefly review the document, adding any contextual comments, before forwarding the transcript to Washington. There, the proceedings would be reviewed by the Judge Advocate General, the army's senior legal officer, whose role was to review in turn the proceedings to determine whether the evidence presented to the court warranted both a conviction and a sentence of death.

If the Judge Advocate General was satisfied on both counts, Article 48 of the Articles of War specified that he must then forward the verdict and sentence to the Commander-in-Chief, US President Franklin Roosevelt, for confirmation. No death sentence could be carried out until this confirmation had been received. While the final decision might therefore be seen to be made in Washington, the bulk of the review, and the bulk of any recommendations, would come from reviewers and review teams based in Australia. The American end was not a rubber stamp, and Eddie's ultimate fate would be determined by legal reviews undertaken in Australia.

The first of these formal reviews was undertaken by Lieutenant Colonel John Stagg, a lawyer in the Judge Advocate General's office at Melbourne Grammar. His report, which was completed by 29 September, found a number of flaws in the proceedings of the court martial. Despite these flaws, Stagg did not believe that any of them constituted a miscarriage of justice by the court.

He recommended that Major General Richard Marshall, then MacArthur's Deputy Chief of Staff, authorise and sign Eddie Leonski's Death Warrant. This Marshall did on 30 September.

On 10 October, a second review of the trial was undertaken by Lieutenant Colonel Nathan Roberts, another army staff legal officer. Roberts, too, was quite critical of some aspects of the trial. He felt strongly that the introduction of the victims' clothing – item by item – should not have been allowed by the Law Member, while crime scene photographs of the victims' exposed genital areas were of questionable legal value. Roberts also found that, without the confessions, the Hosking murder was the only crime for which Leonski could legally be convicted.

Roberts' findings included one which stated that Eddie Leonski had deliberately murdered all three of his victims, with the 'collecting voices' justification being added by Leonski after the crimes had actually been committed. Roberts believed that there may actually have been a sexual motive to the crimes. He also found that Leonski's mental state – and the doctors' assessment of it – was neither adequately challenged nor explored in sufficient depth.

In his conclusion, Lieutenant Colonel Roberts found that both Leonski himself and the trial transcripts should be examined by a board of 'competent' medical officers and that, pending their review, the sentence be confirmed by General MacArthur.

Roberts' report was forwarded to MacArthur on 12 October and two days later General MacArthur himself confirmed the sentence. That confirmation was withheld, in accordance with military law, until a board of review could complete its examination of the trial. That board comprised three lawyers from another branch of the Judge Advocate General's office, none of whom had any previous involvement in the case. They would base their review solely on the trial transcript, and they would complete that review by 26 October. When finalised, their report supported the findings of the original court martial in all respects, and concluded that the three doctors who made up the Medical Board did indeed qualify as expert witnesses and that Leonski's actions were the result of a moral rather than a mental failure.

Colonel George Burt, Assistant Judge Advocate General and MacArthur's chief legal officer, supported the Board's conclusions, which he forwarded to MacArthur, who by then was based in Brisbane. Burt recommended that MacArthur sign and promulgate the execution order. Burt also flew to Brisbane from Melbourne shortly afterwards to confer personally with the general about the case, pointing out a number of flaws and inconsistencies in the board of review's findings, but adding that the original verdict and sentence should not be set aside because of these.

On 4 November 1942, General Douglas MacArthur signed an order directing Major General Richard Marshall, in his capacity as Commander of the United States Service of Supplies in the South West Pacific Area, to have the death sentence imposed on Private Edward Joseph Leonski carried out, 'without undue delay, at such place as determined by you'.

•

Edward Joseph Leonski himself was only dimly aware of what was happening post-trial, and never seems to have taken any great interest in the legal processes that would determine how the rest of his life would be structured and, indeed, just how long the rest of his life would be. Early on, he expressed a passing interest in reviewing his own trial, and Hayford Enwall personally delivered a copy of the court martial transcript to Eddie's cell during August. The only time Eddie seemed to refer to it, though, was when he was visited by Spencer Eddy or Ira Rothgerber, and even then he seemed more interested in their thoughts on his sketches than their thoughts on his future.

In fact, others with no direct stake in the matter seemed to be more concerned about Eddie's fate than the man himself. In late July, one Sydney newspaper reported:

> At a meeting of the Howard Prison Reform League in Sydney, it was urged that the death sentence passed on Private Edward Joseph Leonski in Melbourne recently should be commuted because it was not in harmony with the policy of the present Australian government.
>
> It was urged that if the sentence was not commuted, no Australian citizen should be allowed to carry out the sentence, and that the execution should not take place in Australian territory. Copies of resolutions to this effect have been sent to President Roosevelt, the Prime Minister, Mr. Curtin, and to General MacArthur.

Other priorities were apparent elsewhere. 'A plea that Leonski, instead of being hanged, should be handed over to psychiatrists to study has been made by a leading Melbourne alienist. He said, "To hang Leonski is to throw away valuable material merely to gratify the community's desire for retribution."'

Eddie Leonski's soul was also the object of external players. During the week following his conviction, Leonski was visited by a Catholic priest, Father Tom Shanahan. A Jesuit, Father Shanahan had been a missionary in the Philippines, but had escaped to Australia, where he was commissioned a captain in the US Army Chaplain Corps. For the next seven weeks, Father

Shanahan would try to spend at least an hour in Leonski's cell most nights of the week, sitting and talking with the condemned man.

Through Tom Shanahan, Eddie seemed to rediscover some elements of his childhood religion. He assisted the priest in his preparation for the weekly Mass he conducted in the Watchhouse, even though he couldn't be part of it, and had a private communion in his cell with Father Shanahan each week. On 1 September, Eddie took the sacrament of Penance. Two days later, Father Shanahan was posted to Brisbane with the army unit to which he was attached. His Watchhouse role was taken over by a young local Australian parish priest, Father Kevin Hannan.

•

Eddie Leonski's post-trial life in the City Watchhouse started out in much the same way and at much the same pace as his pre-trial life there. His daily routine varied little, if at all, and the mundane details did not make good reading for the Australian public, so rumours soon started circulating, rumours that became stories, stories that became facts:

> Leonski . . . has been visited regularly at the city watchhouse in the past few weeks by a beautiful young woman to whom he is greatly attached. Leonski is allowed out of his cell to talk to his woman visitor through the grille, at the end of the corridor in the Watchhouse. He has been happier since his visitor came, but it is not known whether they were acquainted before his arrest. He also sends letters to her.

It might have made good copy, but it was just a figment of some writer's imagination. Eddie did correspond with a number of young Australian women, but that was as close as he would ever get to them. In those letters, if the one extant copy is anything to go by, Eddie seems to have taken up where he left off sometime in May. Writing to an unidentified young woman named Rene – he also refers to her as both 'Dovey' and 'Tootsy' – Eddie apologises for his failure to write earlier, 'but my fingers were numb for words'. He refers to, 'the unfortunate circumstances unavoidably prevalent at the time I ran amuck [sic],' and hopes that, 'someday I may be able to account for the diabolical mania that played so tragically with my usual gentlemanly behaviour'.

It is a neat little letter, one that boyfriends and girlfriends and lovers were exchanging all over Australia and beyond at that time. It had its little terms of endearment, its little lover's secrets, and it was signed at the bottom by, 'My mamma's Little Baby for ever and ever, Edward J. Leonski.' The hand that signed it, and that had tried so hard to write a fluffy little lover's note to his Tootsy, was the same hand that had crushed the life out of three other women on the darkened streets of Melbourne one hundred days earlier.

•

There were visitors to Eddie's cell, but those visitors were always men, just as there were conversations, sometimes through a grille, but those conversations were either official, or were the kind of banter that could reasonably be expected to occur between a closely guarded prisoner and his guards.

Changes in Eddie's gaol regime began to occur around the middle of August, small changes that would eventually lead to a whole new lifestyle for the condemned man. Eddie may not even have noticed the first of these when it occurred. The number of armed military policemen watching over him twenty-four hours a

day was reduced from six to two. Those two were placed outside
his cell door and were replaced at regular intervals. The guards
at either end of the cell block corridor, and those outside the
doors at either end of that corridor, were removed, although
reinforcements were always on stand-by at Camp Pell.

Around the middle of August, Eddie was also allowed to
exercise outside his cell, in the women's exercise yard, a twenty-
metre trip down two corridors from his cell. The exercise yard
was relatively large, some five by fifteen metres, with one long
bluestone wall backing onto the Old Melbourne Gaol, and was
a fully enclosed space with a cast-iron and glass roof. Eddie
and his guards were able to spend half an hour there each day.

It was a much larger area than Eddie was used to; he could
walk – on his feet or on his hands – around and around the
space, and actually have a good workout. One of his guards then
gave Eddie a tennis ball, and his exercising took on a whole new
dimension. Back home in New York, handball and baseball had
been two of his favourite sports, and he was now able to indulge
his passion for both. He would throw the ball at the wall to
practise his rebound catches, or would practise handball, again
using the bluestone wall. He would also challenge his guards to
games of handball; none of those who accepted the challenge
was ever able to defeat him.

In early October, another significant change occurred when
Eddie was given both a radio and permission to play it in his
cell. It was a radio donated by an army welfare organisation,
and Eddie was the first prisoner in Victoria who authorities
could remember being allowed one in their cell. It soon became
a prized possession of Eddie's and he quickly made a list of
his favourite stations and programs. He really enjoyed classical
music and when he wanted to relax would search the dial until

he found a station playing it. He also enjoyed popular music and cabaret shows, although they were usually accompanied by Eddie's comments on 'swing' music and 'swinging' shows. If the program was one Eddie thought was particularly good, he would move the radio closer to the spyhole in his door then turn up the volume to share the music with whoever else happened to be in that part of the Watchhouse.

Every Sunday night, when Eddie wrote to his mother, he would tune the radio into a religious program. His mother continued to be central to Eddie's life. She seemed to be the only constant point of reference in his existence, and time and time again he would bring her into what were otherwise general conversations with his guards. Once, following an outburst when he questioned why he had been born to bring so much misery to so many people, he sat down and immediately wrote to her, 'Dear Mother, I want you to be my guardian angel, and to always watch over me. Edward.' Unlike several other letters he wrote while feeling morose, Eddie asked that this one actually be posted to his mother.

Eddie did also express some genuine concerns about his mother. One was about her ability to cope financially after he was gone, although he does not seem to have allotted any of his army pay to her. A second concern was exactly how she would cope when she learned the full extent of his criminality. Again, the concern was for how his mother would actually perceive him after she learned of what he had done, rather than for any reaction to the crimes themselves. The subsidiary themes were just how far away she was – 'she's a long way from me as I sit in this goddam [sic] place' – and how his mother, and no one else, was really able to understand him. From this conviction flowed another one: his mother wouldn't have wanted him to be locked away for the rest of his life, so the death penalty was probably the best solution for everyone.

•

Amelia Leonski also wrote regularly to her son or, more likely, had Helen Leonski write letters to Eddie for her, as she was only semi-literate. Helen had tried to keep most of the news about Eddie from their mother, fearing what it might do to her fragile physical and mental health. Within twenty-four hours of the news of Eddie's arrest breaking in Melbourne, reporters in New York had beaten a path to the Leonskis' tenement. There, Helen had told reporters that she believed there must have been some kind of mistake: 'Eddie is the best one of the family.' She had also said that she would not be passing on the news to her mother, who adored Eddie. Her mother was in poor health, she had said, and she feared that such news might kill her.

It was a monumental task for Helen to keep news of Eddie's crimes from their mother; as well as the blanket coverage in Australia, the story was considered very newsworthy in the United States. *Time* magazine covered the story, it received several mentions in the *New York Times*, while the *New York Tribune* also carried the story prominently. The closest Amelia Leonski would come to learning the whole truth about her son was when Helen only just turned off the radio in time before the announcer began to read the results of Eddie's court martial in Australia.

•

It seemed important to Eddie that he confronted the reality of his own imminent death head-on. His earliest recorded responses to the death penalty he received included, 'Don't worry about me. I have always been ready to die since I was 16 . . . I have been wanting experience and this will be a new experience for me . . . There will be plenty of experiences for me, I suppose, on the other side.' Another time, he was supposed to have said, 'They say I got a severe sentence, but I don't think so. I think I got out of it lucky with death. Death is a wonderful thing.'

At times, Eddie would be almost philosophical about what was to happen: 'I don't want any guy to think I'm afraid to die. I think death is a great thing. You just get jerked to sleep and that is the end of everything.' But, mostly, he would fall back onto the gallows humour that had become one of his characteristics since the time he confessed to the murders. When one of his guards looked glum, Eddie quipped, 'No need for you to look glum. I'm the one who is going to get his neck pulled.' Another time, he smiled, brushed his close-cropped hair, and said, 'I'm fine. They're going to lift my face for me.'

Death was increasingly central to Eddie Leonski's life. As well as writing to his mother weekly, he would, on average, write one or two other letters on most days. As September became October, he began to write more, and would now average two or more letters a day. Many of these were farewell letters to family and friends back in New York City. When discussing his end with his guards – something else that he did on most days – he always stated that, had he been asked, his preference would have been for execution by firing squad rather than by hanging. The choice had not been his, however, and all he could now do was gather as much information as possible on the mechanics of death by hanging.

This interest coincided with his ongoing fascination with Ned Kelly, who himself had been executed by hanging just fifty metres away from where Eddie exercised every day, on the other side of the bluestone wall where Eddie practised his handball. 'That guy could sure dish it out,' was one of his favourite quips whenever the subject of Ned Kelly was raised.

Eddie also developed a new passion, poetry, and specifically the poet Oscar Wilde, after someone gave him a book of Wilde's poems. He became especially attached to *The Ballad of Reading Gaol*, in which Wilde told the story of an English soldier awaiting execution for killing his wife. Eddie would recite by heart his favourite verse of the poem to anyone who showed even the slightest interest:

> *It is sweet to dance to violins*
> *When Love and Life are fair:*
> *To dance to flutes, to dance to lutes*
> *Is delicate and rare:*
> *But it is not sweet with nimble feet*
> *To dance upon the air!*

•

Around 20 October, MacArthur's headquarters received the news from Washington that army authorities there had reviewed the court martial transcript and could see no legal reasons that justified overturning the original verdict and sentence. They believed that President Roosevelt would authorise the execution pending the findings of the legal reviews in Australia if they, too, supported the original findings. The Australian government was informed of this, and a minor brouhaha ensued.

Frederick Shedden, Secretary of the Department of Defence, immediately wrote to MacArthur, saying, 'The Attorney-General is strongly of the opinion that if the death sentence passed on Leonski is to be carried out, it should not be carried out in this country, as it will interfere with morale on account of morbidity.' MacArthur replied to Shedden on 24 October, noting firstly that the case was still under review. If that review confirmed the original verdict and sentence, and Leonski was executed, it would be done without any notification and a simple press release would be issued afterwards. The letter closed with MacArthur's statement that, 'The execution of American soldiers in an expeditionary campaign while on foreign soil has complete precedence as in France during the last war.' And then things began to develop a momentum of their own.

•

During the last week of October there were a couple of interruptions to what had become Eddie's regular routine. Around the middle of that week, he was taken across the road by armed escort to the Russell Street Police Headquarters where he was photographed and fingerprinted. Later in the week, probably during the afternoon of Friday, 30 October, two senior US Army officers visited Eddie in his cell to tell him that his case had been reviewed at the highest levels, and that both the verdict and the sentence had been confirmed. One then read him the formal Warrant of Execution.

The next morning, Eddie was his ebullient self, joking with his guards about preparing to have a facelift at the government's expense.

•

On Wednesday, 4 November, General MacArthur signed the Execution Order and the following day Major General Marshall started to put that order into effect. He appointed Colonel William Purdy as his personal representative overseeing the implementation of MacArthur's order and directed the Commanding Officer of Base Section 4 to undertake the execution of Eddie Leonski on or around 9 November. There were dozens of matters that had to be cleared up, starting with the basic questions of where Leonski would be executed and who would actually execute him. After many months, there was now so much to do, and so little time to do it.

18.

DEATH AT DAWN

After the Warrant of Execution was read to Eddie Leonski in his cell on the Friday evening, he is supposed to have said, 'I hope they get it over and done with in a hurry so I won't have to go on like this.' Any doubts he may have harboured about a long, drawn-out process would have been laid to rest on the Saturday morning when his guards were increased from two to their original complement of six. Later in the morning, he was visited by a US Army medical officer, who gave him a general examination, finishing it off by taking exact measurements of Eddie's height and weight, checking several times that the latter was exactly 175 pounds (79 kilograms). Finally, when Father Hannan called in to visit Eddie on Saturday afternoon, he had another priest with him, Father Tom Shanahan, who had been flown down from Brisbane by the US Army.

•

What Eddie had no way of knowing was the amount of work that his army had done in the background to make certain that his death went according to a predetermined process. He would have found it interesting, as he did most things where he was the centre of attention. Early on in that process, it became obvious that there were no US Army facilities in Australia that were even remotely suitable for a formal execution by hanging. This first problem was solved by the Victorian government, who offered the Americans the use of the execution chamber at Pentridge Prison, located on the outskirts of the city at Coburg. It would be ideal for the purpose. The facilities at Pentridge had been used for all executions in Victoria since 1924, when the gallows, beam and trap had been relocated from the Old Melbourne Gaol. They had also been used for most of the executions carried out at the Old Melbourne Gaol, meaning that Eddie would be executed on the same apparatus as his hero, Ned Kelly.

Within Pentridge, the scaffold was located on the catwalk in 'D' Division, with the condemned cell just a few metres away. Traditionally, prisoners in 'D' Division were moved to other areas of the prison when an execution was to be carried out. This time, however, there was still a degree of secrecy attached to the execution, and so only those in the cells near the scaffold were to be moved and neither they, nor their guards, would be told the reason why. In fact, only the prison governor and some of his senior staff were aware of what was being planned.

There were also issues around who would actually perform the execution. It was decided not to use the official Victorian hangman, as Victoria had surrendered some of its sovereignty and probably did not want to add to its responsibilities at this late stage. Instead, a hangman was sourced from another state, probably South Australia. That hangman was guaranteed anonymity, a guarantee that has lasted over seventy-five years. All that we know about the man is that he was short and solid, and that he brought with him his own tools of the trade. Among these was a coiled nylon rope; it was brand new and it was two centimetres thick.

Sunday, 8 November was just another day for Eddie, with meals and morning exercise, visits from his two priests, music on the radio, writing letters and reading books and magazines. After dinner, as evening came, so did the visitors. Detective Fred Adam was summoned to the City Watchhouse to again formally confirm Eddie Leonski's identity. Sid McGuffie had also learned that Eddie's execution was imminent and he, too, took the opportunity to visit Eddie on that Sunday evening.

Sid McGuffie and Eddie Leonski shared a strange relationship, one that at times veered towards companionship rather than any form of true friendship. When they spoke that Sunday evening, Eddie, as usual, cracked a few of his gallows gags, telling the homicide detective that if he knew any dames that needed strangling, he certainly knew where to send them.

In their conversation, McGuffie asked Eddie exactly how he had killed those three women; Eddie said that he would be happy to give the policeman a demonstration, an offer that Sid accepted. The guards weren't particularly happy about this, but agreed to let the demonstration proceed. Four of the MPs left their weapons in the corridor outside Eddie's cell and accompanied McGuffie into it, lining up in a half-circle along the walls. Another MP stood in the cell doorway, automatic weapon at the ready, while the final guard stood just behind him.

The murderer and the detective sergeant stood face to face. Eddie reached across and took hold of McGuffie's neck with his right hand, firmly, but without applying any great pressure. As he did so, he explained, 'I always set them up with the right hand. Then I would get working with the left hand.'

With this, he grabbed McGuffie's throat with his left hand and squeezed hard, but for just a second. In that second, McGuffie felt the immense strength in Leonski's hands and forearms and was on the edge of blacking out. Almost nonchalantly, Eddie then added, 'I always operate with my left hand. Back in San Antonio, I tried to throttle a dame with my right hand. But I lost my balance and she got away. I made up my mind never to make the same mistake again.' Eddie laughed at this, and was still laughing when McGuffie made his farewells and was escorted from the cell.

After McGuffie departed, Eddie turned on his radio and began listening to the evening service from St Paul's Cathedral, broadcast on the local ABC station. Two American officers ended his reverie when they entered his cell. One of the officers proceeded to read out the charges and the sentence imposed by the court martial. The second then informed Eddie that the sentence handed down by the court would be carried out on the following morning. Eddie's only comment was that he knew that he would not have long to wait after he had been weighed and measured the previous day.

Father Tom Shanahan arrived immediately after the two officers departed, having waited outside while the awful news was delivered to Eddie. Shanahan would later write to Amelia Leonski that her son 'had accepted his sentence with calm and resignation, only wishing that he could suffer more in reparation for his mistakes. His last evening was a splendid manifestation of his faith in Our Lord and His merciful goodness.' Father Hannan then joined Eddie and Shanahan and the three men remained together throughout the night.

At one point during that night, the men were escorted to the exercise yard where they walked and sat and talked, looking at the stars above and discussing in broad detail the nature of life, death and eternity. Eddie did not sleep at all and does not seem to have even rested during those dark hours. After they tired of sitting and talking in the exercise yard, the three men were escorted back to Eddie's cell. There, at 4 a.m. on the morning of Monday, 9 November, the two priests celebrated Mass and Eddie took Holy Communion.

•

All those who spoke to Eddie after he was told of his imminent execution on the Friday night were struck by his calmness and lack of any visible emotion. He had studied the mechanics of execution by hanging and knew that over the weekend of 7–8 November a gallows had been prepared for him somewhere, probably not too far away from where he was spending his last few days and hours of life. He knew that those gallows were being tested over and over again, that hinges and bolts and levers were being oiled, and a rope was being stretched with a weight attached to its end. And he knew that somewhere, maybe even in this very building, a man was doing the calculations which would ensure that his death was quick and clean: a snapped neck – cervical displacement – based on his weight and how far his body would have to drop for that death to occur. Eddie knew that sometimes executioners had miscalculated, and death had been from slow strangulation or by a bloody decapitation. Eddie knew all this and it did not appear to have had the slightest impact on him.

•

At 5.30 a.m. on Monday morning, two military policemen whom Eddie had never seen before entered his cell and ordered him to stand. One produced handcuffs and used them to shackle

Eddie's hands in front of his body. They led him from his cell, with the priests trailing, turning right into the corridor and down a few metres to a heavy door, already open and with other MPs standing on either side of it. There, it was another right turn and a short walk down another corridor to the door that led directly into the Watchkeeper's office. That door, too, was open, with armed guards again on either side.

Eddie paused at the counter in front of the Watchkeeper's desk and thanked the uniformed sergeant seated there for the way he had been treated by the Watchhouse staff. He closed with, 'Goodbye, old timer. This is the end of the long, long trail. Thanks for all you guys did for me. I won't forget.' And then, with a smile, 'I won't forget. But I won't have very long to remember, will I?'

Eddie and his escorts exited the Watchhouse by its main entrance in Russell Street. Waiting for them, parked at the kerb and with its engine running, was a 'Black Maria', a large police van. Eddie and two MPs sat in the enclosed cage in the rear, while other MPs climbed into the front passenger area of the van or into the dark-coloured cars that were parked in front and behind it. Once all the passengers were in, the small convoy headed off, down Victoria Street then up Elizabeth Street and into Royal Parade.

It was still dark, although it seemed to be lightening a bit in the east as the cars and van drove north through light drizzling rain. Had it been light, and had the rear of the van contained windows, Eddie could have noted Melbourne University – where Gladys Hosking had worked – on his right and then, in quick succession, the Parkville Hotel and Gatehouse Street on his left. The overnight brownout was almost gone with the lightening sky, so he might even have been able to see, out there, a kilometre to the left, the lights and tents of Camp Pell.

They continued in a straight line as Royal Parade became Sydney Road and then, suddenly, the impressive bluestone walls of Pentridge Prison rose up on their right. The little convoy pulled into the parking area near the prison's massive front gate just fifteen minutes after leaving the City Watchhouse. As they climbed out of their cars and van, some of them noted that theirs weren't the only vehicles in the car park. There, over in the corner, was a US Army ambulance. On the ground alongside it was a stretcher, assembled and ready to use.

When the rear door of the police van was unlocked and opened, Eddie was assisted out, and then bustled through the main gate and a doorway just inside it. His escorts led him up a flight of stairs and along a catwalk then into a cell at the end of that catwalk. Once inside the cell, Eddie raised his manacled hands to remove his overseas service cap which he threw towards a chair in the corner. 'Well, I guess I won't be needing that darn thing anymore,' he said, seemingly to no one in particular.

•

The arrival of the large group of Americans did not go unnoticed within the prison, and in 'D' Division there were some moments of confusion. The scaffold there had been prepared and tested the previous day, so most of the prison officers in the division were aware that an execution was planned, knowledge that was reinforced when the occupants of the cells nearest the scaffold were moved elsewhere. Those officers had not, however, been informed of either the who or the when, and a number of warders coming off duty were quite shocked when confronted by numbers of uniformed American soldiers and Australian civilians coming into the division. That number included several official witnesses. In an attempt to placate some of the prison officers, they were told that they, too, could witness the execution, provided they remained some distance away and were 'discreet'.

•

Fathers Shanahan and Hannan had entered the condemned man's cell with Eddie, and the three men huddled together and spoke in hushed tones. Quickly and quietly, the priests celebrated a Thanksgiving service with Eddie. When it was over, one of the guards offered Eddie a cigarette, which he accepted with thanks, adding that he hoped that he would have enough time to finish it.

He didn't. He had taken only a puff or two when the same guard patted him on the arm and nodded towards the cell door. A young US Army officer entered and, in a nervous voice, read from a formal document, saying, 'Private Leonski, in the name of the United States, you are now called upon to have the verdict of the court carried out.'

At that, things happened in rapid succession. Eddie dropped the cigarette he was smoking to the cell floor and ground it out under his shoe. One of the guards undid Eddie's handcuffs, asked him to place his hands behind his back, and then put the handcuffs back on. One guard then stood in front of him, with another falling in behind Leonski as they escorted him out of the cell to the scaffold in the middle of the platform at the end of the cell block. He didn't flinch during the short walk, although he couldn't seem to be able to take his eyes off the rope and the noose hanging from the overhead beam just ahead of him.

As he had left the cell with soldiers in front and behind, Eddie was joined by the priests, with Father Shanahan on one side and Father Hannan on the other. The distance from the cell door to the scaffold was short, four metres at most, and during that short walk and the pause when the scaffold was reached, the priests prayed aloud, chanting the Prayer of the Last Blessing. At the conclusion, with Eddie now stationary and silent on the scaffold, Father Shanahan gave him the Apostolic Blessing, holding his crucifix in front of Eddie, who kissed it when the blessing ended.

One of the Army officers then produced a copy of the Warrant of Execution, and read it aloud. It was a brief document, a short legal statement, and reading it took only a few seconds. When he had concluded, the officer asked Eddie if he had anything to say. Eddie's answer was a simple shake of the head.

As that officer stepped back, the executioner stepped forward. Even in those unusual circumstances, he presented an unusual figure – workmen's clothes and dustcoat, leather gloves and leather mask. He worked quickly. Firstly, he placed a black cloth cap on Eddie's head and then he stooped down to pinion Eddie's legs both above and below the knees. Standing up again, he pulled the black cap down, revealing it to be more of a cloth mask, one that covered Eddie's head and fell down almost to his shoulders. Before that mask fell, Eddie nodded his head slightly towards two US Army doctors who stood at the wall behind the hangman. He also turned his head slightly towards Father Shanahan and gave him a faint smile. Both Fathers Shanahan and Hannan were now praying aloud in Latin.

As the black cloth fell down over Eddie's face, the hangman turned to his side, found the rope and noose, and lifted them up before placing the noose, carefully and almost gently, over Eddie's head. As he did so, the military policeman nearest Eddie said quietly, 'I'm sorry, buddy,' to which Eddie replied, also softly, 'It's quite OK, pal. Carry on.'

The hangman, again carefully, adjusted the noose so that it sat quite closely around Eddie's neck, with the knot sitting snugly under the angle of the jaw on the left side of Eddie's neck. Satisfied that everything was as it should be, he stepped back from the trapdoor as the MPs did the same. He grasped a large lever with a locking handle and in one fluid movement squeezed the handle and pulled the lever.

The trapdoor snapped open and Eddie's body dropped from sight in a sudden, brutal cacophony. Amongst that noise was the squeal of the various hinges and levers, the crash of the trapdoor and the snap of the rope as it took the full force of a heavy object falling a short distance. It was the sound of a man dying suddenly and it was a sound that no one there would ever forget.

It was a sound that lasted only a second or so, but which seemed to reverberate for much longer. When it was over, other sounds became clear and somehow more focused; the sound of the two priests praying quietly and the sound of the rope creaking ever so slightly as it swung backwards and forwards a few centimetres, almost as if a gentle breeze was blowing through that awful place.

•

Those who were wearing watches glanced down at them, and were surprised to note that the time was now just after 6 a.m.

•

Under Victorian state law, the body of an executed criminal was required to be left hanging for an hour after execution to ensure that the sentence had been carried out successfully. Again, this requirement of the local law was waived for Eddie Leonski. Two minutes after his body had dropped through the trap, the hangman's rope was loosened and Eddie's still-warm body was lowered to the floor in a screened-off area immediately below the scaffold. There, two US Army medical orderlies placed it on the stretcher they had brought in from their ambulance outside. While one removed the noose and rope from around Eddie's neck before taking off the mask he had been wearing, the second rolled up one of Eddie's sleeves and administered what would have been, in other circumstances, a lethal injection.

Those two medical orderlies were soon joined in their workspace by several other people. The two US Army doctors made their way down to examine the body. Edward Joseph Leonski was officially declared dead seven minutes after the executioner had pulled the trapdoor lever.

Their work done, the two doctors were replaced by the two priests, Shanahan and Hannan, who still had things to do, obligations to fulfil for both the living and the dead. The two completed the last rites over the body of the young man both had come to know well; Father Hannan gave the Sacrament of Extreme Unction, after which he joined Father Shanahan in a prayer for forgiveness of the soul of the dead man. When they had finished, they packed up their vestments and departed. Both had a full day ahead of them.

The soldiers, too, gradually packed up and left. Those who were there in their official capacity as witnesses to the execution signed the necessary paperwork before being escorted out of the prison and to their staff cars in the car park. The executioner quietly collected the tools of his trade and disappeared into the pages of history without anyone really noticing. In more ways than one, it was like he had never really existed. No details of the execution of Eddie Leonski were ever entered into the official records of Pentridge Prison.

In the end, it was just the medical orderlies and Eddie; three young men a long way from home. The orderlies covered Eddie's body on the stretcher with a grey military blanket, making certain that it was tucked in on all sides. They carried the stretcher down the long corridor – MPs ahead and behind them – out through the main door of the prison and across to their ambulance. There, the group probably paused for a short time as no one was in a hurry now. They maybe smoked a cigarette or two and talked about what had just happened as they looked up and around at the new day. The overnight rain had stopped, the clouds were breaking up and the sun was now well clear of the horizon. It looked like it might be a pretty good day. The soldiers helped the orderlies load Eddie's body into the ambulance, the back doors were locked and another little convoy made its way back into the city.

•

Later on the morning of Monday, 9 November 1942, the General Headquarters of the South West Pacific Area Command issued the following statement: 'The sentence imposed by court martial on Private Leonski has been approved by the Board of review and the Commander-in-Chief, and Leonski has been executed. The sentence was carried out today by hanging.'

Still later that day, Australian forces in New Guinea captured the Japanese stronghold of Gorari and, in doing so, isolated the main Japanese forces in that theatre of operations. Still later, in North Africa, American forces moved to secure the beachheads they had seized around Casablanca. There would still be a lot of fighting and a lot of dying before the war was over, but that end was now becoming visible through the fog swirling around the future.

SCHOFIELD BARRACKS POST CEMETERY, HONOLULU

Eddie Leonski's physical journey through life ended on a foreign gallows and at foreign hands shortly after 6 a.m. on the morning of Monday, 9 November 1942. The end of that journey was also the start of a long and tortuous journey for Eddie Leonski's earthly remains.

The ambulance that carried Eddie's body away from Pentridge Prison that Monday morning drove to the Royal Melbourne Hospital in Flemington Road, Parkville, and just a short distance from both Camp Pell and Gatehouse Street, where Eddie had murdered his last victim. Part of the Royal Melbourne Hospital had been given over to the US Army, who had now located their 2nd Base Hospital there. It was to that hospital that Eddie's body was taken, presumably for an autopsy or some kind of post-mortem examination.

The body remained at the hospital for twenty-four hours before it was placed in a steel military coffin and driven, again by ambulance, to Father Kevin Hannan's parish church, where the priest conducted a Requiem Mass for Eddie. After the service, Eddie's coffin was driven out to the Springvale Cemetery, then on the extreme south-eastern outskirts of Melbourne's suburban sprawl. There, it was buried well away from the rest of the graves in what was known officially as the 'Isolated Section'. So isolated, in fact, that the grave diggers there would refer to Eddie as 'The Lone Ranger'.

He was not to remain isolated for long. In December, a month after the first burial, Eddie's remains were reinterred in the American servicemen's section of that same cemetery. There they remained until the end of the Pacific War, when American authorities decided to bring the remains of all American servicemen and women who had been interred in Australian cemeteries together at the one site. That site was the Manson Park Cemetery in Ipswich, Queensland, a town then about an hour's drive to the west of Brisbane.

Two years later, another administrative decision was made, this time to remove all the American war dead from Australia and reinter their remains in cemeteries in their homeland. Eddie Leonski's remains were again disinterred and moved by sea to the Post Cemetery at Schofield Barracks, Honolulu, Hawaii. There, they were buried in Section 9, Row B, Site 8 in a section reserved for general prisoners who died while in military custody.

When Eddie was executed, his family were informed that, should they so desire, his remains would eventually be returned to them in America. There is nothing to suggest they ever responded to this offer. It is also believed that no member of the Leonski family has ever visited his grave.

•

Eddie's execution did not end all the legal processes that had attached themselves to his life. Part of the formal agreement and wider understanding between the governments of

Victoria and the United States was that the Coronial Inquests into the deaths of Eddie's three victims would be suspended until the American military legal process had been completed. This occurred when Eddie was formally declared dead. For the Victorian legal processes to be resumed, the Coroner required a sworn account of the court martial and an official death certificate for Eddie Leonski. In late November, the City Coroner, Mr Arthur Tingate, received both documents.

On Monday, 7 December 1942, the first anniversary of the attack which brought the United States into the war, the legal processes surrounding Eddie Leonski's sixteen-day killing spree were formally ended. Mr Tingate reopened his Coronial Inquest and then accepted into evidence the formal identification of Leonski made by Detective Fred Adam on the evening preceding Eddie's execution, the transcript of his court martial, verdict and sentence, and his official Certificate of Death. Tingate then handed down his findings, which were:

Ivy Violet McLeod died at Albert Park on 2 [sic] May 1942 through a fracture of the skull, laceration of the brain and suffocation.

Pauline Buchan Thompson died at Spring Street on 9 May 1942 through paralysis of the heart following pressure on the neck.

Gladys Lillian Hosking died at Parkville on 18 May 1942 through strangulation.

The Coroner formally recorded that Edward Joseph Leonski, a member of the United States Army, was not subject to the jurisdiction of the Australian courts, but that under the laws of the United States, Leonski was convicted of the unlawful killing of the three women by a general court martial, sentenced to death and executed by hanging on 9 November 1942. Tingate then closed the inquest and the official file on the murder of the three women.

•

In the wake of the evidence concerning Leonski's drinking habits across Melbourne at the time of the offences, the Victorian Cabinet directed the Chief Commissioner of Police, Mr Alexander Duncan, to report on the conduct of the hotels mentioned in that evidence: the Victoria, Bleak House, Astoria and Parkville Hotels. Duncan was also asked to make any general recommendations he thought appropriate to tighten up the *Licensing Act*.

Duncan's inquiry into licensing infringements revealed that there was a widespread culture of Sunday and out-of-hours drinking right across Melbourne's hotels. It also revealed that the Licensing Squad, which was responsible for enforcing the state's drinking laws, contained twelve officers. Those officers, working in teams, were able to visit about fifteen hotels each night. In 1942, in Melbourne City and the adjoining suburb of West Melbourne, there were over 100 hotels, with hundreds more within a ten-kilometre radius. The Duncan Report, too, was formally accepted and then informally shelved. Melbourne's drinking culture continued with barely a hiccup.

•

For all of those directly involved in what was already becoming the folkloric 'Brownout Strangler' case, life went on after the execution of that strangler. The lead investigator in the case, Detective Sergeant Sid McGuffie of the Victoria Police Homicide Squad, continued to work long hours tracking down murderers, but over thirty years of police work were beginning to take their toll. By 1943, his health was beginning to falter and he was transferred out of the high-pressure environment of the Homicide Squad and into the more leisurely pace of the South Melbourne Criminal Investigation Branch.

From South Melbourne CIB, Sid transferred to the regional town of Shepparton in Victoria's north-central region. In January 1946, he was admitted to the Police Hospital in St Kilda Road, Melbourne, for treatment which included surgery on his skull. By February 1947, he was back in charge of the Shepparton police station, but he resigned from the police shortly afterwards. For several years, Sid worked as a private detective – often working jointly with the police – and, following the death of his wife, Lillian, he moved to Brisbane to be close to his daughter and grandchildren. Sid McGuffie died there in 1966.

McGuffie's primary assistant in the case, Detective Fred 'Bluey' Adam had his police career end ignominiously in the 1960s when he was exposed as the bagman in a sophisticated and widespread illegal abortion network which paid large sums of money to ensure police protection.

As 1942 drew to a close, Detective Inspector Harry Carey formally recorded the appreciation of Victoria Police for the assistance of US Army investigators during the hunt for the Brownout Strangler. Carey singled out Captain Clyde Servis and Lieutenant William Johnston for praise.

Anthony 'Joey' Gallo was honourably discharged in July 1945, having been awarded the American Defense Service Medal, the Asiatic Pacific Service Medal and the Good Conduct Medal. After the war he worked as a clerk for the United States Post Office for more than fifty years. In 2004, Joey died at his home in Yonkers, New York, aged eighty-nine.

•

Hayford Enwall, the Trial Judge Advocate, survived the war and returned to his home in Gainesville, Florida. After Melbourne, Enwall had seen service in both New Guinea and the Philippines, but his heart remained in Melbourne. There, in August 1944, the then Colonel Hayford Enwall married Lieutenant Jean Kennett, an Australian Army nurse and poster girl for army recruiting, in a simple service at Christ Church in South Yarra, not all that far from where his office had been at Melbourne Grammar during the time of the Brownout Strangler. Hayford's best man was his legal brother in arms, Colonel John Stagg.

Jean joined Hayford Enwall in Gainesville after the war and the couple raised a family there. Hayford eventually followed in his father's footsteps and became a professor of law at the University of Florida. In the late 1980s, Hayford took part in an oral history program run by the university, and a transcript of his recollections is available online at the university's website. In it, Hayford recalls the Leonski case as being one of the most important in which he had an involvement.

Hayford Enwall passed away in Florida in May 1993. His son, Peter, is also a lawyer, and runs his family law firm. Peter also maintains the family's collection of material related to the Leonski trial – books, a copy of the film *Death of a Soldier* and a bound copy of the trial transcript. Peter has travelled regularly to Melbourne to catch up with cousins living there, one of whom is a former premier of the state, Jeff Kennett.

Ira Rothgerber, Eddie Leonski's junior Defense Counsel, also survived the war, and was a highly decorated combat veteran by the time it ended. Perhaps because the two men were closer in age, Ira and Eddie seem to have enjoyed a different and closer relationship than that which existed between Eddie and his senior Defense Counsel, Spencer Eddy. Leonski quite freely admitted the murders to Ira, for instance, and often added select details he told no others, including the claim that he had post-mortem sexual intercourse with one of his victims.

Like Hayford Enwall, Ira Rothgerber returned to his hometown after the war. Back in Denver, Colorado, he rejoined the law firm that his father had helped to establish. Over time, both Ira's and the firm's reputation and reach grew, and that law firm is now one of the largest in the Mountain States. Ira also involved himself in legal and philanthropic enterprises. Today, the University of Denver hosts an Ira Rothgerber Scholarship, while there is an annual conference on constitutional law named in his honour.

The Rothgerber law firm has its own combination of museum and archives. Prominent among its holdings is Ira's copy of the trial transcript – complete with marginal notes – plus his own notes about the case and the trial. Like Hayford Enwall, Ira Rothgerber, Junior, passed away in 1993.

•

Then there were the by-products and the anomalies that sat around the events in Melbourne in May 1942. The Melbourne newspapers learned of Eddie Leonski's arrest (although not his name) in time for the early editions on Saturday, 23 May. By that evening, there were numbers of American soldiers again on the streets and in the bars and cafés of Melbourne. Those Americans did not seem to be having too much trouble finding female companions either. Leonski's reign of terror was over, and Melbourne seemed to have a good deal of catching up to do.

That catching up would not necessarily involve American officers anymore. By the end of the month, Melbourne's social pages were beginning to suggest that the Americans were now becoming a bit passé. In select circles, the latest thing was to have a soiree that included Dutch officers who had recently escaped from the Netherlands East Indies. Their English was generally as good as the Americans, and many of them were tall and blond. Plus, their uniforms were a particularly divine shade of green . . .

Slightly longer lasting than the society pages' fascination with foreign officers' uniforms was the effect that one American name would have on a generation of young and wilful Australian girls. 'You know,' many a father who sat up late would say to the daughter who arrived home after her curfew, 'they reckon that Leonski bloke may not have acted alone.'

•

The city of Melbourne has changed immeasurably since Eddie Leonski stalked its streets and alleys. The Hotel Victoria on Beaconsfield Parade, across the road from a beautiful bayside beach, is where Leonski spent a large part of the day drinking before he murdered his first victim, Ivy McLeod. From the outside at least, the hotel looks very much as it did on the day Eddie last walked out of its main door. Beaconsfield Parade and Albert Park Beach are also very much as Eddie would have seen them in May 1942. A two-minute walk along the parade towards the city reveals the first changes.

The sea wall at the edge of the beach where Eddie sat and watched Ivy McLeod is still there, a bit higher now. The Bleak House Hotel is no more; there might be some structural remains but the building itself, with its unique history and culture, has been transmogrified into The Beach, a watering hole for the socially mobile, complete with chrome coffee machines and a gaming lounge.

Across the road are the flats where Harold Gibson, the man who disturbed Leonski as he arranged Ivy McLeod's body, departed early that morning. They appear to be little changed on the outside since the 1940s. Between those flats and the hotel are the tram lines and the tram terminus at the end of Victoria Avenue on Beaconsfield Parade. Much of the terminus – the waiting area, the lines themselves – has been restored and it, too, looks very much like it would have looked in 1942. The dry cleaner's and hairdresser's entry alcove, the spot where Ivy was actually murdered, no longer exists. Where it once stood is now the entry doors of a bustling supermarket which occupies all the space the two shops once occupied.

The heart of the city of Melbourne has also changed significantly, and although the streets in their distinctive grid pattern remain the same, few of the buildings that lined those streets in 1942 remain, and those that do serve a different purpose now from what they did then. The American Servicemen's Club is no more, while the Astoria Hotel was demolished many years ago; where it once stood is now part of a much larger international hotel and shopping complex. Neither Eddie nor Pauline Thompson would recognise the part of Spring Street where one killed the other on the steps of a Victorian-era boarding house. The line of stately old mansions of which that boarding house was a part are also long gone, replaced by a mix of upmarket apartments and mid-market hotels, with the odd convenience store thrown in. The alley where Eddie rifled through Thompson's purse is still there, but little else remains the same.

Just to the north of the city centre, the suburb of Parkville, whose localities Eddie Leonski prowled, is the least changed of all. It is a fascinating little enclave. If you ignore the modern cars and their accoutrements, street parking signs and the like, walking through Parkville's streets and lanes in a quiet part of the day evokes images and thoughts of days gone by, not all of them good days either.

The University of Melbourne still occupies a prime position on the eastern side of Royal Parade and, externally at least, its School of Chemistry appears much the same as it did when Gladys Hosking locked its front doors and walked off into the gloom of that Monday night in May 1942. Tin Alley still borders the northern side of the main university campus and, almost exactly opposite where it meets Royal Parade, the Parkville Hotel still stands on the corner of Royal Parade and Morrah Street, welcoming thirsty customers.

Those customers dine and drink in a hotel vastly changed from the one where Eddie Leonski drank his alcohol cocktails, performed his feats of strength and worked himself into a murderous rage. The interior has been gutted and modernised, and the bar that Eddie used to circumnavigate on his hands is long gone. It is now bright and airy, and the customers today would probably have sat in a group a long way away from the customers of yesterday.

'Elizabeth House', Rupert Burns' boarding house, where Eddie paused briefly on his journey to kill Gladys Hosking, is also still there, and has been restored to what it would have been like in its glory days of a century and more ago. Gladys Hosking's boarding house in Park Street is still there, too, looking from the outside very much now as it would have looked then. The main difference there is that Park Street is now called Park Drive. Gatehouse Street is still there, with its lovely mix of terraces and period houses on one side and the green expanses of Royal Park on the other.

If you were able to remove the traffic and the accompanying roundabouts and speed humps designed to slow down that traffic, it would be easy to imagine how the scene presented itself to a butcher carrying a load of meat from the market to his customers at dawn on a frosty morning some seventy-five years ago. Royal Park itself has been redeveloped and redesigned several times over those seventy-five years. Old trees have died and been replaced and young trees have become old. New paths and tracks have been added, while the old ones have been obliterated by time and neglect. Even with old photographs, it is no longer possible to precisely identify where the slit trenches were, or where Gladys Hosking's life ended.

At the bottom of Gatehouse Street, where it meets Flemington Road, a massive medical complex has grown up around the site now occupied by the Royal Children's Hospital. It has also grown considerably in size, with new wings and wards and outbuildings being added regularly over the years. When they are, the land is excavated for the foundations of those buildings. If you visit the site when such work is underway, you may be able to see, just there, a metre or so below the surface, a thick layer of clay that is a peculiar dull yellow colour.

Camp Pell itself no longer exists. It remained a military camp for the duration of the war and at war's end was handed back to the Victorian government. In the late 1940s and early 1950s, Camp Pell became a residential complex for families removed from their homes as the state's Housing Commission undertook a slum clearance program. Its long-term residents renamed the area, 'Camp Hell'. The site was cleared ahead of the 1956 Olympics and its residents accommodated elsewhere.

It was subsequently restored to parklands and sports facilities. One of those sports facilities is the State Netball and Hockey Centre. To reach that centre, you turn off Elliott Avenue onto Brens Drive and head up a slope. About two-thirds of the way up that slope, on either side of the road, are two curious concrete structures, vaguely resembling old-style public telephone boxes. They are the original guard posts that stood at the main entry to Camp Pell. They are also all that remains of what was once Melbourne's largest army camp.

Russell Street Police Headquarters still exists, but it is no longer a police headquarters. Some years ago, the enormous building was sold to private developers who turned the complex into an upmarket apartment block. The entrance used several times a day by Sid McGuffie and Fred Adam is still in place, and alongside it is now a chic little café they would probably at first dismissed as effete, and then fallen in love with. Further up Russell Street to the north is the building that hosted Eddie Leonski's court martial. It, too, is now an apartment block and has been completely refitted inside. A glance through the plate-glass security doors reveals that the stairs that once led to the makeshift courtroom are still in place and still in use.

On the opposite, western side of Russell Street are the remains of what was once Melbourne's main penal precinct. At the northern end of that precinct is the remaining wing of the Old Melbourne Gaol, a somewhat forbidding three-storey bluestone building containing rows of small cells on either side of a wide central corridor. At one end of the building is the execution chamber and scaffold last used there in 1924 and at the other end is an entrance and gift shop, for the Old Melbourne Gaol is now one of Melbourne's premier tourist attractions.

To the south of the gaol is a large open space, once part of the gaol itself but now an open plaza for students from an adjoining university. On the south side of that plaza, opposite the old police headquarters, is the City Watchhouse, in very much the same condition as it would have been in May 1942. If you pay your admission fee at the gaol's entry point, you can join a group 'experience' of the City Watchhouse, a guided tour of the building which replicates the experience of being taken into police custody there.

After entering the building through its main doorway, participants parade past the Watchkeeper's desk, line up to be examined and searched in the corridor which leads to the cells, and then file past an open ablutions area in the main cell block. Men and women are then separated and placed in different cells where a Watchhouse 'sergeant' explains the daily regime of the prisoners held there. The men are locked into Cell Number 6 as the sergeant talks to the women in another cell. Cell 6 is the very cell occupied by Eddie Leonski in the months between his arrest and his execution.

It is a very large cell to be occupied by one man, but then the sergeant tells you that it was designed to house up to seven prisoners. It has changed little since Eddie lived out the last months of his life there. The walls and ceiling are painted that indeterminate institutional green, and are covered with graffiti written by pens that Eddie could only have dreamed about in 1942.

If that paint was removed, slowly and ever so carefully, would Eddie's sketches, doodles and lyrics be revealed? Somewhere underneath all that, is there a stanza of *The Ballad of Reading Gaol* written in Eddie's own hand, waiting to be resurrected?

The tour moves on the short distance to what was the female exercise yard, given over to Eddie's use once a day, and again a lot larger than what was expected. It remains today very much as it would have been during those winter months of 1942, and it is possible to imagine him bouncing a tennis ball off that blue-stone wall, and walking around and around the yard, talking about eternity to Tom Shanahan and Kevin Hannan during his last night on earth. The tour ends soon after that with an opportunity to have a souvenir photograph taken through the bars of one of the holding cells.

Pentridge Prison remains, but only in part. Large areas of its former grounds have been demolished and landscaped to provide space for a housing development, allowed after the prison itself was decommissioned in 1997. Eddie Leonski was one of eleven prisoners executed there between 1927 and 1967. After Victoria abolished capital punishment in 1975, the beam used in every execution for over a century was removed from Pentridge and put into storage. It was reinstalled in its original position in the Old Melbourne Gaol in 2000.

Eddie Leonski died on that beam, as did the hero he found late in his life, Ned Kelly. In fact, the rope attached to that beam would have been placed in much the same position as the rope that was used to execute Ned. Both men were Roman Catholics, and execution protocols in Victoria had it that the rope used to execute Catholics was not placed in the same position on the beam as the ropes that were used to execute Protestants.

If he knew of that, Eddie Leonski may well have appreciated the symmetry of it all. While Eddie's humour always tended towards the vulgar, in his last months and away from the havoc that alcohol wreaked on him, Eddie seemed to seek knowledge for knowledge's sake, whether secular or religious, something that he could add to his bank of experiences. He wasn't one for irony, though, and that was just as well. Eddie Leonski always craved being the centre of attention, always wanted the spotlight to shine his way, even if that spotlight was searching for a psychopathic killer. For that was all that Eddie Leonski was. He killed because he was strong and his victims were weak. He killed because those victims gave him the opportunity to kill, and he took that opportunity. Eddie ultimately died at the end of a rope because he killed and because, given the social and political sensitivities of the time, he had to die. In that lies the ultimate irony of Eddie Leonski's life. For a short time, he gained a principal role on a very large stage, and became known to many more people than a life as an ordinary soldier and son would ever have entailed.

For such a man, craving attention and full of self-importance, the irony is that, at the end, people – large numbers of people – knew precisely who he was. They knew who he was and they knew what he was, but in the end no one really cared about Eddie. They just wanted him dead.

A NOTE ON SOURCES

Most of the material on which this story is based is freely available to the public. The National Archives of Australia holds a complete transcript of the General Court Martial which tried, convicted and sentenced Eddie Leonski, with quite a lot of supporting documentation from the court martial also attached. The newspapers from those dark months also provide a wealth of material. Because US Army authorities wanted the court martial to be fair and transparent, and something of a showcase, they encouraged newspaper reporters and correspondents to report in as much depth as possible. Other primary material is available in scattered places, in odd museums and collections privately held. Where I have used these, I have noted the source of the material.

Three books have been written about the case. One, Ivan Chapman's, is a very good work, reflecting the research and effort of someone to whom writing is a means of communication as well as a way of making a living. The second, by Andrew Mallon, is a lot more impressionistic and a lot less useful – 'He was Leonski, full of darkness, destiny and death' (p. 103) is a good example of Mallon's writing style. I found a third book, by

John Harvey, buried away at the National Library, where it doesn't seem to have been accessed since the early 1990s. It falls neatly between the other two. Harvey's style is quite melodramatic at times, but during the time in question, he seems to have been a reporter (Melbourne *Truth*) attached to General MacArthur's headquarters, and he seems as well to have been able to access persons unavailable to others, most notably Leonski's guards. Where I have been able to check Harvey's material against other sources, it does seem to be accurate.

There was also a film made based on the story, *Death of a Soldier*, released in 1986 and starring James Coburn as Leonski's Defense Counsel. It is a film that takes very large liberties with the truth and creates a persona for Eddie Leonski that grates. At the time of its release it attracted a very mixed response. One person I spoke to took umbrage at Detective Sergeant Sid McGuffie being portrayed as a beer-drinking, piano player in a bar in his off-duty hours. I am uncertain whether it was the beer drinking or the piano playing that was most offensive.

I was also fortunate enough to be able to make personal contact with some people who are quite germane to what happened over seventy-five years ago in Melbourne. Graham McGuffie, Sid's nephew and greatest fan, was very helpful in providing anecdote after anecdote with his illustrious uncle as their centrepiece. Peter Enwall, Hayford's son, corresponded electronically with me from Gainesville, Florida, filling in a lot of little gaps in his father's story. Peter also seems to be a fair interpreter of the music of Hank Williams and Johnny Cash. Meeting him for dinner in Gainesville in June 2013 was one highlight of the journey writing this account was to become. Patrice Hettinger from Rothgerber Johnson and Lyons LLP in

Denver, Colorado, filled a similar role with material her firm holds which was once the property of Ira Rothgerber, Junior.

The staff at the Old Melbourne Gaol was, once again, both friendly and very, very competent, as were the staff at the National Library of Australia and the National Archives. The Melbourne highlight – or at least one of them – was the tour of the City Watchhouse, complete with line-up and lockdown. I suspect the others with me in Cell 6 wondered why I was taking detailed notes and measurements. It was because that was as close as I would ever come to knowing Eddie Leonski, the man whose actions seven decades earlier had terrorised my mother, her sisters and thousands of other young women in Melbourne.

ENDNOTES

1. He's Coming South!

p. 2   ... *Will you help?* ... In what was one of his great speeches, Curtin said: 'We are therefore determined that Australia shall not go, and we shall exert all our energies toward shaping of a plan, with the United States as its keystone, which will give to our country some confidence of being able to hold out until the tide of battle swings against the enemy.' Melbourne *Herald*, 26 December 1941.

p. 3   ... *everyone but themselves* ... See, for instance, the Melbourne *Argus*, 3 January 1942.

p. 4   ... *63 and 44 arrests* ... Melbourne *Argus*, 6 March 1942.

p. 5   ... *substantial American forces* ... McKernan, *All In!*, p. 277. While Curtin did not give any figures, by 'substantial' he meant the 25 000 US servicemen already present in Australia.

p. 7   ... *The 4600 servicemen* ... Included in this number was the anonymous young lieutenant who became an early casualty, killed in a motor vehicle accident caused by confusion over which side of the road was the correct one to drive on.

p. 7   ... *established his headquarters* ... For some months, American intelligence officers believed that there was a real possibility that up to three Japanese divisions were poised to invade northern Australia. The headquarters were therefore established as far south as practical.

p. 7   ... *the average Australian probably knew* ... An academic conference produced an interesting representation of this: 'A graph of America's standing in Australia in the 20th Century would probably show a correlation with the evidence of American power – the visit of the United States fleet in 1908, rising through the problems of the Anglo-Japanese alliance and World War 1 to the Washington conferences of 1921–22, a dip during the trade disputes and American isolationism of the 1920s and 1930s, a sharp rise after the Japanese attack on Pearl Harbor brought America into World War 2 ...' Grant, Bruce, 'The American image in Australia' in Harper, *Pacific Orbit*, p. 208.

p. 10   ... *young and white* ... There were always going to be tensions over
the despatch of non-white troops to Australia because of the extant
White Australia Policy. The Advisory War Council wanted no non-
white troops in Australia but was overruled by Prime Minister
Curtin. The two African-American engineering units that arrived
in Melbourne in February 1942 were cheered by onlookers as they
disembarked.

p. 10   ... *trying not to look* ... Penglase and Horner, *When the War Came to
Australia*, p. 107.

p. 11   ... *They were known as 'Victory Belles'* ... The first group of American
support workers, from the American Red Cross, would not arrive
in Melbourne until the first week of May (Melbourne *Age*, 6 May
1932), and their first recreation club – the American Red Cross
Service Club – would not open in Melbourne until mid-June.

p. 12   ... *apparently very loving* ... Connell, *The War at Home*, p. 115.

p. 12   ... *standard courting armament* ... Chapman, *Leonski: The Brownout
Strangler*, p. 21.

p. 13   ... *identifies a girl* ... Robertson, *Australia at War*, p. 128.

p. 13   ... *sorted them out for us* ... ibid.

p. 13   ... *a man of destiny* ... What made Roosevelt's decision even more
courageous was that MacArthur was regarded with suspicion, if not
enmity, in Washington, where his Republican credentials were viewed
with suspicion by many in Roosevelt's Democrat administration.

p. 15   ... *enlivened the social scene* ... Ever conscious of the media's ability to
both make and break reputations, MacArthur himself would decline
many of the lower end invitations he received, saying that all his
energies were being directed towards defeating the Japanese.

2. Private Leonski

p. 18   ... *as well as technique* ... In her youth, Amelia Leonski had loved
weightlifting, both the training and the competition, a love she
passed on to Eddie.

p. 22   ... *being a trained signalman* ... The 52nd Signal Battalion had originally been constituted on 18 December 1927 as part of the regular
army. Its motto was, and is 'We Transmit'. The battalion was reacti-
vated at Fort Sam Houston on 10 February 1941. Arriving in
Australia on 2 February 1942, it would eventually become known as
'MacArthur's Own'.

p. 23   ... *until he had calmed down* ... This would be seen in a different light
a few months later. United States Military Forces in Australia, *Transcript of Evidence: Leonski Murder Trial*, p. 351.

p. 26   ... *take all of them away* ... Bernstein, ibid., p. 335.

3. Camp Pell

p. 29   ... *a rain of machine-gun fire* ... Floyd Pell was awarded a posthumous
Distinguished Service Cross for his actions that day. The medal
was presented to his father at a service in Ogden, Utah on
1 September 1942.

p. 29   ... *visitors to the site* ... Other US Army camps were sited across Melbourne. The Melbourne Cricket Ground became Camp Murphy, named after another US officer killed in action, while there were temporary encampments at Fawkner Park in South Yarra, the Port Melbourne football ground and at several sites on the Mornington Peninsula. The suburb of Parkville, adjacent to Camp Pell, became the epicentre of the American presence in Melbourne. The Americans snapped up all the private accommodation available in the area for messes and billets.

p. 30   ... *the site was open for business* ... Also handed over to the Americans was the newly completed Royal Melbourne Hospital, on Flemington Road and almost adjacent to Camp Pell. Its first occupants would be the US Army's 4th General Hospital.

p. 30   ... *the eastern end of Camp Pell* ... Eddie's tent was one of those furthest from the Royal Melbourne Zoo, although the animals could be clearly heard on a still night. There is a story, which could perhaps be true, about one of the early arrivals at Camp Pell. In bed on his first night at the camp he could clearly hear the squeals and roars of lions, elephants and monkeys. He wondered what else was out there waiting for him in the Australian bush.

p. 32   ... *a means of communication* ... Melbourne *Age*, 29 April 1942.

p. 33   ... *proposed to the company commander* ... Later that year, Christian Kauffman would transfer into the US Army Air Forces; he would survive the war, ending his service as a lieutenant colonel.

p. 34   ... *his behaviour returned to normal* ... 'Vincent Tuzzio evidence', *Transcript*, op. cit., p. 351.

p. 37   ... *the bayside suburb of St Kilda* ... The following account of the assault on Doreen Justice is taken from Dower, *Crime Chemist: The Life Story of Charles Anthony Taylor, Scientist for the Crown*, pp. 126–29. Charles Taylor had access to Justice's statement to Detective Superintendent Matthews in Sydney some two months later.

p. 40   ... *would not countenance any contact* ... Percy Justice may have had real reasons for not wanting to involve the police with his family. In August 1940, in the Supreme Court in Melbourne, he had been named as a possible co-conspirator in a case involving a plan to embezzle a quarter of a million pounds from an elderly woman. Years later, in 1949, Percy Justice would be convicted, in Brisbane, of the armed robbery in company of three others.

p. 41   ... *'I'm thinking of choking a dame'* ...' Perth *Mirror*, 19 April 1952.

p. 43   ... *That and a massive clean-up job* ... All Melbourne newspapers reported on the storm, and this description is based mainly on the reports published the next day in the *Age* and the *Argus*.

4. Mrs Ivy Violet McLeod

p. 47   ... *a brief holiday in Sydney* ... Melbourne *Herald*, 5 May 1942.

p. 48   ... *It was 11 p.m.* .... Thompson's flat was in a block at 135 Beaconsfield Parade. It was on the ground floor at the front of the block and his bedroom looked out onto Beaconsfield Parade.

p. 48   ... *there might be complications* ... Some years earlier, Ivy had undergone a tubal ligation operation and would not be able to bear children. *Transcript*, op. cit., p. 189.

p. 57 ... *where he turned left* ... *Transcript*, op. cit., p. 26.

p. 60 ... *a severe fracture of the skull* ... In a fall on the Scenic Railway at St Kilda's Luna Park two years earlier, Ivy had sustained a fractured skull. She had subsequently suffered from occasional, and severe, headaches. There was some medical speculation that her death may therefore have been an accidental consequence of the attack.

5. Sid McGuffie, Detective

p. 63 ... *she was identified as* ... Melbourne *Sun*, 4 May 1942. Most of the reporting on the murder followed a similar, sensationalised approach. The *Kalgoorlie Miner* (4 May 1942), for example, opened its story, 'With severe bruising on the head and lower portion of her body, and blood oozing from her mouth ...'

p. 63 ... *Detective Inspector Carey* ... Detective Inspector Harry Carey was one of Victoria's best-known police officers. He was believed to have a photographic memory for faces and had been given the nickname 'The Wolf' by the Melbourne underworld. He had also been given a nickname by his police colleagues, 'Jumbo'.

p. 63 ... *Detectives Mooney and Page* ... Melbourne *Sun*, 4 May 1942.

p. 63 ... *maintain the size and quality* ... Police were in a reserved or protected occupation and could not be conscripted for military service. They were also actively discouraged from volunteering for the armed forces; those who did could expect to lose all their entitlements.

p. 65 ... *when attempting to make an arrest* ... Melbourne *Argus*, 12 January 1915.

p. 66 ... *routine investigation work* ... Sid made a glorious return to the newspapers in 1932: 'When obtaining petrol for his motor car at a garage in Russell Street, City, last night, Detective McGuffie was approached by a man who had just asked the garage attendant for money. The man asked Detective McGuffie for one pound. The detective replied that he was a member of the police force, and he warned the man not to beg. The man rapidly moved his hand to his hip pocket and shouted, "I have shot better men than you." Detective McGuffie seized the starting handle of the motor car and struck the man over the head, felling him to the ground. The detective then picked up the man and drove him to the Melbourne Hospital, where he was admitted with a probable fracture of the skull.' Melbourne *Argus*, 3 March 1932.

p. 66 ... *was the local policeman* ... Bill Graham would die suddenly, while on duty, at the Canterbury police station in July 1928.

p. 71 ... *unconscious in the doorway* ... Melbourne *Sun*, 4 May 1942.

p. 71 ... *and he was hopeful* ... Melbourne *Argus*, 5 May 1942.

p. 71 ... *she had been with him* ... Melbourne *Argus*, 6 May 1942.

p. 71 ... *disarranged her clothing* ... ibid. Police had by now discounted the idea that whoever attacked McLeod had not intended to kill her, but that the attack caused a recurrence of the former injury, the fractured skull.

p. 72   ... *waited until she left* ... ibid.

p. 73   ... *answered a telephone call* ... Harvey, *Journey to the Gallows*, p. 16.

6. Mrs Pauline Buchan Thompson

p. 76   ... *feared it was not to be* ... This must have been particularly difficult for Pauline, who had grown up in a large family, the youngest of ten children.

p. 79   ... *catering specifically and exclusively* ... Officially known as the American Hospitality Bureau, the club was run by an all-volunteer staff that included many expatriate American women. Later in the year, it would amalgamate with the American Red Cross and move to new premises in Spring Street, Melbourne.

p. 80   ... *a new club debuting* ... The Dug Out Club operated in the basement of the Capitol Building in Swanston Street from its opening that night until shortly before Christmas 1945. It was widely regarded as the best, and was certainly the most popular, of Melbourne's servicemen's clubs.

p. 86   ... *they were doing just fine* ... Esther Grunden had known Pauline Thompson for twenty years, although she knew her as Pauline O'Brien. Grunden, who lived at Essendon, would later state that she left the Astoria Hotel at 11.20 p.m., and that Pauline and her American beau were still there when she left.

p. 92   ... *crushed underfoot* ... The necklace had been torn off with such force that beads from it were found in a gutter more than ten metres away from the body.

p. 92   ... *the Government Analyst* ... Charles Taylor's position of Government Analyst no longer exists. Best described as a forensic scientist, Taylor's work is now undertaken by specialist police and civilian forensic officers.

7. The Brownout Strangler

p. 95   ... *May brought with it* ... By 22 May, a rainfall record for the entire month in Melbourne would be broken with the Weather Bureau recording more than ten centimetres of rain to that date. Melbourne *Argus*, 23 May 1942.

p. 95   ... *struck and seriously injured* ... Melbourne *Age*, 5 May 1942.

p. 95   ... *while two wandering horses* ... South Melbourne *Record*, 2 May 1942.

p. 96   ... *the public's lack of response* ... Melbourne *Age*, 5 May 1942.

p. 97   ... *during the identification process* ... The circumstances of Thompson's death gave rise to all sorts of rumours about her behaviour and the state of her marriage at the time of her death. Constable Leslie Thompson became aware of these, and gave a statement to the Melbourne *Truth*: 'I always said she was as true as steel, and anyone who says differently speaks a black and dastardly lie ... We were as happy as man and wife could possibly be ... There were no secrets between us.' Harvey, op. cit., p. 24.

p. 97   ... *no fewer than 12 000 copper coins* ... Melbourne *Age*, 11 May 1942.

p. 98   ... *£1 in her bag* ... Melbourne *Argus*, 11 May 1942.

p. 99   ... *beneath her neck* ... ibid.
p. 99   ... *suggesting that criminal assault* ... ibid.
p. 99   ... *co-opted in the second case* ... ibid.
p. 104   ... *in an almost straight line* ... Neither the Astoria Hotel nor Collins
Place exists today. The entire block where they once stood has been
taken over by a commercial development that also bears the name
'Collins Place'.
p. 105   ... *each one will be interviewed* ... Melbourne *Argus*, 15 May 1942.
p. 106   ... *should inform detectives* ... Melbourne *Argus*, 12 May 1942..
p. 107   ... *green and turquoise beads* ... Melbourne *Argus*, 14 May 1942.
p. 107   ... *anxious to hear from anyone* ... Melbourne *Sun*, 13 May 1942.
p. 107   ... *how accurate the figure was* ... Although this was the first time the
technique had been used in Victoria, New South Wales Police had
tried the same technique earlier in what was known as the Albury
'Pyjama Girl' case. In that instance, the pyjama-clad body of a young
woman was found outside Albury in 1933 – a case that would eventually be solved in 1944.
p. 108   ... *may have known the man* ... See, for example, reports in the *Age*
and *Argus* on both 12 and 13 May, and the *Weekly Times* on 13 May.
p. 109   ... *It wasn't hard to figure out.* ... It was around this time that a number
of newspaper correspondents, and some newspapermen themselves,
began to suggest that they had suspected an American involvement
from the time of the McLeod murder, if only because the crime was
so 'un-Australian'.
p. 110   ... *outside a city apartment house* ... Perth *Daily News*, 16 May 1942.
p. 110   ... *avoid dark lanes and streets* ... Brisbane *Courier-Mail*, 11 May 1942.

8.   Anthony 'Joey' Gallo

p. 114   ... *I killed, Gallo, I killed* ... Most of the material in this chapter is
based on Joey Gallo's written statement and his testimony to the
Leonski court martial, as recorded in the transcript; Gallo's testimony is found on pages 240–257. That testimony was also widely
reported in Melbourne newspapers, although Gallo's name was
suppressed. See, for example, the Melbourne *Sun*, 17 July 1942.
p. 119   ... *an evil killer, Mr Hyde* ... In the film, *Dr Jekyll and Mr Hyde*, which
Eddie might have seen in Melbourne, Hyde strangles a girl as she
sings to him. 'You have a marvellous voice. I want to hear that voice.
I want that voice,' says Hyde.
p. 120   ... *There is nothing to worry about.* ... Anthony Gallo, sworn statement.
NAA A 472 W7493 Part 3 – Trial Exhibits
p. 121   ... *you want me to give myself up* ... ibid.
p. 122   ... *Late in the afternoon* ... As well as later newspaper reports, the
Kathleen Elliott and other attacks are reported in some detail in
Dower, op. cit.

9.   Miss Gladys Lillian Hosking

p. 128   ... *into the gathering darkness* ... Melbourne *Age*, 18 May 1942.
p. 128   ... *much to consider* ... On Tuesday, 19 May, an African-American
soldier named J. W. Floyd was arrested by Brisbane detectives and

charged with assault and battery and rape. Handed over to US Army authorities, Floyd faced a general court martial on charges that carried the death penalty in wartime. On 30 July 1942, Floyd was found not guilty of rape but guilty of assault and battery and sentenced to six months imprisonment at hard labour. Melbourne *Argus*, 31 July 1942.

p. 129 ... *the Perth Concert Artists* ... Perth *Mirror*, 23 May 1942.

p. 130 ... *more than purely secretarial duties* ... She told friends that getting the job at the university had been the happiest day of her life. She was also so highly regarded at Fintona that they gave her leave of absence to take up the university position, hoping that she would return to them one day.

p. 131 ... *a long letter to her father* ... The letter was later summarised in the Melbourne *Argus*, 21 May 1942. It is also quoted in Chapman, op. cit., and Harvey, op. cit.

p. 131 ... *it interferes with my war work* ... ibid.

p. 131 ... *the soldiers in the camp* ... Lismore *Northern Star*, 22 May 1952.

p. 136 ... *had lied about his age* ... Seymour, by then nineteen years old, was attached to a training battalion.

p. 142 ... *the low rail fence* ... The park fence along Gatehouse Street comprised fence posts with a small iron pipe running between them approximately one metre above the ground. The body they were looking at was about eight metres beyond the fence and twelve metres from the Gatehouse Street kerb.

p. 142 ... *with their clothes like that* ... *Transcript*, op. cit., p. 37. Harvey, op. cit., p. 30 also contains a detailed description of the discovery.

p. 144 ... *a handbag and purse* ... Gladys Hosking's unopened bag was later found to contain over four-and-a-half pounds in notes and coins, her identity card, a bank passbook, university papers and private letters.

p. 145 ... *her stockings and shoes were still in place* ... A detailed examination would later reveal that Gladys Hosking had been wearing a grey suit, grey cardigan, blue and maroon vest, slate blue button blouse, flesh-coloured stockings, black shoes and a black overcoat over a slip, brassiere and underpants. She was carrying a black umbrella and a large envelope-type black bag.

p. 146 ... *and had subsequently run* ... George was one of several Aboriginal trackers then based at the Bundoora Police Depot. He was driven to the scene by one of the depot's senior officers, a senior constable named Haygarth. Melbourne *Argus*, 20 May 1942.

10. A Mud-Bespattered Body

p. 152 ... *the clothing ... was disarranged* ... Melbourne *Herald*, 18 May 1942.

p. 153 ... *had been criminally assaulted* ... Melbourne *Argus*, 20 May 1942.

p. 154 ... *Melbourne's browned-out streets* ... Sydney *Truth*, 24 May 1942.

p. 154 ... *time for one good blast* ... Melbourne *Argus*, 25 May 1942.

p. 154 ... *in the hope of entrapping him* ... Brisbane *Courier-Mail*, 11 May 1942.

p. 155 ... *where the brownout is severe* ... Mackay *Daily Mercury*, 20 May 1942.

p. 155 ... *several points of dissimilarity* ... Melbourne *Herald*, 18 May 1942.

p. 161 ... *the end of the trail* ... This sequence of events has been reconstructed from Joey Gallo's statement and evidence he offered at
Leonski's subsequent court martial.

p. 162 ... *by events elsewhere in the camp* ... There was some subsequent
confusion about the exact timings around Gallo coming forward to
report Leonski to authorities, with some reports suggesting that it
was actually made the next day, i.e. after Leonski had been arrested.
It was unable to be located anywhere in the National Archives.

11.   The Right to Remain Silent

p. 170 ... *tried in Australia under US law* ... In Federal Parliament the
following week, when the applicability of the Act was raised, Archie
Cameron, the mercurial former leader of the Country Party, came to
Prime Minister Curtin's aid by asking the rhetorical question, 'Would
we want Australian troops in Egypt to be subject to Egyptian law?',
Darian-Smith, *On the Home Front*, p. 148.

p. 171 ... *agreed to this proposal* ... For a more detailed explanation see
Melbourne *Argus*, 25 May 1942.

p. 171 ... *had to be built from the ground up* ... The same process would be
followed in the proceedings against Private J. W. Floyd in Brisbane,
but those proceedings would begin sometime after Leonski's trial.

p. 174 ... *Captain Clyde Servis* ... Servis is referred to in several accounts of
the Leonski story, but a search of available records online located
only one serviceman named Clyde Servis, and his period of service
(no pun intended) did not commence until after the Leonski episode.

p. 178 ... *McGuffie followed up* ... Again, the bulk of this chapter is a recon-
struction of events based on interview material, newspaper reports
and evidence presented at Leonski's court martial.

12.   Without Fear of Punishment or Hope of Reward

p. 191 ... *at least one of them* ... Melbourne *Argus*, 22 May 1942.

p. 194 ... *decided to let Eddie wait* ... These scenes are based on contemporary
interviews, newspaper reports and court martial testimony.

p. 194 ... *monitoring the Leonski interviews* ... Johnston was a member of the
813th Military Police Company, based at Camp Pell. The 813th, and
its sister unit, the 814th, were responsible for general MP duties, and
also for providing bodyguards for General MacArthur and guards
for his headquarters.

p. 200 ... *'That is my life.'* ... *Transcript*, op. cit., p. 285.

p. 203 ... *taking definite action* ... Melbourne *Argus*, 23 May 1942. See also
Sun News-Pictorial and Melbourne *Age*.

13.   The Uniform Code of Military Justice

p. 207 ... *held in close confinement* ... Melbourne *Argus*, 25 May 1942.

p. 210 ... *court martial in Melbourne* ... *Argus*, 27 May 1942.

p. 210 ... *agreement between the countries* ... *Argus*, 28 May 1942.

p. 211 ... *comfortable with the outcome* ... ibid.

p. 211 ... *to take up more secular responsibilities* ... Hayford Enwall's father
was anything but ordinary. Swedish by birth, he was a sailor who

had been part of a crew that mutinied against a cruel captain, taking over their ship and sailing it to San Francisco. There the captain was gaoled pending charges being laid. Most of the sailors who mutinied signed on to other ships and sailed away; without witnesses, the charges against the ship's captain were dropped. Enwall's father stayed in San Francisco, where he studied to become a Methodist minister. Peter Enwall, 6 June 2013.

p. 212 ... *the two had never met* ... Hayford Enwall was extremely aware of the impact the Brownout Strangler killings had made in Melbourne. Shortly after arriving there, he had met a young Melbourne woman who had joined the WAAAF, introduced at a cabaret by a mutual friend. He and Jean Kennett, the young woman, had already fallen deeply in love.

p. 213 ... *attracted enormous public attention* ... See, for example, Melbourne *Argus*, 29 May 1942.

p. 214 ... *sensational American trials* ... Charters Towers *Northern Miner*, 10 June 1942.

p. 214 ... *and Melbourne city becomes Carlton* ... The building, located at 370 Russell Street, is still there. It was probably chosen because of its proximity to the City Watchhouse, its position at the edge of the CBD and because it could be easily secured.

p. 217 ... *He would then fold* ... Leonski was first allowed to exercise outside his cell on the day before his trial commenced.

p. 217 ... *the history of the gang* ... The book was probably J. J. Kenneally's, *The Inner History of the Kelly Gang and Their Pursuers*. First published in 1929, it was a well-written and sympathetic account of the rise and fall of the gang.

p. 222 ... *crucial in determining the outcome* ... Peter Enwall, 6 June 2013.

14. The Medical Board

p. 224 ... *to determine his mental status* ... Rockhampton *Central Queensland Herald*, 18 June 1942.

p. 224 ... *until that board had reported* ... Transcript, op. cit., p. 7.

p. 225 ... *neurologist and psychiatrist* ... Another Henry Maudsley, Harry's great uncle, had founded the Maudsley Hospital for mental disorders, in London.

p. 226 ... *six private sessions with Leonski* ... Transcript, op. cit., pp. 10–11.

p. 226 ... *As could be expected* ... The following section is based on all the Board members' reports – all were called as witnesses and examined and cross-examined – as well as the consolidated Medical Board report.

p. 230 ... *because of his prowess* ... Chapman, op. cit., p. 153.

p. 231 ... *was not then, and had never been, insane* ... Transcript, op. cit., p. 12.

p. 231 ... *bedridden for several days* ... The wisdom of selecting a large panel of officers for the court martial was also validated during the adjournment when one member, Colonel John Creham, was posted to northern Australia in late June; he would take no further part in the proceedings.

p. 234 ... *an attractive southern accent* ... Rockhampton *Morning Bulletin*, 20 July 1942.

p. 235 ... *everything else was irrelevant* ... *Transcript*, op. cit., pp. 17–18.

15. Evidence-in-Chief

p. 239 ... *an apology of sorts* ... *Transcript*, op. cit., p. 66A.

p. 241 ... *the matter would be dealt with* ... There was an unusual exchange around this point. Reading between the lines, it appears Spencer Eddy believed that Leonski had been offered some kind of deal if he confessed to the murders. No evidence for this was offered and there was no follow-up.

p. 246 ... *does not imply insanity* ... *Transcript*, op. cit., p. 296.

p. 247 ... *a chilling, 'Yes, sir.'* ... ibid., p. 279.

p. 248 ... *with psychopathic personalities* ... ibid., p. 302.

p. 250 ... *is in a mental hospital* ... Melbourne *Sun*, 17 July 1942.

16. For the Defence

p. 253 ... *a recent illness* ... This was the allergic reaction to the yellow fever inoculations he had first suffered during the adjournment after Leonski's arraignment.

p. 254 ... *and had cried about it* ... Leonski's breakdown at Fort Sam Houston in San Antonio was seen as a significant turning point in his mental deterioration brought on, so it seemed, by his imminent separation from those he loved, most notably his mother. Rothgerber returned to it with two witnesses. See, *Transcript*, op. cit., pp. 323 and 325.

p. 256 ... *the passage of time* ... Charles Taylor, in his evidence about the scientific aspects of the case, said that he had been unable to match the blood found on Leonski's clothes with Thompson's blood because it had dried out too much to be amenable to typing.

p. 257 ... *any other held in Australia* ... Rockhampton *Morning Bulletin*, 20 July 1942.

p. 257 ... *is also on trial* ... *Transcript*, op. cit., p. 364. Enwall's closing argument was widely reported throughout Australia and, on paper at least, it remains an extremely powerful speech. See, for example, the *Sydney Morning Herald*, 18 July 1942.

p. 257 ... *you are vicious underneath* ... *Transcript*, op. cit., p. 365.

p. 260 ... *to be hanged by the neck until dead* ... *Transcript*, op. cit., p. 388.

p. 261 ... *I guess that's that* ... Harvey, op. cit., p. 76.

p. 261 ... *immediately once it was available* ... While the US Army did not immediately make a copy of the transcript available to the Victoria Police, it did send a copy to the Commonwealth Attorney-General, and also offered to pay the expenses of the police witnesses. The offer was declined.

p. 262 ... *and he gave his funny little laugh* ... *West Australian*, 21 July 1942.

17. Killing Time

p. 266 ... *as determined by you* ... Chapman, op. cit., p. 213.

p. 267 ... *and to General MacArthur* ... *Sydney Morning Herald*, 31 July 1942. Founded in the United Kingdom in 1866, the Howard League for

Penal Reform still exists and remains active in criminal and prison law reform, most notably in England and Wales.

p. 267 ... *the community's desire for retribution* ... Broken Hill *Barrier Miner*, 20 July 1942.

p. 268 ... *sends letters to her* ... ibid., 3 November 1942.

p. 269 ... *my usual gentlemanly behaviour* ... Letter dated 3 August, 1942; Australian National Maritime Museum Collection, 00017256.

p. 271 ... *posted to his mother* ... Perth *Mirror*, 8 August 1942.

p. 271 ... *in this goddam place* ... ibid.

p. 272 ... *Amelia Leonski also wrote regularly* ... Father Tom Shanahan returned one of her last letters to Eddie after the war.

p. 273 ... *plenty of experiences for me* ... These quotes are taken from the Broken Hill *Barrier Miner* (23 July 1942) and the Rockhampton *Morning Bulletin* (20 July 1942).

p. 273 ... *Death is a wonderful thing* ... Perth *Mirror*, 8 August 1942.

p. 273 ... *the end of everything* ... Harvey, op. cit., p. 78.

p. 273 ... *lift my face for me* ... Both stories are from a lengthy article published in the Perth *Mirror* on 8 August 1942.

p. 274 ... *To dance upon the air!* ... Harvey, op. cit., p. 79.

p. 275 ... *a momentum of their own* ... All these notes and letters are held in the Leonski court martial transcript folder in the Australian Archives.

18. Death at Dawn

p. 277 ... *go on like this* ... Chapman, op. cit., p. 213.

p. 278 ... *probably South Australia* ... Ivan Chapman believed that the executioner was actually brought over from Western Australia but, logistically, this would have been difficult. Where the executioner is mentioned in other sources, it is usually with the addition of 'South Australian' as a descriptor. A story published almost a decade later suggested that the hangman had carried out five previous executions, *Brisbane Telegraph*, 16 June 1950.

p. 280 ... *the same mistake again* ... Chapman, op. cit., p. 221. Chapman was told this story directly by Sid McGuffie.

p. 280 ... *His merciful goodness* ... ibid, p. 233.

p. 282 ... *very long to remember* ... Harvey, op. cit., p. 80.

p. 285 ... *It's quite OK, pal.* ... Darian-Smith, op. cit., p. 148.

p. 288 ... *Leonski has been executed* ... The official statement was quoted widely in newspapers across Australia. See, for example, the Melbourne *Herald*, 9 November 1942.

Postscript: Schofield Barracks Post Cemetery, Honolulu

p. 296 ... *a bit passé* ... Moore, *Over-sexed, Over-paid and Over Here*, p. 146.

BIBLIOGRAPHY

Adam-Smith, Patsy, *Australian Women at War*, Penguin, Melbourne, 1984.

Bolt, Andrew (Ed.), *Our Home Front: 1939–45*, Wilkinson, Melbourne, 1995.

Buckton, Henry, *Friendly Invasion: The American Occupation of Britain 1942–45*, Phillimore & Company, Chichester, 2006.

Chan, Gabrielle, (Ed.), *War on Our Doorstep*, Hardie Grant, Melbourne, 2003.

Chapman, Ivan, *Leonski: The Brownout Strangler*, Hale and Iremonger, Sydney, 1982.

Connell, Daniel, *The War at Home: Australia 1939–1949*, ABC, Sydney, 1988.

Darian-Smith, Kate, *On the Home Front: Melbourne in Wartime, 1939–1945*, Melbourne University Press, 2009.

Day, David, *John Curtin: A Life*, HarperCollins, Sydney, 1999.

Dean, Peter (Ed.), *Australia 1942: In the Shadow of War*, Cambridge University Press, Melbourne, 2013.

Dower, Alan, *Crime Chemist: The Life Story of Charles Anthony Taylor, Scientist for the Crown*, John Long, London, 1965.

Esthus, Raymond A., *From Enmity to Alliance: U.S.–Australian Relations 1931–1941*, University of Washington Press, Seattle, 1964.

Haldane, Robert, *The People's Force: A History of the Victoria Police*, Melbourne University Press, 1995.

Harper, Norman (Ed.), *Pacific Orbit: Australian–American Relations Since 1942*, F. W. Cheshire, Melbourne, 1968.

Harvey, John R., *Journey to the Gallows*, Invincible Press, Sydney, 1947.

Horner, David, *High Command: Australian and Allied Strategy 1939–45*, Allen and Unwin, Sydney, 1982

Kaplan, Alice, *The Interpreter*, Free Press, New York, 2005.

Lloyd, Clem and Hall, Richard, *Backroom Briefings: John Curtin's War*, National Library of Australia, Canberra, 1997.

Mallon, Andrew, *Leonski, The Brown-out Murders*, Outback Press, Melbourne, 1979.

McKernan, Michael, *All In!: Australia during the Second World War*, Nelson, Melbourne, 1983.

——*The Strength of a Nation: Six Years of Australians Fighting for the Nation and Defending the Homefront in WWII*, Allen & Unwin, Sydney, 2008.

McKerrow, John, *The American Occupation of Australia, 1941–45: A Marriage of Necessity*, Cambridge Scholars Publishing, Newcastle upon Tyne, 2013.

Moore, John Hammond, *Over-sexed, Over-paid and Over Here: Americans in Australia, 1941–45*, University of Queensland Press, Brisbane, 1981.

Penglase, Joanna and Horner, David, *When the War Came to Australia*, Allen & Unwin, Sydney, 1992.

Porter, Trevor, *Executions in the Colony and State of Victoria 1842–1967*, Aimsetters, Adelaide, 2002.

Potts, E. Daniel and Potts, Annette, *Yanks Down Under, 1941–45*, Oxford University Press, Melbourne, 1985.

Ralph, Barry, *They Passed This Way: The United States of America, the States of Australia and World War II*, Kangaroo Press, Sydney, 2000.

Robertson, John, *Australia at War 1939–1945*, Heinemann, Melbourne, 1981.

Thompson, Peter A., and Macklin, Robert, *The Battle of Brisbane: Australians and the Yanks at War*, ABC, Sydney, 2000.

Williamson, Kristin, *The Last Bastion*, Lansdowne, Sydney, 1984.

Wurth, Bob, *1942: Australia's Greatest Peril*, Pan Macmillan, Sydney, 2008.

Wyatt, Ray, *A Yank Down Under: From America's Heartland to Australia's Outback*, Sunflower University Press, Manhattan, KS, 1999.

Monographs

Hore, Monique, 'The Hangman's Journal, Part IV', *Herald-Sun*, 7 June 2012.

Hyde, Penny, 'The Prosecutor and the Perpetrator: Murder in Melbourne', Australian National Maritime Museum, <anmm.blog/2012/11/23/the-prosecutor-and-the-perpetrator-murder-in-melbourne/>, 23 November 2012, accessed 30 May 2017.

United States Military Forces in Australia, *Transcript of Evidence: Leonski Murder Trial* and *Exhibits*, Melbourne, 1942, National Archives of Australia, A472 W7493 Parts 1–5.

Newspapers

Advertiser	Adelaide
Age	Melbourne
Argus	Melbourne
Barrier Miner	Broken Hill
Central Queensland Herald	Rockhampton
Courier-Mail	Brisbane
Daily Mercury	Mackay
Daily News	Perth
Herald	Melbourne
Mercury	Hobart
Miner	Kalgoorlie
Mirror	Perth
Morning Bulletin	Rockhampton
Northern Miner	Charters Towers
Northern Star	Lismore
Record	South Melbourne
Sun News-Pictorial	Melbourne
Sydney Morning Herald	Sydney
Telegraph	Brisbane
Truth	Melbourne
Truth	Sydney
Weekly Times	Melbourne
West Australian	Perth

ACKNOWLEDGEMENTS

I would firstly like to thank my family and friends, again, for their ongoing support and encouragement to tell stories they know mean something to me. Pam is at the heart – literally – of that group which includes our children and their partners, our grandchildren and those we value as both friends and in-laws. The latest grandchild, Archie Tor Fowlie, arrived as this story moved from plan to reality. Thanks, as well, to my sister Laraine, who continues to inspire me by assuring me that I am probably the best writer in the family.

Professionally, staff at three of Australia's greatest institutions were unfailingly polite and helpful as I worked my way through this story. The Research Centre at the Australian War Memorial, the National Library of Australia and the National Archives of Australia make it easier to be an Australian writer than it might otherwise be. Alexander Fax, Kristen and David, and their bookshop, have again been helpful and supportive – thank you. My agent, Sarah McKenzie of Hindsight Literary Agency, her partner Michael, and Matthew Kelly and Tom Bailey-Smith at Hachette Australia all personify professionalism with a very human touch; I thank them all for their assistance as the story of Eddie Leonski and his victims moved its way from thought to paper.